OUTDOORS

TAKE A HIKE
LOS ANGELES

ANN MARIE BROWN & JULIE SHEER

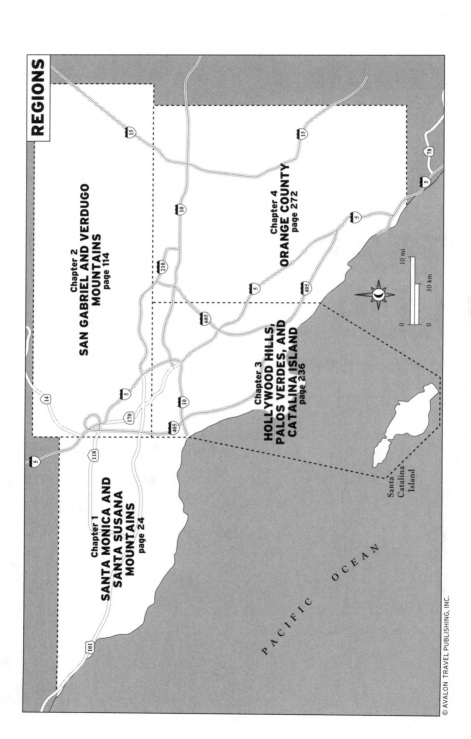

REGIONS

Chapter 2
SAN GABRIEL AND VERDUGO
MOUNTAINS
page 114

Chapter 4
ORANGE COUNTY
page 272

Chapter 3
HOLLYWOOD HILLS,
PALOS VERDES, AND
CATALINA ISLAND
page 236

Chapter 1
SANTA MONICA AND
SANTA SUSANA
MOUNTAINS
page 24

PACIFIC OCEAN

Santa Catalina Island

0   10 mi

0   10 km

© AVALON TRAVEL PUBLISHING, INC.

Contents

Best Waterfall Hikes
Best Historical Hikes
Best Hikes for Families
Best Wildflower Hikes

Best Hikes for Geology Buffs
Best Coastal Hikes
Best Summit Views
Best Butt-kickers

Food and Water
Trail Map
Extra Clothing
Sunglasses and Sunscreen

Flashlight
First-Aid Kit
Emergency Supplies

Including:
Big Sycamore Canyon
Caballero Canyon
Calabasas Peak
Castro Crest

Cheeseboro and Palo Comado Canyons
Cold Creek Canyon Preserve
Devil's Canyon
Eagle Rock
Escondido Canyon Falls

Chapter 2 **San Gabriel and Verdugo Mountains**

Including:

How to Use This Book

ABOUT THE MAPS

This book is divided into chapters based on regions that are within close reach of the city; an overview map of these regions precedes the table of contents. Each chapter begins with a region map that shows the locations and numbers of the trails listed in that chapter.

Each trail profile is also accompanied by a detailed trail map that shows the hike route.

For a directory of map symbols, please see page 295.

ABOUT THE TRAIL PROFILES

Each profile includes a narrative description of the trail's setting and terrain. This description also typically includes mile-by-mile hiking directions, as well as information about the trail's highlights and unique attributes.

The trails marked by the **BEST** symbol are highlighted in the authors' Best Hikes list.

Options

If alternative routes are available, this section is used to provide information on side trips or note how to shorten or lengthen the hike.

Directions

This section provides detailed driving directions to the trailhead from the city center or from the intersection of major highways. When public transportation is available, instructions will be noted here.

Information and Contact

This section provides information on fees, facilities, and access restrictions for the trail. It also includes the name of the land management agency or organization that oversees the trail, as well as an address, phone number, and website if available.

ABOUT THE ICONS

The icons in this book are designed to provide at-a-glance information on special features for each trail.

- 🏔 The trail climbs to a high overlook with wide views.
- 🦌 The trail offers an opportunity for wildlife watching.
- 🌸 The trail features wildflower displays in spring.
- 🏖 The trail visits a beach.
- 💦 The trail travels to a waterfall.
- 🏛 The trail visits a historic site.
- 🐕 Dogs are allowed.
- 🚌 The trailhead can be accessed via public transportation.

ABOUT THE DIFFICULTY RATING

Each profile also includes a difficulty rating. The ratings are defined as follows:

Easy: Easy hikes are five miles or less round-trip and have less than 700 feet of elevation gain (nearly level). They are generally suitable for families with small children and hikers seeking a mellow stroll.

Easy/Moderate: Easy/Moderate hikes are between four and eight miles round-trip and have 500–1,200 feet of elevation gain. They are generally suitable for families with active children above the age of six and hikers who are reasonably fit.

Moderate: Moderate hikes are between five and nine miles round-trip and have 1,000–2,000 feet of elevation gain. They are generally suitable for adults and children who are fit.

Strenuous: Strenuous hikes are between 5 and 10 miles round-trip and have 1,800–2,800 feet of elevation gain. They are suitable for very fit hikers who are seeking a workout.

Butt-kicker: Butt-kicker hikes are between 7 and 14 miles round-trip and have 3,000 feet or more of elevation gain. These hikes are suitable only for advanced hikers who are very physically fit.

The level of difficulty for any trail can change considerably due to weather or trail conditions. Always phone ahead to check on current trail and weather conditions.

INTRODUCTION

Authors' Note

We are nature lovers, wildlife watchers, committed hikers, and card-carrying members of conservation organizations. We have been known to drop everything when the timing of the wildflower bloom is just right, or rainy weather has made the waterfalls flow. When it comes to scheduling, the first thing that goes on our calendars is outdoor time in the mountains or at the coast.

This being the case, it may seem odd that we chose to write a hiking book about a large urban area populated with 10 million-plus people. But as many of its residents know—but most outsiders don't—Los Angeles is a surprisingly wild metropolitan area. How many U.S. cities can brag of having a 650,000-acre national forest located on its borders? Or a 20-mile-long island just 20 miles off its coast? Those are in addition to a national park, nearly a dozen state parks, a wealth of open space areas managed by nonprofit agencies, and too many county, city, and regional parks to count. Although grizzly bears no longer roam the area as they did 150 years ago, coyotes still gallop across the grasslands, bighorn sheep wander the high mountains, and mountain lions and bobcats stalk their prey.

If you hike much around Los Angeles, you will be awed by the beauty and grace of wind-sculpted Jeffrey pines and 1,000-year-old limber pines. You'll wonder at the sight of rare and precious wildflowers, some of which grow here and nowhere else in the world. Your ears will be filled with the sound of crashing surf against high palisades and rocky shores. You'll gaze at waterfalls coursing down basalt cliffs and pouring over sandstone precipices. You'll stand on mile-high—and much higher—mountain summits and look down thousands of feet to the L.A. basin and Mojave Desert below. In autumn, you'll watch sycamores and big leaf maples turn bright gold, and in winter, you'll see snow fall on the Angeles Crest's high peaks and ridges.

Quite possibly, you'll wind up spending some of the best days of your life on L.A. trails. Speaking of hiking, take a look out the window. Chances are good that it's a nice day for a walk. See you out there.

—Ann Marie Brown and Julie Sheer

Best Hikes

◖ Best Waterfall Hikes

Escondido Canyon and Falls, Santa Monica and Santa Susana Mountains chapter, page 52.

Trail Canyon Trail, San Gabriel and Verdugo Mountains chapter, page 126.

Sturtevant Falls and Big Santa Anita Canyon Loop, San Gabriel and Verdugo Mountains chapter, page 150.

Fish Canyon Falls, San Gabriel and Verdugo Mountains chapter, page 156.

Cooper Canyon, San Gabriel and Verdugo Mountains chapter, page 188.

◖ Best Historical Hikes

West Mandeville Fire Road to San Vicente Mountain Park, Santa Monica and Santa Susana Mountains chapter, page 98.

Sam Merrill Trail to Echo Mountain and White City, San Gabriel and Verdugo Mountains chapter, page 135.

Eaton Saddle to Mount Lowe, San Gabriel and Verdugo Mountains chapter, page 171.

Big Horn Mine, San Gabriel and Verdugo Mountains chapter, page 206.

Bridge to Nowhere and The Narrows, San Gabriel and Verdugo Mountains chapter, page 216.

◖ Best Hikes for Families

Wildwood Canyon Loop, Santa Monica and Santa Susana Mountains chapter, page 41.

Stough Canyon to Verdugo Fire Road, San Gabriel and Verdugo Mountains chapter, page 123.

Gabrielino Trail, San Gabriel and Verdugo Mountains chapter, page 132.

Vetter Mountain Lookout, San Gabriel and Verdugo Mountains chapter, page 177.

Scrub Jay Trail, Hollywood Hills, Palos Verdes, and Catalina Island chapter, page 253.

◖ Best Wildflower Hikes

La Jolla Canyon Loop, Santa Monica and Santa Susana Mountains chapter, page 26.

Wildwood Canyon Loop, Santa Monica and Santa Susana Mountains chapter, page 41.

Nicholas Flat Trail, Santa Monica and Santa Susana Mountains chapter, page 44.

Stunt High Trail, Santa Monica and Santa Susana Mountains chapter, page 76.

West Fork National Recreation Trail, San Gabriel and Verdugo Mountains chapter, page 212.

◖ Best Hikes for Geology Buffs

Castro Crest, Santa Monica and Santa Susana Mountains chapter, page 58.

Backbone Trail in Hondo Canyon, Santa Monica and Santa Susana Mountains chapter, page 79.

Towsley and Wiley Canyons, Santa Monica and Santa Susana Mountains chapter, page 102.

Geology Trail and Foot Trail, San Gabriel and Verdugo Mountains chapter, page 117.

Burkhart Trail to the Devil's Chair, San Gabriel and Verdugo Mountains chapter, page 197.

◖ Best Coastal Hikes

Point Dume Beach Walk, Santa Monica and Santa Susana Mountains chapter, page 50.

Point Vicente Beach Walk, Hollywood Hills, Palos Verdes, and Catalina Island chapter, page 256.

Two Harbors West End Road, Hollywood Hills, Palos Verdes, and Catalina Island chapter, page 261.

Cottonwood-Black Jack Trail to Little Harbor, Hollywood Hills, Palos Verdes, and Catalina Island chapter, page 264.

El Moro Canyon Trail, Orange County chapter, page 277.

◖ Best Summit Views

Los Liones Trail to Parker Mesa Overlook, Santa Monica and Santa Susana Mountains chapter, page 88.

Mount Williamson, San Gabriel and Verdugo Mountains chapter, page 191.

Mount Islip, San Gabriel and Verdugo Mountains chapter, page 194.

Vincent Gap to Mount Baden-Powell, San Gabriel and Verdugo Mountains chapter, page 203.

Mount Baldy, San Gabriel and Verdugo Mountains chapter, page 229.

◖ Best Butt-kickers

Stone Canyon Trail to Mount Lukens, San Gabriel and Verdugo Mountains chapter, page 129.

Fish Canyon Falls, San Gabriel and Verdugo Mountains chapter, page 156.

Vincent Gap to Mount Baden-Powell, San Gabriel and Verdugo Mountains chapter, page 203.

Ice House Canyon to Ice House Saddle, San Gabriel and Verdugo Mountains chapter, page 226.

Mount Baldy (the Hard Way), San Gabriel and Verdugo Mountains chapter, page 229.

Hiking Tips

WHAT TO CARRY WITH YOU
Food and Water
There's nothing like being hungry or thirsty to spoil a good time, or to make you anxious about getting back to the car. Even if you aren't the least bit hungry or thirsty when you park at the trailhead, you may feel completely different after 45 minutes or more of walking. A small day pack or fanny sack can keep you happily supplied with a quart or two of water and a few snacks. Always carry more than you think you'll need. If you don't bring your own water, make sure you carry a water filter or purifier so you can obtain water from a natural source, such as a stream or lake. Never, ever drink water from a natural source without first filtering or boiling it. The risk to your health (from *Giardia lamblia* and other microorganisms) is too great. And remember, in the Mediterranean climate of Southern California, it's unwise to depend on finding natural water sources. A spring or creek that flows with fervor in March may be completely dry by July.

Trail Map
Get a current map of the of the park or public land where you plan to hike. Maps are available from a variety of resources, including the managing agency of most parks, and from private sources, such as Tom Harrison Maps or Trails Illustrated. All their contact information is in the Resource guide at the end of this book.

Extra Clothing
On the trail, conditions can change at any time. Not only can the weather suddenly turn windy, foggy, or rainy, but your own body conditions also change: You'll perspire as you hike up a sunny hill and then get chilled at the top of a windy ridge or when you head into shade. Because of this, cotton fabrics don't function well in the outdoors. Once cotton gets wet, it stays wet. Generally, polyester-blend fabrics dry faster. Some high-tech fabrics will actually wick moisture away from your skin. Invest in a few items of clothing made from these fabrics, and you'll be more comfortable when you hike.

Additionally, always carry a lightweight jacket with you, preferably one that is waterproof and also wind-resistant. Put it in your day pack or tie it around your waist. If your jacket isn't waterproof, pack along one of the $2, single-use rain ponchos that come in a package the size of a deck of cards (available at most drug stores and outdoor stores).

If you are hiking in the mountains, carry gloves and a hat as well. You never know when you might need them.

Sunglasses and Sunscreen

The dangers of the sun are well known. Wear both sunglasses and sunscreen, and/or a hat with a wide brim. Put on your sunscreen 30 minutes before you go outdoors so it has time to take effect, and don't forget about your lips. Coat them with lip balm with a high SPF to protect them.

Flashlight

Just in case your hike takes a little longer than you planned and darkness falls, bring at least one flashlight. Mini-flashlights are available everywhere, weigh almost nothing, and can save the day—or night. Our favorites are the tiny squeeze flashlights, about the shape and size of a quarter, which you can clip on to any key ring (the Photon Micro-Light is a popular brand). Since these flashlights are so small, carry two or three. That way you never have to worry about the batteries running out of juice.

First-Aid Kit

Unless you're trained in first aid, nothing major is required here, but a few large and small Band-Aids and moleskin for blisters, antibiotic ointment, ibuprofen, and an ace bandage can be valuable tools. Also, if you or anyone in your party is allergic to bee stings or anything else in the outdoors, carry their medication. If you are hiking where you might be bothered by mosquitoes, bring a small bottle of insect repellent.

Emergency Supplies

Many hikers think that if they are just going for a day hike, they don't need to carry anything for emergencies. Think again. Ask yourself this question, "What would I need to have with me if I broke my ankle and had to spend the night outdoors?" Aside from food, water, and other items previously listed, always carry a few basic supplies that will get you through an unplanned night outdoors. Of great use is a Swiss Army–style pocket knife—one with several blades, a can opener, a scissors, and a tweezers on it. Matches in a waterproof container and a candle will ensure you can always build a fire if you need to. A lightweight space blanket or sleeping bag made of foil-like mylar film will keep you warm (these can be purchased at outdoors stores, weigh next to nothing, and come in a package about the size of a deck of cards). A whistle and small signal mirror can help you get found if you ever get lost. And if you know how to use a compass, carry one.

MOUNTAIN LIONS, TICKS, AND RATTLESNAKES

All three of these creatures deserve your respect, and it's good to know a little bit about them. Chances are high you will never see a mountain lion, but you just might run into a tick or a snake somewhere.

Mountain lions are almost everywhere in California, but they are very shy and secretive animals, and as a result, are rarely seen. When they do show themselves, they get a lot of media attention. If you're hiking in an area where mountain lions or their tracks have been spotted, remember to keep your children close to you on the trail and your dog leashed. If you see a mountain lion, it will most likely vanish into the landscape as soon as it notices you. If it doesn't, make yourself appear as large and aggressive as possible. Raise your arms, open your jacket, wave a big stick, and speak loudly and firmly or shout. If you have children with you, pick them up off the ground, but try to do so without crouching down or leaning over. (Crouching makes you appear smaller and more submissive, like prey.) Don't turn your back on the cat or run from it, but rather back away slowly and deliberately, always retaining your aggressive pose and continuing to speak loudly.

Ticks are a common problem in the Southern California outdoors, especially in the spring months. The easiest way to stay clear of ticks is to wear long pants and long sleeves when you hike, and tuck your pant legs into your socks. But this system isn't fail-proof. The darn things sometimes find their way onto your skin no matter what you do. Always check yourself thoroughly when you leave the trail, looking carefully for anything that's crawling on you. Check your clothes and also your skin underneath. A good friend can be a useful assistant in this endeavor.

Of 850 tick species in the world, 49 are found in California. About one to six percent of the Western black-legged ticks found in the Los Angeles area carry Lyme disease. Most tick bites cause a sharp sting that will get your attention. But rarely, ticks will bite you without your noticing. If you've been in the outdoors, and then a few days or a week later start to experience flulike symptoms such as headaches, fever, muscle soreness, neck stiffness, or nausea, see a doctor immediately. Tell the doctor you are concerned about possible exposure to ticks and Lyme disease. Another early tell-tale symptom is a slowly expanding red rash near the tick bite, which appears a week to a month after the bite. Caught in its early stages, Lyme disease is easily treated with antibiotics, but left untreated, can be severely debilitating.

Eight rattlesnake species are found in California. These members of the pit viper family have wide triangular heads, narrow necks, and rattles on their tales. Rattlesnakes live where it's warm, usually at elevations below 6,000 feet.

If you see one, give it plenty of space to get away without feeling threatened. If you're hiking on a nice day, when rattlesnakes are often out sunning themselves on trails and rocks, keep your eyes open for them so you don't step on one or place your hand on one. Be especially on the lookout for rattlesnakes in the spring, when they leave their winter burrows and come out in the sun. Morning is the most common time to see them, as the midday sun is usually too hot for them.

Although rattlesnake bites are painful, they are very rarely fatal. More than 100 people in California are bitten by rattlesnakes each year, resulting in only one or two fatalities on average. About 25 percent of rattlesnake bites are dry, with no venom injected. Symptoms of bites that do contain venom usually include tingling around the mouth, nausea and vomiting, dizziness, weakness, sweating, and/or chills. If you should get bitten by a rattlesnake, your car key—and the nearest telephone—are your best first aid. Call 911 as soon as you can, or have someone drive you to the nearest hospital. Don't panic or run, which can speed the circulation of venom through your system.

Except for a handful of rattlesnake species, all other California snakes are not poisonous. Just give them room to slither by.

POISON OAK

Poison oak is the bane of hikers everywhere, but you can avoid it with a little common sense. Learn to recognize and avoid *Toxicodendron diversilobum,* which produces an itching rash that can last for weeks. If you can't readily identify poison oak, at least remember the old Boy Scout motto: Leaves of three, let them be. But be wary: poison oak disguises itself in different seasons. In spring and summer when in full leaf, it looks somewhat like wild blackberry bushes. In late summer, its leaves turn bright red. But in winter, the plant loses all or most of its leaves and looks like clusters of bare sticks. Poison oak is poisonous year-round.

To avoid poison oak, stay on the trail and watch what you brush up against. If you know you have a bad reaction to poison oak, wear long pants and long sleeves, and remove and wash your clothes immediately after hiking. If you have been exposed to poison oak, you can often prevent a rash from developing by washing thoroughly with soap and water, or a product like Technu, as soon as possible. If you do develop poison oak rash, a relatively new product on the market can help you get rid of it. The product is called Zanfel, and although it costs a small fortune (about $30–40 a bottle), it is available at pharmacies without a prescription. You simply pour it on the rash and the rash vanishes, or at least greatly diminishes. Many hikers consider this product to be the greatest invention since lightweight hiking boots.

GETTING LOST AND GETTING FOUND

If you're hiking with a family or group, make sure everybody knows to stay to-gether. If anyone decides to split off from the group for any reason, make sure they have a trail map with them and know how to read it. Also, be sure that everyone in your group knows the key rules about what to do if they get lost:

• Whistle or shout loudly at regular intervals.

• "Hug" a tree or a big rock or bush. Find a noticeable landmark, sit down next to it, and don't move. Continue to whistle or shout loudly. A lost person is easier to find if they stay in one place.

HIKING WITH DOGS

Dogs are wonderful friends and great companions. But dogs and nature don't always mix well. Bless their furry little hearts, most dogs can't help but disturb wildlife, given half a chance. Even if they don't chase or bark at wildlife, dogs leave droppings that may intimidate other mammals into changing their normal routine. Kept on a leash, a dog can be the best hiking companion you could ask for.

Dogs are allowed on some trails in Los Angeles and not on others. For many dog owners, it's confusing. When using this book, check the information listing under each trail write-up to see whether or not dogs are permitted on a specific trail. Always call the park or public land in advance if you are traveling some distance with your dog. Here is a general guideline to park rules about dogs:

In most state parks around Los Angeles, dogs are not allowed at all on hik-ing trails. In the Santa Monica Mountains National Recreation Area, which is managed by the National Park Service, dogs are allowed on-leash. Ditto for most lands managed by the Santa Monica Mountains Conservancy, and at most L.A. County and L.A. city parks. Always follow and obey a park's spe-cific rules about dogs. When the rules state that your dog must be leashed, that usually means he or she must be on a six-foot or shorter leash. Don't try to get away with carrying the leash in your hand while your dog runs free; rangers are not fooled by this and may give you a ticket.

In Angeles National Forest, dogs are allowed, and in many areas they are allowed off-leash. Check for regulations in special wildlife management areas, such as where bighorn sheep are found, because in those areas, dogs must be leashed. Even if your dog is allowed off-leash, he or she should still be under voice control, for his or her safety more than anything. The outdoors presents many hazards for dogs, including mountain lions, rattlesnakes, ticks, porcupines, black bears, and a host of other potential problems. Dogs are frequently lost in national forest areas. Keeping your dog close to your side or on a leash in the national forests will help you both have a worry-free trip and a great time.

PROTECTING THE OUTDOORS

Take good care of this beautiful land you're hiking on. The basics are simple: Leave no trace of your visit. Pack out all your trash. Do your best not to disturb animal or plant life. Don't collect specimens of plants, wildlife, or even pine cones. Never, ever carve anything into the trunks of trees. If you're following a trail, don't cut the switchbacks. Leave everything in nature exactly as you found it, because each tiny piece has its place in the great scheme of things.

You can go the extra mile, too. Pick up any litter that you see on the trail. Teach your children to do this as well. Carry an extra bag to hold picked-up litter until you get to a trash receptacle, or just keep an empty pocket for that purpose in your day pack or fanny sack.

If you have the extra time or energy, join a trail organization in your area or spend some time volunteering in your local park. Anything you do to help this beautiful planet will be repaid to you, many times over. For more information or materials, please visit www.LNT.org or call 303/442-8222 or 800/332-4100.

SANTA MONICA AND SANTA SUSANA MOUNTAINS

© ANN MARIE BROWN

BEST HIKES

❰ Best Waterfall Hikes
Escondido Canyon and Falls, **p. 52**

❰ Best Historical Hikes
West Mandeville Fire Road to San Vicente Mountain
Park, **p. 98**

❰ Best Hikes for Families
Wildwood Canyon Loop, **p. 41**

❰ Best Wildflower Hikes
La Jolla Canyon Loop, **p. 26**
Wildwood Canyon Loop, **p. 41**
Nicholas Flat Trail, **p. 44**
Stunt High Trail, **p. 76**

❰ Best Hikes for Geology Buffs
Castro Crest, **p. 58**
Backbone Trail in Hondo Canyon, **p. 79**
Towsley and Wiley Canyons, **p. 102**

❰ Best Coastal Hikes
Point Dume Beach Walk, **p. 50**

❰ Best Summit Views
Los Liones Trail to Parker Mesa Overlook, **p. 88**

The best-known, and most frequently visited, mountain range in the Los Angeles region is not the dramatic peaks of the rugged San Gabriel Range, but rather a gentler stretch of sloping peaks along the coast: the Santa Monica Mountains. The range begins near Hollywood and continues 46 miles west to Point Mugu, averaging seven miles in width. Much of the public land in these mountains is part of L.A.'s only national park – the Santa Monica Mountains National Recreation Area – but other portions are divided into several state parks: Topanga, Malibu Creek, Leo Carrillo, Point Mugu, and Will Rogers. Several smaller parklands are managed by nongovernment agencies: the Santa Monica Mountains Conservancy and the Mountains Restoration Trust. This patchwork of parklands is crisscrossed not just by trails but also by roads, making it easy to access its more than 100 trailheads from either the inland side (U.S. 101) or the coast (Highway 1).

The trails in the Santa Monicas travel across chaparral- and sage-covered hillsides, oak and sycamore woodlands, and native grasslands. The range is well known for its springtime wildflower displays and also for its heat in summer. Rocky sandstone and volcanic outcrops poke up here and there, adding variety to the landscape. Ocean views are plentiful and wildlife sightings common. Deer, bobcat, coyotes, and a huge variety of songbirds and raptors are commonly seen. Hiking trails are generally well marked and relatively gentle in grade.

The parklands become wilder and more remote the farther west you travel. Although you are never far from the crowds at Topanga State Park or Temescal Gateway Park on the east side of the range, you can often find solitude far to the west at Point Mugu State Park, just over the Ventura County line. Not only are there fewer hikers, but there is also much less development. Here you will find trails where you can walk all day and never see a single highway or mega-mansion.

This region also contains a few scattered parklands to the north, as far away as the rapidly expanding Santa Clarita Valley. Here, in a little-known range called the Santa Susana Mountains, lie some of L.A.'s least-known nature preserves. Although the range is similar to the Santa Monicas in many ways, particularly wildlife and weather, hikers will note one conspicuous absence in the Santa Susanas: chaparral is a scarce commodity. Instead, oak woodland and grasslands dominate the ridges and canyons. Because of the rapid expansion and development of land in this region of Los Angeles, the small parks and preserves here are particularly significant for wildlife, and for city-weary nature lovers.

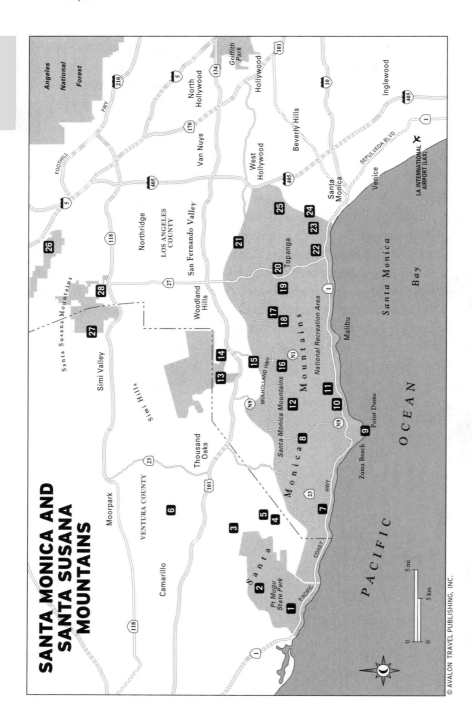

SANTA MONICA AND
SANTA SUSANA
MOUNTAINS

© AVALON TRAVEL PUBLISHING, INC.

Santa Monica and Santa Susana Mountains Hikes

1 LA JOLLA CANYON LOOP   BEST ☾
Point Mugu State Park

Level: Easy/Moderate   **Total Distance:** 5.5 miles round-trip

Hiking Time: 2.5 hours   **Elevation Gain:** 750 feet

Summary: A flower-filled loop past a waterfall, duck pond, and grassland savannah in the more remote western region of the Santa Monica Mountains.

In a beauty contest of all the parks in the Santa Monica Mountains, Point Mugu State Park would win hands down. Maybe it's because Point Mugu is a little farther west on the highway, closer to Oxnard than it is to Los Angeles. Maybe it's the park's wildflowers, waterfall, well-built trails, and serene coastal views. Whatever the reason, Point Mugu always feels more wild and pristine than its eastern neighbors.

The popular La Jolla Canyon Loop at Point Mugu is both a great day hike and/or an easy backpacking trip with an overnight stay at La Jolla Valley walk-in camp. (Backpackers must register in advance at neighboring Sycamore Canyon Campground.) Most people make the trip as a mellow half-day hike.

Start at the Ray Miller Trailhead and follow the wide gated road, which narrows almost immediately. The trail travels through an open valley that is continually refreshed by ocean breezes blowing up the canyon. In only 0.8 mile, you arrive at a small, two-tiered waterfall. A few railroad-tie stair steps lead up to the quiet pool between the two cascades, where you can easily rock-hop across.

In the early spring months, the canyon walls in a quarter-mile stretch both before and after the waterfall are blanketed with blooming giant coreopsis. These giant "sunflowers on steroids" are common on the Channel Islands but much less so on the mainland. The bright yellow flower stalks can reach

© ANN MARIE BROWN

Stalks of giant coreopsis line the trail in La Jolla Canyon.

as high as seven feet tall, but in the plant's nonblooming, dormant stage, you could easily walk right by them without giving a second glance.

Almost all of the work on this trail occurs in the first mile. As you climb, the canyon gets narrower and rockier, and, hidden amid the chaparral, you'll see rock caves that were once used by Native Americans. At a fork at 1.2 miles, go right (left will be the return of your loop). The trail's grade lessens considerably as you travel through a shady stretch lined by trees and tree-sized ceanothus. At a second junction, go left and wander past a small tule- and cattail-lined duck pond.

Less than 0.5 mile from the pond, you arrive at La Jolla Valley walk-in camp, situated near a high meadow filled with native bunch grasses. The campsites are hidden among clumps of tall coastal sagescrub. Campsite 1 is the best of the lot; it has a picnic table with a high view of the duck pond. In terms of wildflowers, you'll find all the usual suspects: mariposa lilies, morning glories, monkeyflower, brodiaea, paintbrush, and blue-eyed grass, among others. From the camp, bear left on the dirt road that runs just north of it, which narrows to a double-track path through the grass. In a short distance, a trail heads off to the left; take this if you want to cut 0.4 mile off your trip, or continue straight ahead for the com-plete 5.5-mile loop. Going straight provides a view of acres of gently sloping grasslands, punctuated by the radar antennae–covered summit of Laguna Peak (off-limits to hikers). Another 0.7 mile brings you to a junction with Chumash Trail heading right; go left to complete your loop. The path circles through more native grasses, offering wide-reaching ocean views, back to La Jolla Can-yon Trail. Turn right to head back the final mile to your car.

Options

Add on a detour around Mugu Peak on Chumash Trail and Mugu Peak Trail, which will add 1.5 miles to your loop. Mugu Peak at elevation 1,266 feet has a few planted pine trees and a sublime ocean view.

Directions

From U.S. 101 in Agoura Hills, exit at Kanan Road and drive 12.5 miles to Highway 1/Pacific Coast Highway on the Malibu coast. Turn west (right) and drive 14.8 miles to the La Jolla Canyon trailhead parking area on the right (one mile west of Big Sycamore Canyon Campground).

Information and Contact

A $4 day-use fee is charged per vehicle. Dogs are not allowed. A trail map is available for a fee at the entrance kiosk at Sycamore Canyon Campground, one mile south on Highway 1. A map of Point Mugu State Park is also available for a fee from Tom Harrison Maps, 800/265-9090, www.tomharrisonmaps.com. For more information, contact Point Mugu State Park, 9000 W. Pacific Coast Highway, Malibu, CA 90265, 805/488-5223 or 805/488-1827.

2 BIG SYCAMORE AND SERRANO CANYON LOOP
Point Mugu State Park

Level: Strenuous

Hiking Time: 5 hours

Total Distance: 10.0 miles round-trip

Elevation Gain: 1,400 feet

Summary: An all-day hike through some of the most remote land in Point Mugu State Park, with a guarantee of fine scenery and solitude.

Many seasoned L.A. hikers say you just can't "get lost" in the Santa Monica Mountains any more. There are too many roads, too many trails, and too much private property splitting up the open spaces. Here's a place at Point Mugu State Park where at least you can feel like you've gotten lost.

First, you'll want to come prepared. Most of the year this is a simple loop hike, but, in the wettest months, you'll have numerous stream crossings to negotiate. The water flow in Big Sycamore Canyon is not usually deep, but the stream flow can be very wide, requiring you to either take off your shoes and wade barefoot, or wear Tevas or other river shoes. There's no way to get by with rock-hopping. Second, you might want to bring a field guide with you for plant identification. There is an incredible amount of foliage variety on this hike. You'll travel through a sycamore-lined canyon, oak savannah, chaparral, grassy meadows, and finally a lush riparian corridor.

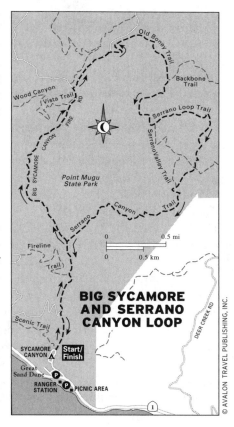

BIG SYCAMORE AND SERRANO CANYON LOOP

© AVALON TRAVEL PUBLISHING, INC.

Bikes are allowed on part of this loop (Big Sycamore Canyon only), but this isn't much of a concern. The riders we have met here have been very courteous.

Start at the wide gate at the end of Sycamore Canyon Campground and walk

© ANN MARIE BROWN

A piece of rusted machinery lies amid the grasslands in Serrano Canyon.

up the mostly level Big Sycamore Canyon Fire Road. True to this canyon's name, an abundance of sycamore trees line the path, and they have grown to grand proportions. In spring, the canyon blooms with big patches of sticky monkeyflower, morning glories, and lupine. Just past the second stream crossing, 1.1 miles from the start, you'll see the Serrano Canyon Trail turnoff on the right. Bypass it for now; this is the return of your loop. Ignore the numerous other side trails as well, and just stick to the wide dirt road through the middle of the canyon.

You have about eight stream crossings to make on Big Sycamore Canyon Trail. You'll complete your travel on this trail 0.6 mile past the Wood Canyon Fire Road turnoff. Here, a total of 3.7 miles from your start, is a small sign on the right for the Old Boney Trail turnoff, which is also a part of the Backbone Trail. The level, mellow grade you have been following ends abruptly with a turn on Old Boney. The trail is narrow and often overgrown, and it rises upward very quickly, cutting through a dense thicket of aromatic chaparral. You'll gain 1,000 feet in only 1.5 miles. After winter rains, the trail is usually badly eroded, with a deep cut down the middle from water runoff. In no time at all you have great views of Big Sycamore Canyon below you, but you may be huffing and puffing too hard, or sweating too profusely on these sun-baked slopes, to enjoy them.

You'll pass a junction with the Backbone Trail heading left; stay straight and climb some more. An array of spring wildflowers (nightshade, yarrow, Indian paintbrush, and more) graces this steep ridge and makes the ascent less punishing. A third of a mile later, you reach a high point on the ridge at 1,200 feet, capped by a beautiful meadowy grassland that makes an ideal picnic spot. Go ahead, have lunch, you deserve it. If it's a clear day, you'll have views down into both canyons—Big Sycamore and Serrano—and a peek at the ocean to the west. It is truly a blessing that there aren't condominiums or mega-mansions all over these hills.

It's almost all downhill from here. A third of a mile past your high lunch spot, bear left on the Serrano Loop Trail (unsigned). The trail descends and then rolls through a series of gorgeous meadows—what appears to be an endless expanse of grass punctuated by purple brodiaea in spring. You'll pass by the remains of a piece of old machinery, perhaps an engine for a tractor. After looping around these lush grasslands, you'll head south (right) and wind up on Serrano Canyon Trail, now joining its stream. This creek is exactly the opposite of what you saw in Big Sycamore Canyon. Instead of a wide swath of free-flowing water, Serrano Canyon is a boulder-choked, narrow, rushing watercourse. Along its edges are a huge variety of sylvan flora, from shady sycamores and oaks to ferns and poison oak. Poking out from the greenery are some odd-shaped volcanic outcrops. This stream is much easier to cross, even in the wet months, as it rarely reaches more than three feet wide. This is good news, since you must cross it more than a dozen times. At times, the creekbed simply becomes the trail.

Too soon, this leg on Serrano Canyon Trail is completed, and you are deposited back on Big Sycamore Canyon Trail only 1.1 mile from your car. Turn left and walk out this final mile with a smile on your face, knowing you have done something extraordinary with your day.

Options
Skip most of the fire road and take a simple out-and-back walk on Serrano Canyon Trail (the turnoff is 1.1 miles up the fire road).

Directions
From U.S. 101 in Agoura Hills, exit at Kanan Road and drive 12.5 miles to Highway 1/Pacific Coast Highway on the Malibu coast. Turn west (right) and drive 13.8 miles to Big Sycamore Canyon Campground at Point Mugu State Park. Park to the left of the entrance kiosk in the day-use lot, then walk to the far end of the campground to access the trailhead.

Information and Contact
A $10 day-use fee is charged per vehicle. Dogs are not allowed. A trail map of Point Mugu State Park is available for a fee at the campground entrance kiosk or from Tom Harrison Maps, 800/265-9090, www.tomharrisonmaps.com. For more information, contact Point Mugu State Park, 9000 W. Pacific Coast Highway, Malibu, CA 90265, 805/488-5223 or 805/488-1827.

3 SYCAMORE CANYON FALLS AND OLD CABIN SITE
Santa Monica Mountains National Recreation Area

Level: Easy/Moderate

Hiking Time: 3 hours

Total Distance: 6.8 miles round-trip

Elevation Gain: 750 feet

Summary: Easy access to the inviting trails of Point Mugu State Park from the inland side, just a few miles off U.S. 101.

The Santa Monica Mountains National Recreation Area Rancho Sierra Vista/Satwiwa Site is the very long name for the back door to Point Mugu State Park. It's a mouthful to say, but all you need to remember is Satwiwa, which means "the bluffs," the name of the Chumash Indian village that once existed here. Another thing worth remembering is that Point Mugu's back door is only a couple miles off U.S. 101, so there's no need to drive all the way to the coast to access these lovely trails.

Because of its location in the backyard of Thousand Oaks and Newbury Park, the Satwiwa Site is a popular place for after-work exercise and casual weekend hikes. A variety of loops and out-and-back routes are

SYCAMORE CANYON FALLS AND OLD CABIN SITE

possible, but, if you are visiting in the winter or spring months, you will probably want to go see the waterfall in Sycamore Canyon. The small fall is set in a lovely sandstone grotto, surrounded by ferns and sycamore trees. Shortly beyond the fall are the remains of an interesting piece of Santa Monica Mountains history. The trail to reach them both shows off aromatic chaparral, spring wildflowers, and an oak- and sycamore-lined stream. Canine lovers take note: dogs are allowed on the trails of Satwiwa Site but are not allowed past the Point Mugu State Park border.

Start from the trailhead at the junction of Wendy Drive and Potrero Road, following the Wendy Trail as it quickly ascends. (Pick up a trail map at the signboard before you start; there are multiple junctions to negotiate.) The simplest way to reach the waterfall is to follow a series of a half-dozen "lefts." The route will take you uphill first along Wendy Trail for 0.3 mile, then along the east side of the Satwiwa Loop Trail, past an old windmill and a junction with the Hidden Valley Overlook Trail, and then finally into Point Mugu State Park. Here, you finally quit climbing and head downhill on a wide dirt road, the Old Boney Trail.

Where Upper Sycamore Canyon Trail comes in sharply from the right, stay left on Old Boney Trail and cross the creek (an easy rock-hop even in winter and spring). You are now about two miles from your car. Walk about 100 yards and then make one final left. In about 50 yards of easy stream scrambling, you're at Sycamore Canyon Falls. The water pours, or trickles if it hasn't rained lately, over a series of sandstone ledges, artfully accented by huge woodwardia ferns, smaller sword ferns, and an overhanging canopy of sycamore and big-leaf maple leaves. The waterfall isn't huge or particularly forceful but rather more Zenlike in its appeal, dancing its way through a half dozen miniature pools and cascades.

After a visit, backtrack 50 yards to the start of the waterfall spur trail and head left. You'll switchback uphill, continuing on Old Boney Trail and gaining 450 feet. In 0.9 mile, where the trail forks, bear left. Less than 0.5 mile

© ANN MARIE BROWN

Large, spreading oaks line the creek below Sycamore Canyon Falls.

farther, you'll reach the stone remains of a herdsman's cabin. It was built sometime in the early 1900s when this area was used for cattle grazing. The cabin burned in a wildfire in the 1950s, and all that is left is a tall chimney and some scattered rocks from foundation walls. It's a good spot for a lunch break before retracing your steps to the trailhead.

Options

Loop aficionados can backtrack 0.3 mile from the old cabin site to Old Boney Trail, turn left, hike 1.4 miles to Fossil Trail, turn right, and hike one mile to Big Sycamore Canyon Fire Road. From there, it's a right turn and about two miles back to your car via the fire road and Wendy Trail. This makes a loop hike of just over eight miles.

Directions

From U.S. 101 in Thousand Oaks, exit on Wendy Drive and drive north for 2.9 miles to where Wendy Drive ends at Potrero Road. Park here and begin hiking at the signboard.

Information and Contact

There is no fee. Dogs on leash are allowed only on part of this loop; dogs are not allowed once you enter Point Mugu State Park. Free trail maps are available at the trailhead, or you can download one at www.nps.gov/samo/pphtml/maps.html. A map of Point Mugu State Park is available for a fee from Tom Harrison Maps, 800/265-9090, www.tomharrisonmaps.com. For more information, contact Santa Monica Mountains National Recreation Area, 401 West Hillcrest Drive, Thousand Oaks, CA 91360, 805/370-2301, www.nps.gov/samo.

4 THE GROTTO
Santa Monica Mountains National Recreation Area

Level: Easy

Total Distance: 3.4 miles round-trip

Hiking Time: 1.5 hours

Elevation Gain: 500 feet

Summary: A volcanic rock garden on the West Fork Arroyo Sequit creates a watery playground in summer and an awesome roar in winter.

Is it a waterfall or a boulder playground? It just depends on when you show up. Circle X Ranch's "the Grotto" is a rugged jumble of volcanic rocks, many as big as Volkswagens, over which the West Fork of Arroyo Sequit tumbles (or, in summer, lazily dribbles). Perhaps this boulder garden should be called the Playground instead of the Grotto, because in low water you can spend all day climbing around it, making use of millions of possible handholds and footholds. In high water, don't even attempt exploring. A slip on these rocks could mean a broken ankle or worse.

If it's your first visit, you'll notice that Circle X Ranch is a different ball of wax from the coastal parks in the Santa Monica Mountains. Located at a higher elevation, it's generally much warmer. Behind it looms a remarkable backdrop of craggy peaks, including Sandstone Peak, the highest summit in the Santa Monica Mountains at 3,111 feet. But down in the Grotto lies a lush riparian environment, overgrown with oaks, bay laurel, sycamores, and ferns. During the wet season, the noise of running water through the Grotto's jumble of boulders can be deafening. The splashing cascades create great echoing sounds as they bounce around the rocks. Soon after a rainstorm is by far the best time to hike here, when the creeks and cataracts in and around the Grotto are full and lively.

After a brief walk downhill from the Circle X Ranch ranger station parking lot, you access the Grotto by following the Grotto Trail from the ranch's group campground. The 1.3-mile trail makes a moderate descent on a pleasant grade. The 500-foot elevation loss must be gained back

© ANN MARIE BROWN

At the Grotto, a boulder playground of volcanic rock creates mini-waterfalls in the wet season.

on the return trip, but fortunately there is a good amount of shade along the route. Only 0.3 mile beyond the campground you meet up with Canyon View Trail coming in from the left. In a few footsteps, you cross over the brink of 35-foot-high Botsford Falls, named by the legions of Boy Scouts who frequent the Circle X Campground. After a stint through a lovely grassland meadow, the trail moves close to the water again. Another short stretch of trail and you come upon an overlook revealing two more waterfalls, one about 100 yards from the trail and a second 0.5 mile distant, across the canyon.

Keep traveling gently downhill on this charming pathway, and soon you emerge just above the sycamore-shaded Grotto. When the water is high, the trail disappears and you must boulder-hop to get a good look. Just keep heading downstream as far as it is safe to travel, then stand back and listen to the water roar. In the dry months, on the other hand, you can scramble around to your heart's content on these inviting volcanic rocks.

Options

To lengthen this hike, start at either of two trailheads on Yerba Buena Road, about one mile east of Circle X Ranch, and follow Canyon View Trail either 1.5 miles or 0.6 mile (depending on which trailhead you use) to the group campground and the Grotto Trail, then continue as above.

Directions

From Highway 1/Pacific Coast Highway in Malibu, drive northwest for 10 miles to Yerba Buena Road, 1.5 miles past Leo Carrillo State Park. Turn right and drive 5.3 miles up Yerba Buena Road to the entrance to Circle X Ranch on the right. Park by the ranger station, then follow the trail to the group campground. The Grotto Trail begins at the group camp.

Information and Contact

There is no fee. Dogs on leash are allowed. A free trail map is available at the Circle X Ranch visitor center, or you can download one at www.nps.gov/samo/pphtml/maps.html. A map of Point Mugu State Park, which includes Circle X Ranch, is available for a fee from Tom Harrison Maps, 800/265-9090, www.tomharrisonmaps.com. For more information, contact Santa Monica Mountains National Recreation Area, 401 W. Hillcrest Drive, Thousand Oaks, CA 91360, 805/370-2301, www.nps/gov/samo. Or contact Circle X Ranger Station at 310/457-6408.

5 SANDSTONE PEAK LOOP
Santa Monica Mountains National Recreation Area

Level: Moderate   **Total Distance:** 6.0 miles round-trip

Hiking Time: 3 hours   **Elevation Gain:** 1,300 feet

Summary: Climb to the tallest peak in the Santa Monica Mountains on this scenic loop hike near Circle X Ranch.

Take a drive on Yerba Buena Road, and you'll see some wild-looking volcanic outcrops towering over the hillsides. Take a walk on the Mishe Mokwa Trail, and you'll get an even better look at these strange rock formations, plus a chance to summit the highest peak in the Santa Monica Mountains, 3,111-foot Sandstone Peak.

The peak is accessible via two trails that form a loop—the Mishe Mokwa Trail and a fire road. Plenty of hikers in a hurry just head up the fire road, tag the summit, and head back down, but then they miss all the beauty of the meandering Mishe Mokwa Trail. Far better to go the long way—take your time heading uphill on Mishe Mokwa, enjoying wildflowers and rocky views, then make a quick descent on the fire road.

The trail begins at a small dirt parking area on Yerba Buena Road. The first half hour is a pleasant ascent through chapparal and spring wildflowers, including ceanothus, purple nightshade, Chinese houses, morning glories, and monkeyflower. The shrubby plants alternate with occasional copses of bay laurel and oak, where delicate ferns grow in the shady spots. In about a mile

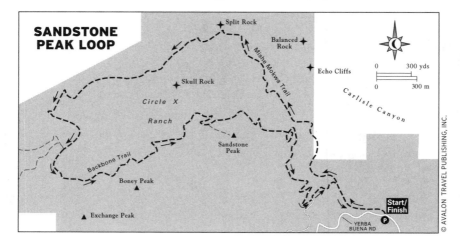

© ANN MARIE BROWN

hikers on the summit of 3,111-foot Sandstone Peak (a.k.a. Mount Allen)

of travel, a distinct outcrop named Balanced Rock comes into view on the op-posite wall of the canyon; you'll have no trouble identifying it. Rock climbers can be seen plying their trade on this and some of the other canyon formations. The Mishe Mokwa Trail surface gives you a clue as to why rock climbing is so popular here—the volcanic rock underfoot is rough in texture but solid, not crumbly or slippery. It makes for easy walking and safe climbing.

At 1.9 miles, you reach a stream crossing (may be dry in summer) and, on the far side, the Split Rock picnic area in a shady grove of oaks and sycamores. You will have no trouble picking out split rock, either; it is aptly named. It is a long-standing hiker's tradition to walk through the cleft in the rock, so go ahead, take your turn. A short spur trail leads from here to Balanced Rock, if you wish to get a close-up look at it.

Beyond Split Rock, Mishe Mokwa Trail now heads west and climbs again past hillsides dotted with still more huge volcanic outcrops. The trail is fairly exposed over the next mile, with much less shade than you enjoyed previously. You'll pass by a couple water towers as the path widens. At a junction 3.2 miles from your start, head left to join the Backbone Trail, now following a wide road.

In slightly less than a mile you'll reach a spur trail leading to Inspiration Point, a view-filled spot dedicated to a 17-year-old Boy Scout. It's worth the short detour just to take a look at the direction marker on top, which gives you some perspective on the remarkable view. The marker points out the Palos Verdes Peninsula, San Nicholas Island, San Clemente Island, Catalina Island, Mount Baldy, and many other landmarks. Yes, this is an inspiring spot, but an even better perspective awaits on 3,111-foot Sandstone Peak. Head back to the fire road, continue a few hundred feet, then follow the spur trail on your right up to the summit. This is the steepest part of your entire hike—some people even use their hands to help them up the final stretch.

A plaque on the summit may take you by surprise—it names this peak Mount Allen. Don't think you're in the wrong place; Sandstone Peak is known by two different names. Despite one of them, the peak is not sandstone at all, but a type of volcanic rock. But why concern yourself with geology or semantics when the view will steal your attention. Sandstone Peak's vista is sublime, especially on a clear day. Island-loving romantics will thrill to the fact that six different Channel Islands are in sight here, even Santa Cruz and Santa Rosa Islands, far to the north. The high peaks of the San Gabriel Mountains and the Ventura/Ojai backcountry can also be seen, as well as the often-hazy L.A. basin. A summit register allows you to pen a few clever words and leave your mark for posterity.

To finish out the loop, just continue on the fire road, which twists and turns steeply downhill. Don't miss the left turnoff to head back to the Mishe Mokwa Trailhead; if you stay on the fire road, you'll end up at a parking lot full of cars that don't look like yours.

Options
The Backbone trailhead is located 0.7 mile south on Yerba Buena Road. You can pick up Canyon View Trail on the south side of the road and follow it 1.5 miles to connect to the Grotto Trail. From that junction, the Grotto Trail travels one mile to the Grotto (see The Grotto listing in this chapter).

Directions
From Highway 1/Pacific Coast Highway in Malibu, drive northwest for 10.0 miles to Yerba Buena Road, 1.5 miles past Leo Carrillo State Park. Turn right and drive 3.9 miles up Yerba Buena Road to the Mishe Mokwa trailhead on the left (not the Backbone trailhead, which is 0.7 mile before the Mishe Mokwa trailhead).

Information and Contact
There is no fee. Dogs on leash are allowed. Download a park map from www.nps.gov/samo/pphtml/maps.html. A map of Point Mugu State Park, which includes the Sandstone Peak area, is available for a fee from Tom Harrison Maps, 800/265-9090, www.tomharrisonmaps.com. For more information, contact Santa Monica Mountains National Recreation Area, 401 West Hillcrest Drive, Thousand Oaks, CA 91360, 805/370-2301, www.nps.gov/samo.

6 WILDWOOD CANYON LOOP BEST ☾
Wildwood Park

🦌 🌼 🌿 🐕

Level: Easy | **Total Distance:** 3.2 miles round-trip
Hiking Time: 1.5 hours | **Elevation Gain:** 500 feet

Summary: An easy loop just off U.S. 101 offers spring wildflowers and a year-round waterfall.

With its proximity to U.S. 101, Wildwood Park is a perfect place for harried commuters to take a break from their cars and get back to nature. In the early morning and after-work hours, you'll see plenty of joggers and dog walkers here. Trails interweave throughout the park, so you can put together a different route every time you visit.

A popular, easy loop begins at the Arboles trailhead in Thousand Oaks. Take the trail by the signboard, Mesa Trail, and head due west across a wide grassland prairie. The first thing you'll notice is the looming rock formation to the north known as Mountclef Ridge, a volcanic outcrop that resulted from a series of eruptions which occurred some 30 million years ago. You'll see more of this craggy rock throughout the park, but, at least in the spring months, your attention will quickly be diverted to the myriad wildflowers that bloom in these grasslands. From late February to early June, you'll wander amid mariposa lilies, goldfields, tarweed, larkspur, lupine, wild onion, Indian paintbrush, tidytips, blue-eyed grass, and shooting stars.

One mile from the parking lot, turn left on the trail signed for Lizard Rock, then, in about 50 yards, turn left again on Stagecoach Bluff Trail. You'll

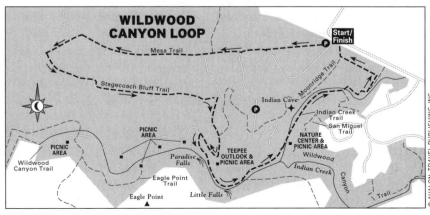

make an easy, level circle around the grassland mesa, enjoying more wildflowers and a few peeks down into Wildwood Canyon. Where the trail ends at a T junction with a dirt road, turn right and head downhill into the canyon. In about 200 yards, you'll come to a tepee display and another T junction. Turn right on Tepee Trail and follow the signs to Wildwood Falls, also called Paradise Falls. A series of stair steps leads you past a few picnic tables to the base of the impressive, 70-foot-tall falls. You may catch a telltale whiff of sulphur, a clue that the waterfall is fed by an underground spring and thus runs year-round, although less enthusiastically in summer and fall. The basalt of the waterfall's cliff was formed by the same volcanic action that created Montclef Ridge.

Wildwood Falls, Wildwood Canyon Park

© ANN MARIE BROWN

Enjoy the coolness of the falls, then follow Wildwood Canyon Trail upstream to the waterfall's brink and beyond. Wildwood Creek slips and slides over rocks in its rush to leap over the waterfall; a chain-link fence keeps hikers from tumbling down the steep drop-offs. The presence of year-round water makes this area a haven for wildlife; keep on the lookout for mule deer, rabbits, coyotes, and numerous songbirds and raptors. The park's impressive wildlife list includes 60 species of birds, 37 species of mammals, and 22 species of amphibians and reptiles.

Near a major junction of trails by the small Meadows Cave nature center, pick up Indian Creek Trail and follow it out for 0.5 mile out of the canyon and back uphill to Avenida de Los Arboles, the road you drove in on. Turn left and follow the trail that parallels the road for a short distance, which brings you back to within a few feet of your car.

Options

For a longer, wilder hike in Wildwood Park, stay on Mesa Trail past the first Lizard Rock turnoff and follow it as it joins with Box Canyon Trail. Bear left at a second turnoff for Lizard Rock 0.5 mile farther (careful—it's easy to miss) and climb very steeply to the rock, a basalt outcrop at a high point of 931 feet. From there, hike east, descending steeply into Wildwood Canyon. Follow Wildwood Canyon Trail to the waterfall and then loop back on Indian Creek Trail as above. This will add two more miles and another 800 feet of elevation gain to your hike.

Directions

From U.S. 101 in Thousand Oaks, take the Lynn Road exit and head north. Drive 2.5 miles to Avenida de los Arboles, then turn left. Drive 0.9 mile and make a U-turn into the Arboles parking lot on the left side of the road.

Information and Contact

There is no fee. Dogs on leash are allowed. A free trail map is available at park trailheads. For more information, contact Conejo Recreation and Park District, 403 West Hillcrest Drive, Thousand Oaks, CA 91360, 805/381-2741 or 805/495-6471, www.crpd.org.

7 NICHOLAS FLAT TRAIL   BEST ℂ
Leo Carrillo State Park

🏕 🦌 🌸

Level: Moderate	**Total Distance:** 7.0 miles round-trip
Hiking Time: 3.5 hours	**Elevation Gain:** 1,700 feet

Summary: A climb from sea level to a high point in Leo Carrillo State Park, where a tranquil pond is a haven for birds and wildlife.

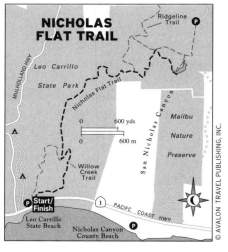

Leo Carrillo State Park is probably best known for its scenic beach—sculpted with sea caves, tunnels, and tidepools, and crowded with surfers, swimmers, and sunbathers—and popular car campground. Only in recent years has this park graduated from a "state beach" designation to a "state park" designation. But there are rewards at Leo Carrillo for hikers and nature lovers as well. The Nicholas Flat Trail is the park's best hiker's pathway, a fairly steep trail that climbs to a pond at Nicholas Flat, where red-wing blackbirds and other songbirds like to spend their days. Because of the substantial ascent involved, you'll quickly leave behind most of the campers and beachgoers that crowd the lower reaches of the park.

The trail begins a few yards from the entrance kiosk at the park's campground. (You'll probably want to park on the highway to avoid the $10 day-use fee here.) Almost immediately you come to a trail fork, with Nicholas Flat Trail on the left and Willow Creek on the right. Although Nicholas Flat will be your trail for most of the day, take Willow Creek Trail now. The two paths join again less than a mile away, and, in this stretch, Willow Creek Trail is a better choice. The grade is mellower and the scenery is much better because your ears aren't assaulted by the noise of motorcycles on Muholland Highway, and your eyes are shielded from the sight of the campground below. Follow the meandering Willow Creek Trail as it switchbacks uphill along flower-filled canyon slopes, then, where it meets with Nicholas Flat Trail again, take the short left spur signed for "Ocean Vista." This overlook delivers on its promise and is a wonderful spot to look for passing gray whales from December to April.

After a few wistful glances at the sea, continue uphill on the Nicholas Flat Trail (after leaving the overlook, go straight at the four-way junction). The climb gets steeper from here, and you'll gain 1,200 feet as you climb along an extended ridgeline, but you are rewarded with many more spectacular vistas along the way (just turn around and take a look), plus, in spring, a bonanza of wildflowers—mariposa lilies, poppies, golden yarrow, and popcorn flower among them.

At 2.7 miles from the start, after the trail has attained its highest point, you reach a junction of trails, shortly followed by another junction. Follow the signs, and you'll come out at the man-made pond at Nicholas Flat after a total 3.5 miles of hiking. If you've seen the small pond at nearby La Jolla Canyon in Point Mugu State Park, the size of this pond will surprise you. Originally used for cattle ranching, the huge pond is mostly tule-lined except for its southwest edge, which has some large boulders you might want to climb around on. Unfortunately, they are jealously guarded by poison oak, so use caution. The best place for nontoxic seating is under a live oak on the pond's northeast side. Sit still for a moment, and you'll notice that the pond is a very birdy place. Red-winged blackbirds, starlings, mallards, coots, and myriad other species can be seen by those willing to wait and watch. A small, lightweight pair of binoculars would come in handy here.

the western edge of the tule-lined pond at Nicholas Flat

If the best spots around the pond are already taken, you can follow a half-mile loop around the grasslands at Nicholas Flat and pick another spot for a rest and a picnic lunch. A spider web of paths crisscross the area, so make sure you have your bearings so you know where to find the main trail for your return. With a little exploring, it becomes obvious that a nearly vertical wall of rock on the south side of the pond, where San Nicholas Canyon rises straight up from the ocean, has created this high plateau and a natural dam for the pond.

When it's time to start making your way back down the hill, the best part of the trip is about to start. Not only is the route entirely downhill except for a brief initial climb, but you can look forward to nearly nonstop ocean views all the way.

Options

With a shuttle car, you can turn this into a one-way hike downhill. Drive one car up Decker Road to the left turnoff for Decker School Road. Turn left there and follow Decker School Road to its end. This is the upper end of the Nicholas Flat Trail. Follow it 0.4 mile to the pond, then head right on either of two trails to continue down to the campground entrance and your waiting shuttle car.

Directions

From U.S. 101 in Agoura Hills, exit at Kanan Road and drive 12.5 miles to Highway 1/Pacific Coast Highway on the Malibu coast. Turn west (right) and drive eight miles to Leo Carrillo State Park. Turn right into the park entrance and park in the day-use lot (fee charged), or park for free on Pacific Coast Highway just outside the park entrance. The Nicholas Flat Trail begins by the entrance kiosk on the inland side of the highway.

Information and Contact

A $10 day-use fee is charged per vehicle, or you can park for free on Pacific Coast Highway. Dogs are not allowed. A trail map is available for a fee at the campground entrance station or from Tom Harrison Maps, 800/265-9090, www.tomharrisonmaps.com (the Point Mugu State Park map includes Leo Carrillo State Park). For more information, contact Leo Carrillo State Park, 35000 W. Pacific Coast Highway, Malibu, CA 90265, 805/488-5223, 805/488-1827, or 818/880-0350, www.parks.ca.gov.

8 NEWTON CANYON FALLS AND ZUMA RIDGE

Santa Monica Mountains National Recreation Area

Level: Moderate

Total Distance: 6.8 miles round-trip

Hiking Time: 3.5 hours

Elevation Gain: 500 feet

Summary: A short jaunt to three waterfalls followed by a longer stroll on the Backbone Trail to Zuma Ridge.

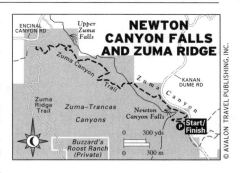

Waterfalls that are easy to reach are in short supply in Southern California. Many require hours of bushwhacking to spots that aren't on any map. The first waterfall on this trip is ideal for those hiking with small children and water-loving dogs. The second and third falls are, well, more of an adventure. And whether you are the adventuring type or not, afterward you'll enjoy taking a 2.5 mile out-and-back hike on the Backbone Trail through Zuma Canyon.

Winter and spring are ideal for hiking to Newton Canyon Falls, which runs all year but is especially impressive following a good rainy season. The trailhead is along Kanan Dume Road, at a parking pullout with a big Backbone Trail sign. There is also a brand-new bus shelter and sign for the National Park Service's ParkLink Shuttle, which began operating in 2005 and transports hikers and bikers to and from a number of shuttle stops in the Santa Monica Mountains National Recreation Area.

There are two Backbone trailhead signs on opposite sides of the parking lot. You want the one on the right (north) side, for the Zuma Canyon Trail, which leads to Zuma Ridge Motorway. The other trail goes east on the Backbone, toward Latigo Canyon.

Right away the trail begins to descend into Newton Canyon, a little slice of watery paradise parallel to and just below Kanan Dume Road. The cool and shady canyon is lined with ferns and other lush vegetation, including sunflowers and miner's lettuce.

The trail switchbacks downhill to the left, crosses Newton Canyon Creek, and in only about 10 minutes of walking you'll note a left turnoff. Follow it downhill and you find yourself on top of a 25-foot waterfall, where Newton Creek slides down a vertical, moss-covered limestone face. Big boulders above the fall's lip make a nice picnic spot, but watch your footing; it's a two-story drop to the fall's base. To access the base by walking, not falling, descend on one of the spur trails just beyond the waterfall's crest, then head upstream a few yards. The watery scene is set in a rounded rock grotto, where small sandstone caves surround the fall. With all the leafy trees, winding vines, ferns, and thick moss, you might think you are someplace in the tropics, not the near-desert of Los Angeles.

Follow the creek downstream from this upper fall for about 100 yards to the top of Lower Newton Canyon Falls, being careful to avoid ticks and abundant poison oak. You'll have to do some boulder-hopping, which can be easy or difficult, depending on how much water is in the stream. This lower fall is taller than the upper but has less water flowing over it. By late spring, every inch of it is covered with greenery, like a Rose Parade float. You can hardly see the water through the leaves.

Now do some soul-searching. It's up to you and your scrambling abilities whether you want to go any farther. There is plenty of risk involved in climbing down to the base of Lower Newton Falls because the slope is nearly vertical and

© JULIE SHEER

the brink of Newton Falls

often muddy, especially after recent rains. Even experienced climbers can slip and fall. If you can safely manage the drop, you'll gain access to Zuma Canyon, at the point were Zuma and Newton creeks join. Head to the right (east) for five more minutes of stream scrambling to Zuma Canyon Falls. Although it's only 25 feet tall, its setting is a piece of artwork. The fall drops over a sandstone ledge surrounded by small caves and ferns, and it has a double pool—two basins divided by a rock ledge—at its base. In high water, the waterfall's flow spills from one pool to the next. When the stream warms up, swimming is best in the lower, deeper pool.

Those who don't want to make the descent to Zuma Falls, or those who do but still have energy to burn afterwards, should return to the main trail above Upper Newton Canyon Falls (the first one you visited). Head left on the Backbone Trail to continue along Zuma Canyon to Zuma Ridge, 2.5 miles farther. Compared to the adventure you just had, this trail is a simple walk in the park, with a mellow grade and plentiful canyon views. The trail meets up with Zuma Ridge Trail just 0.4 mile from Encinal Canyon Road, so you can make this a one-way hike if you can arrange a shuttle car. Otherwise, just head back the way you came for a total 6.8-mile round-trip.

Options
The other segment of Backbone Trail that starts at the Kanan Road Trailhead is a 2.5-mile stretch that travels east (it crosses over the tunnel on Kanan Road), to the Latigo Canyon Trailhead. From there, you can continue hiking into Castro Crest.

Directions
From Highway 1/Pacific Coast Highway in Malibu, turn north on Kanan Dume Road and drive 4.3 miles to the Backbone Trail trailhead, which is on the left, just past the tunnel.

Alternatively, from U.S. 101 in Agoura Hills, exit at Kanan Road and drive 7.6 miles south to the trailhead on the right.

Public transportation: The Kanan Trailhead for the Backbone Trail is a shuttle stop on the National Park Service's new ParkLink shuttle system. For information, call 888/734-2323, www.parklinkshuttle.com.

Information and Contact
There is no fee. Dogs are allowed. Download a park map from www.nps.gov/samo/pphtml/maps.html. A detailed trail map of Zuma/Trancas Canyons is available for a fee from Tom Harrison Maps, 800/265-9090, www.tomharrisonmaps.com. For more information, contact the Santa Monica Mountains National Recreation Area, 401 W. Hillcrest Drive, Thousand Oaks, CA 91360, 805/370-2301, www.nps.gov/samo.

🄈 POINT DUME BEACH WALK   BEST ◖

Point Dume State Preserve

Level: Easy   **Total Distance:** 4.0 miles round-trip

Hiking Time: 2 hours   **Elevation Gain:** 100 feet

Summary: Hike to a high ocean overlook at Point Dume, then explore tide-pools and hidden coves along a scenic stretch of Malibu coastline.

Located just a few miles south of popular Zuma Beach is another strip of sand that is decidedly un-Zuma. That means you won't find hot dog stands or volleyball nets here, but you will find a vast network of rocky tidepools, a high and inspiring ocean overlook, and the chance to spot gray whales up close during their winter and spring migration.

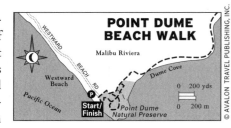

Although the beach and preserve are owned by the state, they are accessed by parking at Westward Beach, which is managed by L.A. County. This means, unfortunately, that you must pay a hefty parking fee, even heftier in the summer months. It also means less people—the parking fee discourages many visitors, and the short walk to reach Point Dume's tidepools, sheer cliffs, and brayed-tan sand keeps others away.

You might notice an interesting piece of trivia at the parking lot. If the large lifeguard tower looks familiar, it's because it was used in the opening scenes of the popular television show Baywatch.

Right from the trailhead, at the far end of the parking lot, you'll be treated to an intriguing sight. Rock climbers are often seen repelling off the high cliffs on the east end of Westward Beach. Enjoy their acrobatics as you ascend up the railroad-tie stair steps that start the trail. When you reach the top of the sandy bluff, you'll find a boardwalk-lined overlook and a Point Dume historical marker. The point was named after a religious figure by a British naval commander in the late 18th century. But it's the ocean view from this high triangle of land that will take your breath away, if the bluff climb hasn't already. In spring, the bluff tops are colored yellow with the cheerful blooms of giant coreopsis and prickly pear cactus.

From this high point, trails branch out in several directions, but you simply parallel the ocean's edge. The trail is lined with rope to keep people from

© ANN MARIE BROWN

searching for tidepool creatures at Point Dume Beach

straying off the path and destroying the fragile vegetation. Only 0.3 mile from your start, you reach a staircase that leads down to the beach on the far side of the point. Hopefully you planned your visit for a very low or minus tide. If so, your trip will now slow down to a crawl, as there is much treasure hunting to be done in the reef (but remember that all these sea creatures are protected—look all you want, but don't remove anything from its rocky home). Starfish, sea urchins, and hermit crabs are common here.

Beyond the tidepools, you can continue walking down the sandy beach for another mile, enjoying towering sandstone cliffs, views of Catalina Island, and the entire expanse of Santa Monica Bay. Your walk ends at Paradise Cove Resort, a popular film location and the site of a beachside restaurant and private fishing pier. From here, turn around and retrace your steps back to Westward Beach.

Directions

From U.S. 101 in Agoura Hills, exit at Kanan Road and drive 12.5 miles to Highway 1/Pacific Coast Highway on the Malibu coast. Turn west (right) and drive 0.9 mile to the Westward Beach Road turnoff on the left. Turn left (south) and drive 1.3 miles to the far end of the last parking lot, where the trail begins.

Information and Contact

A $6 day-use fee (varies by season) is charged per vehicle. Dogs are not allowed. No trail map is available. For more information, contact California State Parks, 1925 Las Virgenes Road, Calabasas, CA 91302, 818/880-0350, www.parks.ca.gov.

⑩ ESCONDIDO CANYON AND FALLS   BEST ☾
Escondido Canyon Natural Area

🌿 🕸️ 🐾

Level: Easy/Moderate

Hiking Time: 2 hours

Total Distance: 4.2 miles round-trip

Elevation Gain: 250 feet

Summary: A stroll through a sylvan canyon to the tallest and most beautiful of all the waterfalls in the Santa Monica Mountains.

This is a strange and wonderful waterfall hike. The strange part? You have to walk a mile just to reach the trailhead, following a paved road through an opulent neighborhood of gargantuan Malibu homes. As you walk by these mansions dressed in your hiking clothes, you half expect a resident to ask if you are looking for a job raking leaves or pulling weeds. But, no, they are accustomed to hikers wandering by.

The wonderful part? The payoff is access to a charming sylvan footpath in Escondido Canyon, where a huge, multitiered limestone waterfall awaits—the highest cataract in the Santa Monica Mountains.

Start your trip at the well-signed hikers' parking lot at the start of Winding Way. Walk up the paved road for one mile, gaining ocean views as you climb. Try not to gawk

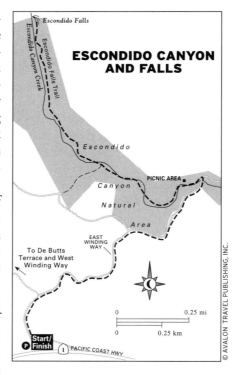

too much at all the affluence. When you reach the trail sign for the Santa Monica Mountains Conservancy lands, veer off to the left, heading into the canyon.

Walk upstream, ignoring all trail junctions and keeping close to the creek. You'll cross it a half dozen times, and, if the water is running high, you will have no choice but to get your feet wet. The lush canyon trail is nearly level, extremely well maintained, and gorgeous to boot. Most of the path is shaded by sycamore trees, but coastal sage scrub and wildflowers make an appearance, too. On a spring day, there isn't a more pleasant walk anywhere in the Los Angeles basin.

In 0.5 mile, you'll catch a glimpse of the big waterfall far ahead, tucked into the back of a high box canyon. One look will be enough to make you quicken your pace. Fifteen minutes later you'll be standing at the base of the lower tier of Escondido Canyon's limestone fall, oohing and aahing at the 50-foot length of streaming water pouring over a wealth of ferns and moss. Horsetail ferns grow around its base, and a couple of rope swings hang from a sycamore tree. The rotten-egg smell of sulphur, coming from the spring that gives birth to this stream, is often very noticeable here.

the upper tier of Escondido Falls

© ANN MARIE BROWN

If your scrambling skills are good, don't stop here. That big cataract you saw a half mile back is still waiting above this one, and it is accessible by following the use trail on the right side of the fall. This easy stroll through the canyon now becomes an adventure, and it's a good idea to know your limits before you start. Ask yourself a few questions: Is the slope dry? Are you wearing solid lug-soled boots? Are you comfortable with off-trail scrambling? If you answered yes to all of the above, a careful 15-minute ascent using both hands and feet will get you to the upper fall, an immense limestone tier that is 150 feet high. Along the way, you'll pass a middle cascade about 15 feet high. The scrambling becomes more challenging on the final push to the upper fall.

A common remark heard at this spot on one April day was simply "wow." Yes, this is a "wow" waterfall. You'll want to kick off your shoes and wade into its shallow pool. If you do, be careful not to step on the giant newts who make their home here. They are unusually large water babies, appropriately oversized to match this amazing cataract.

Options

If after visiting Escondido Falls you are hankering for a little more exercise, drive 2.4 miles west on Highway 1/PCH to a right turn on Bonsall Drive, across from Westward Beach Road. Drive to the end of the road and the trailhead for Lower Zuma Canyon, where you can choose from several trail options. Our suggestion is a loop on Ocean View and Canyon Trails, followed by an out and back on Zuma Canyon Trail, about four miles total.

Directions

From U.S. 101 in Agoura Hills, exit at Kanan Road and drive 12.5 miles to Highway 1/Pacific Coast Highway on the Malibu coast. Turn left (east) and drive 1.4 miles to Winding Way East. Turn left, then left again immediately into the well-signed parking lot.

Information and Contact

There is no fee. Dogs on leash are allowed. Download a free trail map at www .lamountains.com (click on Hiking Trails and scroll down to Escondido Canyon). A map of Malibu Creek State Park, which includes Escondido Canyon Natural Area, is available for a fee from Tom Harrison Maps, 800/265-9090, www.tomharrisonmaps.com. For more information, contact the Santa Monica Mountains Conservancy, 5750 Ramirez Canyon Road, Malibu, CA 90265, 310/589-3200 or 310/858-7272, www.lamountains.com.

11 SOLSTICE CANYON AND SOSTOMO TRAIL LOOP

Santa Monica Mountains National Recreation Area

Level: Strenuous

Total Distance: 6.3 miles round-trip

Hiking Time: 3 hours

Elevation Gain: 1,800 feet

Summary: An easy "walk in the park" followed by a more strenuous loop to a high, remote ocean overlook.

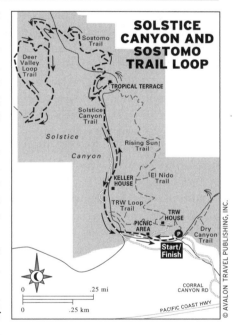

Solstice Canyon is one of the loveliest canyons in the Santa Monica Mountains, a range that has no shortage of lovely canyons. Solstice Creek is a playful year-round watercourse that flows beneath a canopy of spreading oaks and big sycamores, including some remarkably large and old trees. The lower trails in Solstice Canyon are popular with families and casual weekend walkers, but the upper trails are much less visited and much more wild. Why not see them both on this 6.3-mile ramble around the park?

From the parking area, walk up the paved road, called Solstice Canyon Trail, which parallels Solstice Creek. The creek makes fine company along the way, as do the many bunches of orange sticky monkeyflower and colorful but nonnative mustard. Where the road reaches a T junction, bear right and continue up the canyon. The paved road becomes more broken and rustic looking as you travel, until eventually it dissolves into dirt.

Pass by the 1865 Keller house, a small stone cottage that's the oldest in Malibu. It's now a private residence. Continue past the left turnoff for Sostomo Trail and Deer Valley Loop for a short distance to the ruins of Tropical Terrace, the 1950s home of the Fred and Florence Roberts family. This beautiful home and its exotic, terraced gardens were destroyed by a fire in 1982, although its foundations, flagstone walkways, and fireplaces remain. It is obvious that the gardens were resplendent in their heyday. Even now an array of overgrown palm trees, birds-of-paradise, and other tropical plants thrive among the native sycamores. The Roberts also kept giraffes, camels, and exotic birds. Be sure to walk past the house ruins to see Tropical Terrace's natural waterfall, a 30-foot-high cascade on Solstice Creek.

After a pause to admire the cataract and the remains of the Roberts' home, backtrack 100 feet to the Sostomo Trail fork. A turnoff onto this trail suddenly changes this hike from an easy stroll to a strenuous (but worthwhile) trek. You'll face a lot of "up" over the next 1.3 miles, but it takes place on a beautiful single-track trail, complete with plentiful shade and solitude.

old stone cabin ruins along the Sostomo Trail Loop

Sostomo Trail ascends immediately, passing a landslide resulting from the heavy rains of the winter of 2005. After a steady climb over 0.5 mile, the trail levels out and crosses Solstice Creek. An abandoned cabin can be seen by the stream crossing, in a forest thick with oaks and bay laurel. Sostomo Trail continues its ascent, and, near the top amid an abundance of ceanothus, California fuschia, and other soft chaparral plants, you'll notice a lone pine tree growing on the right side of the trail, peculiarly out of place.

A half mile past the last stream crossing you'll pass alongside a fence marking private property and then begin a steep downhill tromp to cross Solstice Creek once more—your first break from climbing in a while. The sylvan setting at the crossing makes a photogenic spot, with big woodwardia ferns drooping their fronds over deep, clear pools. Take a break here before beginning yet another stage of ascent. A few yards beyond the creek crossing is the remains of another stone-walled cottage.

You'll reach the beginning of the 1.3-mile Deer Valley Loop Trail at 3.4 miles from the start. Go left first to hike the loop in the easiest direction. In less than a half mile, the tunnel of dense foliage surrounding the trail opens out to offer a spectacular, and surprising, ocean view. You've been in the shady forest for so long that you may have forgotten you how close the coast is. Choose a view-filled spot along this open stretch to have your lunch.

When you get back on the trail, your loop soon junctions with a dirt road coming in from the west, but your trail turns sharply right to circle back. In another 0.5 mile you'll be back at Sostomo Trail, where you turn left to retrace your steps back to Tropical Terrace, then go right to head back to your car.

Options
On your return trip, take Rising Sun Trail back to the trailhead from Tropical Terrace instead of backtracking on Solstice Canyon Trail. Cross the creek below the waterfall to join Rising Sun Trail.

Directions
From U.S. 101 in Agoura Hills, exit at Kanan Road and drive 12.5 miles to Highway 1/Pacific Coast Highway on the Malibu coast. Turn left (east) and drive 3.6 miles to Corral Canyon Road. Turn left and drive 0.2 mile to the park entrance on the left. Turn left and drive 0.3 mile to the parking area.

Public transportation: Solstice Canyon Park is a shuttle stop on the National Park Service's new ParkLink shuttle system. For information, call 888/734-2323 or visit www.parklinkshuttle.com.

Information and Contact
There is no fee. Dogs on leash are allowed. A free trail map is available at the trailhead, or you can download one at www.nps.gov/samo/pphtml/maps.html. A map of Malibu Creek State Park, which includes Solstice Canyon, is available for a fee from Tom Harrison Maps, 800/265-9090, www.tomharrison-maps.com. For more information, contact Santa Monica Mountains National Recreation Area, 401 W. Hillcrest Drive, Thousand Oaks, CA 91360, 805/370-2301, www.nps.gov/samo.

12 CASTRO CREST   BEST ◖
Santa Monica Mountains National Recreation Area

🏕 🌼 🐴

Level: Easy   **Total Distance:** 5.2 miles round-trip

Hiking Time: 2.5 hours   **Elevation Gain:** 350 feet

Summary: An appealing segment of the Backbone Trail with ocean views and otherworldly rock formations.

This excellent hike would be twice as good if it could be turned into a loop hike. You can try to make a loop—many hikers do—but only if you are not intimidated by giant gates, yellow "no trespassing" signs, and barbed wire. (More on this later.) As it is, an out-and-back hike on the Backbone 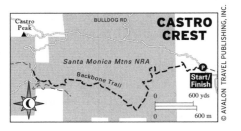 Trail is still satisfying. Castro Crest is a scenic chunk of National Park Service land that butts up against Malibu Creek State Park to the northeast. Several trails lead into the park.

Start by driving up the twisting, steep Corral Canyon Road from Malibu. This is probably the most scenic, circuitous five miles of driving in the Santa Monicas, so keep your eyes on the road, then park in the dirt lot at road's end. Two trailheads are on the left (west) side of the lot. The trailhead on the right (north) is the Castro Fire Road, also known as Castro Peak Motorway. In a perfect world you would return on this road to close out a loop, but, as you hike the Backbone, you'll see in about 2.8 miles why you can't finish the loop.

Instead, for an out-and-back hike, you'll want the Backbone Trail, on the left. The trail descends into upper Solstice Canyon. You'll hike along a shaded creek, crossing it several times. The forest is heavily wooded in spots, alternating with open canyon views. In the spring, the area surrounding the trail is like an overgrown cottage garden, with natural bouquets of larkspur, lupine, monkeyflower, phacelia, and mariposa lily.

As you begin to ascend out of the canyon, you'll glimpse some sandstone outcroppings. A few radio towers come into view, ahead and to the right. When you reach the top of the ridge at 2.6 miles, the trail flattens and the views expand. Castro Peak is directly north and Sandstone Peak to the west; the blue Pacific Ocean beckons to the south.

Here, your options narrow. If you continue heading north (right) on Castro

Fire Road, you'll run into the aforementioned gates and blaring yellow and red signs. Technically, about 200 yards of trail are on private land, owned by someone who also owns some of the radio towers on the surrounding peaks. Unfortunately, a dispute between the landowner and the National Park Service turned nasty in 2003 and 2004, spurring the owner to put up the gate, signs, and even barbed wire. The animosity is mostly toward the Park Service, as evidenced by one of the signs, which reads in red letters, "No Trespassing—this especially applies to NPS Rangers!". There is enough room to walk around the gate, and many trail users do just that. The return on Castro Fire Road is only 2.2 miles (a bit shorter than hiking out and back on Backbone Trail).

If you obey the signs and retrace your steps on Backbone Trail, be sure to hike the Castro Fire Road as a separate trip someday, leaving from the parking lot on the trailhead to the right. There is 575 feet of gain from that direction, with views toward Westlake Village. The rock formations at the top are well worth the hike. Eroded pink rock stacks look like something from another planet. Caves, tilted rock, and stone layers embedded in sandstone are clearly visible—a geologist's dream.

Hopefully some day everyone's differences will be ironed out, the gates and nasty signs will come down, and hikers can enjoy the loop hike they deserve.

© JULIE SHEER

Unique sandstone formations can be seen on the Castro Fire Road.

Options

When you reach the ridge top at Castro Fire Road, you can continue west on the Backbone Trail at a small sign across the road on the left. From here it is 1.4 miles to Latigo Canyon. If you hike up the Castro Fire Road from the trailhead, you can head into Malibu Creek State Park by turning right on Bulldog Motorway, 0.8 mile from the trailhead. From there, it is about four miles to the *M.A.S.H.* television show site.

Directions

From U.S. 101 in Agoura Hills, exit at Kanan Road and drive 12.5 miles to Highway 1/Pacific Coast Highway on the Malibu coast. Turn left (east) and drive 3.7 miles to Corral Canyon Road. Turn left and drive 5.2 miles until the road ends. Park in the trail-head lot.

Information and Contact

There is no fee. Dogs on leash are allowed. A trail map of Malibu Creek State Park, which includes Castro Crest, is available for a fee from Tom Harrison Maps, 800/265-9090, www.tomharrisonmaps.com. For more information, contact the Santa Monica Mountains National Recreation Area, 401 W. Hillcrest Drive, Thousand Oaks, CA 91360, 805/370-2301, www.nps.gov/samo.

13 CHEESEBORO CANYON TRAIL TO SULPHUR SPRINGS

Cheeseboro and Palo Comado Canyons

Level: Easy/Moderate   **Total Distance:** 6.2 miles round-trip

Hiking Time: 3 hours   **Elevation Gain:** 500 feet

Summary: Enjoy easy canyon and hillside hiking in a pastoral setting of ecological interest near Agoura Hills.

Cheeseboro and Palo Comado Canyons are lands abundant with hiking opportunities. A number of out-and-back and loop hikes are possible, along with connecting trails to the newer Las Virgenes Open Space Preserve, directly to the east. Cheeseboro Canyon Trail is the canyon's main byway, an old ranch road left over from when this area was heavily grazed. Before the 150 years of ranching history, the canyons were home to Chumash Indians for thousands of years. Grizzly bears once thrived here, but they were killed off by ranchers.

Today, you'll see hillsides covered with grasses and peppered with valley oaks and coast live oaks. In the spring, the grasslands are vibrant green and the hillsides are painted yellow with black mustard, a non-native plant that, along with other introduced European annuals such as wild oats and thistle, has adapted

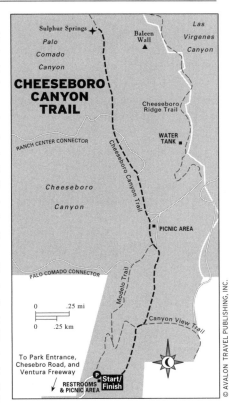

well to our Mediterranean climate and supplanted much of the native vegetation. The mustard is Cheeseboro's signature springtime plant and certainly provides a welcome burst of color, but, unlike native plants, mustard doesn't hold up eroding slopes, and its dried stalks contain a chemical that can prevent other plants from growing. Interpretive signs in the park explain ongoing revegetation efforts designed to replace mustard and other introduced plants with native grasses and shrubs, in order to restore this land to its natural, pregrazed state.

You will also see plenty of native birds in the canyon. Hawks soar overhead, and, if you keep an eye out along the trail, you're bound to see bright yellow goldfinches clinging to the taller strands of grass. Bird-watchers flock to this canyon in fall, winter, and spring. Cheeseboro has one of the largest concentrations of raptor nesting sites in California. In the mornings and evenings, watch for mule deer grazing in the meadows and on the hillsides, and coyotes roaming the grasslands.

Dogs and horses are popular at Cheeseboro and, because the trails here are mostly fire roads, they are extremely popular with mountain bikers. The best seasons to hike here are fall through spring, as the inland canyons bake in the summer.

Cheeseboro Canyon Trail is a fire road from the trailhead until it hits Sulphur Springs, where it turns into single-track trail. After a gentle ascent at the start, the trail remains mostly level for the first mile. At the junction with a connector to Cheeseboro Ridge Trail, at about 1.5 miles, stay to the left. The trail soon joins a creek, which in most years is dry by midspring but can be impassable after extremely heavy rains. Along the trail is a lovely forest of valley and live oaks. A little over three miles in, you'll detect a rotten egg odor. This is Sulphur Springs, where there isn't much to see, but the aroma is noticeable. Make this your turnaround point, then retrace your steps to your car.

Options

You can hike a loop on Cheeseboro Canyon and Palo Comado Canyon Trails by heading north on Cheeseboro Canyon Trail for 2.5 miles. Turn left on the 1.1-mile Ranch Center Connector, then left (south) on Palo Comado Canyon Trail for about three miles to Modelo Trail.

Cheeseboro Canyon is lush with vegetation in the spring.

© JULIE SHEER

Turn right and go one mile, then turn right on Modelo Spur 0.7 mile to the parking lot. This is an 8.3-mile loop.

Directions
From U.S. 101 in Agoura Hills, exit on Chesebro Road. Go one block and turn north on Palo Comado Canyon Road. Drive 0.3 mile to Chesebro Road and turn right. Continue 0.7 mile to the Cheeseboro Canyon entrance. Turn right and drive 0.2 mile to the parking lot.

Information and Contact
There is no fee. Dogs are allowed. Free trail maps are available at the kiosk at the trailhead, or you can download a map at www.nps.gov/samo/pphtml/maps.html. For more information, contact the Santa Monica Mountains National Recreation Area, 401 W. Hillcrest Drive, Thousand Oaks, CA 91360, 805/370-2301, www.nps.gov/samo.

14 EAST LAS VIRGENES CANYON TRAIL TO LASKY MESA

Las Virgenes Canyon Open Space Preserve

🏕 🚴 🌸 🐴

Level: Easy   **Total Distance:** 5.5 miles round-trip

Hiking Time: 2.5 hours   **Elevation Gain:** 500 feet

Summary: Easy trails lace through native grassland and oak savannahs in the former Ahmanson Ranch – the newest addition to the Santa Monica Mountains Conservancy cluster of protected lands.

It's hard to imagine how a homely flower could help save nearly 3,000 acres of open space. But that's what happened when environmentalists raised a stink over a potential development at Ahmanson Ranch, which would have plopped 3,000 new homes on ranch land and possibly have led to the demise of the San Fernando Valley spineflower, a

species that was thought to be extinct until it was rediscovered on the ranch in the 1990s. The ranch is also home to other endangered species, including the California red-legged frog, southwestern willow flycatcher, and southern steelhead trout.

The long battle over the land ended in 2003, when the state of California paid $150 million to purchase the 2,983-acre ranch, which over the years had been used for livestock grazing and film shoots. Now, 15 miles of trails run through the property, with more being planned. If you've hiked at nearby Cheeseboro Canyon, you'll probably experience déjà vu when hiking at Ahmanson. The rolling hills, oak and sycamore woodlands, and myriad species of birds are reminiscent of those of Ahmanson's park neighbor to the west. And just like at Cheeseboro, the hillsides are vibrant green after winter rains but tend to bake in the summer. Fall through spring are the best times to hike here, thanks to more pleasant temperatures.

The hike through East Las Virgenes Canyon to Lasky Mesa is relatively level and a good introduction to this beautiful property. Park on the street where Las Virgenes Road ends and access the trail at the sign for Las Virgenes Canyon Open Space. For most of the hike, you'll be on East Las Virgenes Canyon Trail, a fire road which runs partly alongside East Las Virgenes Creek, a tributary of Malibu Creek. The preserve contains a large portion of the headwaters of Malibu Creek.

Some environmentalists believe that steelhead trout from the ocean used to swim about 10 miles up Malibu Creek to spawn in the East Las Virgenes tributary, something they haven't done since Rindge Dam was erected in the lower part of Malibu Canyon in the 1920s. One of the arguments that helped save Ahmanson Ranch as parkland was that runoff from homes would pour into Malibu Creek, endangering any remaining steelhead.

Less than 0.5 mile from the trailhead, you'll cross the creek, an easy rock-hop only several feet wide. A few minutes ahead is a trail junction, marked only with arrows and the word "trail." Turn right to continue on East Las Virgenes Canyon Trail. Now you'll ascend slightly, leaving the creek's riparian habitat. The terrain opens up. Head-high thickets of thistle and mustard line the trail, surrounded by the park's rolling oak-covered hills. You're likely to spot a variety of birds ranging from hummingbirds to hawks. Swallows targeting insects dive-bomb like jet fighters.

In about 20 minutes, you'll come to a fork marked by a small brown hiking sign, a trash can, and a doggie bag dispenser. Stay to the right on the fork. A little less than two miles from the trailhead is the right turnoff for Lasky Mesa, marked only by a sign with arrows. You'll head slightly downhill, then back up toward the mesa, which is named for silent filmmaker Jesse Lasky. Another short hop over the creek, and just ahead you'll see the broad, grassy mesa rising to 1,391 feet. The mesa's north slope supports the second largest and most ecologically diverse native grasslands in the Santa Monica Mountains. This habitat is important for many wildlife species and provides high-quality nesting habitat for raptors. Keep your eyes peeled for the red-tailed hawks often seen swooping over the trail.

You'll pass through two old metal fence posts and continue past a sign on the left for the Mary Wiesbrock Loop Trail, named for a woman who was instrumental in preserving the Ahmanson property. Save this loop for later and head straight for now. It is breezy and quiet on top of the mesa, with mountain views to the northeast and an occasional plane from Burbank Airport buzzing overhead.

The trail dead-ends at another loop trail sign. Turn left here onto a gravel pathway. Ahead are a few buildings remaining from the days of silent filming, and views of the west end of the San Fernando Valley. Veer left when you get to the next loop trail sign. Stay on the loop and turn right, heading back to the main trail at the final loop sign. When you return to East

Las Virgenes Canyon Trail, go left. If it's a warm day, you'll appreciate the ocean breeze as you head west back to the trailhead.

Options

Instead of turning right to go to Lasky Mesa, you can continue east on East Las Virgenes Canyon Trail until it ends at Victory Boulevard in Woodland Hills, where another trailhead is located. From the Las Virgenes Canyon trailhead, it is six miles roundtrip. You can also head north into Las Virgenes Canyon; instead of turning right on East Las Virgenes Canyon Trail less than 0.5 mile from the trailhead, turn left and head north into Las Virgenes Canyon. You can also head into Cheeseboro Canyon by going this way; the connector is a little over a mile from the trailhead.

Mustard and oaks are abundant on the trail to Lasky Mesa.

Directions

From U.S. 101 in Calabasas, exit at Las Virgenes Road and head north 1.4 miles until the road ends at the trailhead. Park on either side of the road.

Information and Contact

There is no fee. Dogs are allowed. A trail map is available from the City of Calabasas at www.cityofcalabasas.com/hikingtrails.html. For more information, contact the City of Calabasas, 818/878-4225; or the Santa Monica Mountains Conservancy, 5750 Ramirez Canyon Road, Malibu, CA 90265, 310/589-3200 or 310/858-7272, www.lamountains.com.

15 TALEPOP TRAIL
Malibu Creek State Park

🔦 🦌

Level: Easy   **Total Distance:** 3.9 miles round-trip

Hiking Time: 2 hours   **Elevation Gain:** 450 feet

Summary: Enjoy rolling hills, grasslands, and solitude in Malibu Creek State Park's lightly used northeast corner.

It is hard to imagine what the Chumash Indians would think of Southern California these days, with its strip malls, oxygen bars, and multitude of Starbucks. One place they might approve of is the relatively undeveloped northeast corner of Malibu Creek State Park, where their village of Talepop once stood. Talepop was a tiny burg of about 40 inhabitants—much smaller than other Chumash coastal villages with populations as large as 1,000 people. The Chumash lived in this area from approximately 5,000 B.C. to the early 1800s.

The Talepop Trail and Las Virgenes Fire Road bisect some of the park's finest grasslands. This loop takes hikers through two canyons and along Las Virgenes Creek, a tributary of Malibu Creek, the largest watershed in the Santa Monica Mountains.

The loop begins in Juan Bautista de Anza Park in Calabasas, heads west and then south on Talepop Trail, then returns north on Las Virgenes Fire Road. To get to the trail from the parking lot at De Anza Park, go to the far western end of the lot, past the picnic area. On a short trail leading away from the lot, signs explain the Las Virgenes Creek habitat. The creek is one of three wildlife corridors between Simi Hills to the north and the Santa Monica Mountains. At one time, before Rindge Dam was installed in the 1920s, many biologists believe steelhead trout traveled up the creek to spawn.

The trail follows the creek, and you'll soon see a state park boundary marker.

equestrians on a ride along Las Virgenes Trail, heading towards Talepop Trail

Stay to the left and follow this connector trail. Generally more grassy than flowery, this lush meadow area has big clumps of vibrant orange California poppies lining the trail in the spring. Take a right over a small footbridge across the creek. Just ahead you'll see a large oak tree that marks the Talepop/Las Virgenes Trail junction. Going left here takes you to Las Virgenes Fire Road, the return leg of the hike. Instead, look ahead, just past and to the right of the tree, where there is a small brown sign for the Talepop Trail hidden among a tangle of foliage. Follow that path.

Talepop Trail begins switchbacking uphill from the creek. Follow the trail up a ridge, which provides views down into Liberty Canyon. A little over 1.5 miles from the start is the junction with Liberty Canyon Trail. Take a left on Liberty Canyon, go 0.2 mile, then left again for 0.1 mile on a short spur that also connects to the Grasslands Trail. At this junction, you'll see the only structure on this hike, White Oak Farm, an old homestead that used to be a working farm. Just south of the farm is Sepulveda Adobe, a historic 19th century structure left over from the Spanish Colonial era.

Turn left (north) on Las Virgenes Fire Road (still called Talepop Trail on the brown trail marker) and head 1.2 mostly level miles back to the connector to De Anza Park, just past the big oak.

Options

At the junction of Talepop Trail and Liberty Canyon Trail, turn right (north) on Liberty Canyon and follow it 1.1 miles to Phantom Ranch Trail. Turn left (west) and hike 1.8 miles to Mulholland Highway. Come back the way you came; this detour adds 380 feet of elevation gain.

Directions

From U.S. 101 in Calabasas, exit at Lost Hills Road and head south one mile to Juan Bautista de Anza Park on the right. Turn right and park in the lot.

Alternatively, from Highway 1/Pacific Coast Highway in Malibu, turn north on Malibu Canyon Road. Drive 7.6 miles and turn left onto Lost Hills Road. Make a U-turn at the first street on the left, Calabasas Road. Turn right into Juan Bautista de Anza Park and park in the lot.

Information and Contact

There is no fee. Dogs are not allowed. A trail map is available for a fee at the Malibu Creek State Park visitor center (only open on weekends), or from Tom Harrison Maps, 800/265-9090, www.tomharrisonmaps.com. For more information, contact State Parks, Angeles District, 1925 Las Virgenes Road, Calabasas, CA 91302, 818/880-0367 or 818/880-0350, www.parks.ca.gov.

16 VISITOR CENTER TO REAGAN RANCH

Malibu Creek State Park

Level: Easy | **Total Distance:** 5.0 miles round-trip
Hiking Time: 2.5 hours | **Elevation Gain:** 350 feet

Summary: Enjoy Malibu Creek State Park's natural beauty on a series of lesser-used trails, with options to join the crowds at the park's more popular attractions.

Maybe you've seen the mandatory highlights of Malibu Creek State Park—the *M.A.S.H.* television show set, Century Lake, the Rock Pool—and now it's time to explore the quieter side of this jewel of the Santa Monica Mountains. This hike strings together several trails in the park's more remote northwestern corner. It's also possible to extend the trek by visiting Century Lake and those other hotspots, too.

Start by parking in the last lot, just before the campground. Then set off on Crags Road, the main fire road that leads to the park's most popular attractions. In 0.5 mile, you can take a left and cross a bridge over Malibu Creek to the visitor center (open weekend afternoons only), which has maps, fun exhibits on the park's habitat, and a docent to answer your questions.

Or skip the visitor center and continue on High Road, which is lined with oak and sycamore trees and populated with a variety of birds. It borders the creek for 0.6 mile, ascending 215 feet. You'll see a turnoff for Century Lake, but save it for the return leg of the hike. Instead, turn right on Lookout Trail, a quiet and lovely one-mile trek that ascends gradually 250 feet above Cen-

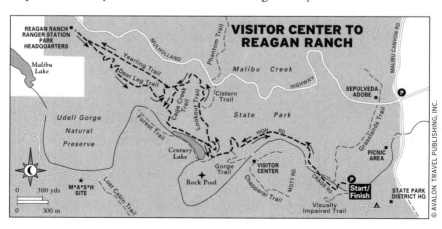

© JULIE SHEER

view of Century Lake near the Crags Road/Lookout Trail junction

tury Lake. You'll be treated to views of the reservoir and the park's distinctive pinkish, volcanic, chaparral-covered peaks.

As well marked as the park's trails generally are, the Yearling Trail is a bit tricky to find. At an unsigned fork, follow the white arrow painted on the ground, heading right. The trail briefly skirts busy Mulholland Highway, but there's still ample opportunity to get a sense of the area's natural beauty. Stay on Yearling Trail to Reagan Ranch. A meadow adjacent to the trail is brilliant green after winter rains and fills with a kaleidoscope of colorful flowers in the spring, including California poppies, lupine, mustard, and wild roses.

The Reagan Ranch is not open to the public, but the site has some interesting history. A home owned by President Ronald Reagan is now a park ranger station. A barn and a few other buildings still stand. Make this your turnaround, then start back on Yearling Trail, but, after about 200 yards, take a detour onto Deer Leg Trail, which parallels Yearling for 0.5 mile. Deer Leg leads you into dense woods adjacent to Udell Gorge Natural Preserve. Along the shady trail, there's a picnic table and stone trough in a sylvan setting near Udell Creek—a sharp contrast to the mostly arid, rocky park. After boulder-hopping across the creek, it's a short uphill back to Yearling Trail. Turn right on Yearling, then, in about 200 yards, turn right again on Cage Creek Trail, which in 0.4 mile delivers you to Century Lake. The lake was formed in 1901, when a dam was built by a local country club, which used the resulting reservoir for sailing, fishing, and hunting. The lake has silted up and is now a winter migratory stop for waterfowl.

Turn left on Crags Road to return to High Road, following signs back to the visitor center and the start of the hike. But to add some mileage and take in another historic site, go right on Crags Road from the lake to the *M.A.S.H.* television series set, a little under a mile away. Not much is left from the original set (many of the props are now on display at the Smithsonian), except a truck that was burned in a wildfire. If you look hard, you can also spot the old helicopter pad where the character Hawkeye examined the wounded.

Options

The detour to the *M.A.S.H.* site adds about 1.6 miles to the hike. If you are heading straight back to the visitor center, you can also add a 0.25-mile detour to the Rock Pool via the Gorge Trail.

Directions

From Highway 1/Pacific Coast Highway in Malibu, turn north on Malibu Canyon Road. Drive six miles and turn left at the signed entrance for Malibu Creek State Park, just before Mulholland Highway. Park in the last lot on the left.

Or, from U.S. 101 in Agoura Hills, exit at Las Virgenes Road and drive south four miles to the Malibu Creek State Park entrance on the right, just beyond the junction with Mulholland Highway.

Information and Contact

An $8 day-use fee is charged per vehicle. Dogs are not allowed. A trail map of Malibu Creek State Park is available for a fee at the park entrance station or visitor center, or from Tom Harrison Maps, 800/265-9090, www.tomharrisonmaps.com. For more information, contact State Parks, Angeles District, 1925 Las Virgenes Road, Calabasas, CA 91302, 818/880-0367 or 818/880-0350, www.parks.ca.gov.

17 CALABASAS PEAK
Santa Monica Mountains Conservancy Lands

🏕 🌸 🐕

Level: Easy/Moderate   **Total Distance:** 4.0 miles round-trip

Hiking Time: 2 hours   **Elevation Gain:** 950 feet

Summary: Catch a sunset from 2,163-foot Calabasas Peak, accessible via a wide fire road from Mulholland Highway.

Looking for somewhere to go after work for some quick aerobic exercise and a little peace and quiet? The fire road to Calabasas Peak is within easy reach of either U.S. 101 or Highway 1/Pacific Coast Highway, and a hike of under an hour will bring you to its 2,163-foot summit. Bring a flashlight with you so you can stay on top to watch the sun set, then hike back down on the wide, easy dirt road as darkness falls.

By most summit standards, Calabasas Peak is not so high. But since there are no peaks anywhere near it that are higher, Calabasas offers a stunning clear-day vista that includes the Santa Monica Mountains, the San Fernando Valley, and the high peaks of the San Gabriel Mountains.

From the parking area alongside Stunt Road, cross the road and begin hiking at the white gate signed for Calabasas Peak. The chapparal-covered slopes offer no shade (another reason to save this hike for the evening hours, or get an early start in the morning) but provide open vistas of neighboring Cold Creek Canyon. You'll pass some tilted sandstone slabs and rounded, cave-ridden outcrops as you gain elevation. Three-quarters of a mile from the start is a saddle at 1,530 feet, where a bench is in place for the weary, and telephone lines are strung overhead. Here, another dirt road on the right leads down to Red Rock Canyon Park. Stay straight on your fire road and continue the

© ANN MARIE BROWN

Water-sculpted sandstone formations add interest to the trail to Calabasas Peak.

gradual ascent, passing more interesting rock formations along the way. The trail's grade gets steeper as you go.

Shortly before you reach the summit of Calabasas Peak, a right spur leads to a high point dotted with sandstone boulders. This spot offers its own fine view, but it isn't a complete 360 degrees because Calabasas Peak is in the way. Continue along the fire road for 50 yards more, now on a completely level grade. An obvious left spur leads uphill from the fire road for another 50 yards to Calabasas Peak's brushy summit. A four-foot-high metal pole marks the spot. (The fire road continues north, past the summit, so, if you start to head downhill, you missed the spur trail.)

A survey marker on top of the peak reads "Dry Canyon" and a coffee-can summit register is buried amid a pile of rocks. A quick read through the register reveals that butterflies are attracted to this chaparral-clad peak in the spring months (several hikers noted seeing them). Although there is an amazing amount of development in view to the west, including some hillsides that have been completely leveled off by large-scale grading, something beautiful can be seen to the northwest—the newly acquired lands of Ahmanson Ranch, which are now public parklands. Far to the east, of course, is the looming presence of Mount Baldy, usually snow-capped in winter and early spring.

Options

From the saddle 0.75 mile up the Calabasas Peak Trail, turn right and follow the fire road into Red Rock Canyon Park. The trail leads downhill for 1.25 miles to the park, which is famous for—you guessed it—its red rock formations.

Directions

From U.S. 101 in Calabasas, exit on Las Virgenes Road and drive 3.2 miles. Turn left on Mulholland Drive and drive four miles. Turn right on Stunt Road and drive one mile to a large pullout on the right (at mile marker 1.0). Park here; the fire road to Calabasas Peak begins across the road from the pullout.

Alternatively, from Highway 1/Pacific Coast Highway in Malibu, turn north on Malibu Canyon Road. Drive five miles and turn right (east) on Mulholland Highway. Drive four miles to Stunt Road and turn right. Drive one mile to a large pullout on the right.

Information and Contact

There is no fee. Dogs are allowed. A trail map of Malibu Creek State Park, which includes Calabasas Peak, is available for a fee from Tom Harrison Maps, 800/265-9090, www.tomharrisonmaps.com. For more information, contact the Santa Monica Mountains Conservancy, 5750 Ramirez Canyon Road, Malibu, CA 90265, 310/589-3200 or 310/858-7272, www.lamountains.com.

18 STUNT HIGH TRAIL BEST ◖

Stunt Ranch/Cold Creek Canyon Preserve

🏔 🌼 🐴

Level: Easy/Moderate   **Total Distance:** 4.4 miles round-trip

Hiking Time: 2 hours   **Elevation Gain:** 765 feet

Summary: Wildflowers abound in the spring and Cold Creek flows year-round on this scenic trail near an environmental studies reserve in the Santa Monica Mountains.

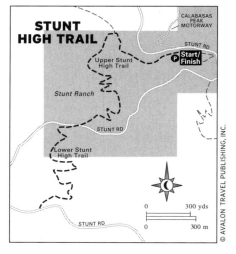

Amidst the patchwork quilt of land ownership that is the Santa Monica Mountains sits 310-acre Stunt Ranch. Located just east of Topanga State Park and adjacent to Red Rock Canyon Park, Stunt Ranch is such a gem of biological diversity that UCLA made part of it a nature reserve and outdoor classroom in 1995. The area serves as an outdoor laboratory in which students from UCLA and other universities undertake research on stream ecology, bird behavior, and post-fire regrowth and erosion.

The hike described here, Stunt High Trail, cuts through the western portion of the ranch and is the only trail at Stunt Ranch open to the public. The UCLA-owned land is accessible only with advance permission or on a docent-led hike. Cold Creek Docents (818/591-1701) lead public hikes in Stunt Ranch once or twice a month.

Most of the vegetation and all of Stunt Ranch's buildings were destroyed in the 1993 Malibu/Topanga fire, which consumed more than 17,000 acres and destroyed more than 300 structures in the mountains near Topanga Canyon. A small cabin built by the Stunt family, who homesteaded here in the late 1800s, also burned down. An education center at Stunt Ranch is in the process of being rebuilt, and the flora has bounced back well from the fires. In many areas it's hard to tell that anything ever burned.

It's a good idea to carry a detailed map on this hike, as the trail crosses twisty Stunt Road several times. Most of the junctions are signed, however, and the out-of-bounds UCLA reserve property is clearly marked. Parking is

© ANN MARIE BROWN

Monkeyflower is a common bloom seen on the Stunt High Trail.

at a pullout on the right side of Stunt Road, a mile from Mulholland Highway. There's an outhouse at the trailhead and a doggie-bag dispenser if you're hiking with Fido.

There's plenty for hikers to enjoy on the High Trail. The path immediately parallels Cold Creek, which originates on the north face of 2,805-foot Saddle Peak, one of the highest points in the Santa Monica Mountains. The creek flows year-round, a rarity in this arid range, and is part of the Cold Creek watershed of Malibu Creek, considered one of the most pristine and biologically diverse of the range. The creek flows mightily in years of heavy rain. Hiking alongside it beneath a canopy of spreading oaks provides one of the most bucolic experiences possible in these mountains.

A short distance from the start, the trail turns away from the creek and ascends slightly. The trail soon forks, and a small wooden sign points the way to the UCLA reserve. Turn left to remain on Stunt High Trail. The habitat quickly changes from riparian woodland to grassland. There are good views of the distinctive pink outcrops of the surrounding sandstone peaks. Lizards scurry across the trail. A lush meadow brimming with spring wildflowers lines both sides of the trail. The grasses are dotted with colorful blooms, including lupine, monkeyflower, Catalina mariposa lily, and pretty blue sprays of fiesta flower.

About one mile into the hike, the trail comes to a paved, UCLA service road, marked with a Trail Crossing sign. Cross here and pick up the Stunt High Trail again on the far side. In less than a half mile, the trail runs into Stunt Road.

There's a big reserve sign to the left and pullout parking for hikers wishing to start the trail here. Watching for traffic, take a right and cross the road. You'll pick up the trail at mile marker 1.94, about 500 feet west of where you crossed.

The trail ascends several stairs amid thick woods. From this point on, the vegetation changes markedly. You'll climb through head-high thickets of chaparral. The shadeless trail meanders this way for 0.9 mile. On the return, you'll get good views of 2,163-foot Calabasas Peak, and, in the foreground, the distinctive bulbous stone formation referred to as Seal Rock.

The end of the trail is anticlimactic. It once again hits Stunt Road, where there's a small parking pullout. Across the road is the Backbone Trail (see Options, below). Reverse your steps to return to the Stunt High Trail trailhead, having gained a new appreciation for this special land and the fact that it is being protected for all to enjoy.

Options

You can access the Backbone Trail from the top of Stunt High Trail. After reaching Stunt Road the final time, take a right and go downhill along the street for about 800 feet. Just past mile marker 2.92, cross the road. A chain-link gate with a small brown sign marks the Backbone Trail. You can go around the gate and take this Backbone segment west to Piuma Road, 3.2 miles away, with an elevation loss of 1,165 feet. Or take the Backbone Trail east from this point for 1.1 miles to Saddle Peak, with an elevation gain of 800 feet.

Directions

From U.S. 101 in Calabasas, exit on Las Virgenes Road and drive 3.2 miles. Turn left on Mulholland Drive and drive four miles. Turn right on Stunt Road and drive one mile to a large pullout on the right (at mile marker 1.0).

Alternatively, from Highway 1/Pacific Coast Highway in Malibu, turn north on Malibu Canyon Road. Drive five miles and turn right (east) on Mulholland Highway. Drive four miles to Stunt Road and turn right. Drive one mile to a large pullout on the right.

Information and Contact

There is no fee. Dogs on leash are allowed. A trail map of Malibu Creek State Park, which includes Stunt Ranch, is available for a fee from Tom Harrison Maps, 800/265-9090, www.tomharrisonmaps.com. For more information, contact Mountains Restoration Trust, 3815 Old Topanga Canyon Road, Calabasas, CA 91302, 818/591-1701, www.mountainstrust.org. Or contact UCLA's Stunt Ranch Reserve, 310/206-3887.

19 BACKBONE TRAIL IN HONDO CANYON

BEST

Topanga State Park

Level: Strenuous

Total Distance: 9.0 miles round-trip

Hiking Time: 5 hours

Elevation Gain: 1,600 feet

Summary: Wildflowers and unique sandstone formations highlight this lesser-used stretch of the Backbone Trail in Topanga State Park.

Hondo Canyon has a little something for everyone. Flower lovers will enjoy the spring blooms along the trail's eastern end. Geologists marvel at the sedimentary rock and embedded marine remains at Fossil Ridge near the trail's western end. Water lovers can look forward to a creek and ocean views. And people who don't want a lot of company may very well have the trail to themselves.

Hondo Canyon is at the far west side of Topanga State Park, a slice of land wedged between the more popular main part of the park and Cold Creek Canyon Preserve to the west. The Backbone Trail runs through the canyon. The nine-mile round-trip is fairly strenuous, so many hikers do a shuttle, leaving one car on Old Topanga Canyon Road on the east end and one at the Saddle Peak Road/Schueren Road intersection at the west end. If you start the hike at Saddle Peak, you have a one-way hike of 4.5 miles with 1,620 feet of elevation loss.

To do the round-trip and burn some calories, start at Old Topanga Canyon Road and make your way west. Park at a pullout less than 0.5 mile from Topanga Canyon Boulevard, just past the mostly organic Inn of the Seventh Ray restaurant, a Topanga Canyon institution. The small pullout on the left is near a horse crossing sign and some speed bumps.

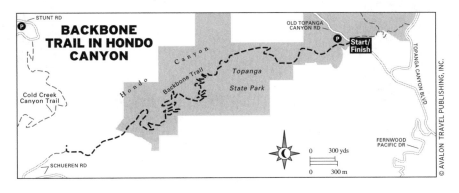

Start hiking on the Backbone Trail along lush Topanga Creek, which is lined with oaks and sycamore. You'll be in and out of the shade, ascending through a grassy meadow. In the spring, pink mariposa lilies, big purple wands of bush sage, and pale orange monkeyflowers line the trail. A few houses are scattered along the canyon, and before long the tilted pink sedimentary rock of the Sespe Formation comes into view. The formation was created 40 million years ago, in a floodplain that arose following a long period when the land that is now the mountains was covered by a shallow sea.

The trail switchbacks up through the chaparral. Watch for rattlesnakes sunbathing in rock indentations on the trail. Just when it seems like the climb might never end, you'll spot some radio towers on the peaks ahead. Right before the trail spits you out at Saddle Peak Road is a Backbone Trail sign and a marker pointing to Saddle Peak and Hondo Canyon. Turn right there, toward the Saddle Peak trailhead, now about a mile away. The trail is fairly faint and tends to be overgrown after a heavy rainy season. It heads southwest, parallelling the road below. Soon there's a view of Flores Canyon in Malibu directly south, a few large houses with fabulous views, and the blue Pacific Ocean beyond.

In about 0.75 mile, you'll come upon a short stretch of trail informally called Fossil Ridge. Look closely at some boulders on the right side of the trail, and you'll see shells embedded in the rock. They are fossils left from when this land was under water.

© ANN MARIE BROWN

From March to May, look for the delicate blooms of mariposa lily in the grasslands along the Backbone Trail.

During the last quarter mile, you'll see some power lines and then the trail ends at a fire road. Turn left there and go through a gate to a pullout parking area at the Saddle Peak/Schueren/Stunt Road intersection, directly ahead and to the right.

If you've arranged a shuttle, this is the end of the road. Otherwise, continue back to Topanga and treat yourself to a cosmic meal at the Inn of the Seventh Ray.

Options

You can continue on the Backbone Trail from Saddle Peak Road, making a right on Stunt Road and walking about 100 feet to a car pullout on the right side. Directly across the street is a faint, unmarked trailhead, but a well-graded trail. Take that along the ridge and around a water tank for 0.8 mile and 335 feet of elevation gain. From there, you can turn left off the Backbone Trail to detour along a short spur to 2,805-foot Saddle Peak. At that junction, you can also pick up the Backbone Trail again heading north; it's 1.1 miles and 800 feet of elevation loss to Stunt Road and a trailhead for the Stunt High Trail. Bring a map to help with navigation.

Directions

From Highway 1/Pacific Coast Highway at Topanga Beach, turn north on Topanga Canyon Boulevard. Drive 4.1 miles and turn left on Old Topanga Canyon Road. Drive 0.3 mile to the trailhead, which is at a small turnout on the left side of the road, just past a horse crossing sign and some speed bumps.

Information and Contact

There is no fee. Dogs are not allowed. A trail map of Topanga State Park is available for a fee at the Trippet Ranch Visitor Center, or from Tom Harrison Maps, 800/265-9090, www.tomharrisonmaps.com, or from National Geographic/Trails Illustrated, 800/962-1643, www.trailsillustrated.com. For more information, contact Topanga State Park, 20825 Entrada Road, Topanga, CA 90290, 310/455-4196 or 310/455-2465.

_E ROCK LOOP

.....ga State Park

Level: Moderate

Hiking Time: 3 hours

Total Distance: 6.2 miles round-trip

Elevation Gain: 1,200 feet

Summary: Visit Topanga State Park's mammoth sandstone formation on this scenic loop on a combination of fire roads and single-track.

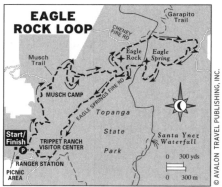

The Trippet Ranch area of Topanga State Park is a busy place crowded with picnickers and casual strollers on weekends. But if you want a little quiet nature time, make your getaway by picking up Musch Trail from the far end of the parking lot (follow the paved trail for about 70 yards to its start). You'll soon leave most of the crowds behind. Musch Trail is a single-track, hikers-only path that travels through a mix of oak and bay forest, grassy meadows, and chaparral. Although the trail is much more shaded than the fire roads that lead from Trippet Ranch, keep in mind that it can still be very hot around here on summer days. This inland region is one of the consistently hottest in the Santa Monicas; it doesn't catch the cool ocean breezes that the more southern reaches get. An early start is a requirement on warm days, or, better yet, plan your hike for winter or early spring.

In one mile you reach Musch Camp, a pleasant hike-in camp that is surrounded by meadows. A restroom and horse corral are located here. From the camp, the trail just gets better—flower-filled grasslands and oak groves await. Look for mariposa lilies, blue-eyed grass, and owl's clover in bloom in March, April, and May. Musch Trail gently descends to cross over a small seasonal creek under a dense oak canopy, then climbs back up on the far side.

Two miles from the start you reach Eagle Junction, where your trail meets up with a passel of fire roads. Take a hard left on Eagle Rock Fire Road. Your main destination, Eagle Rock, is now a half mile away. (The "other" left also goes to Eagle Rock, but save it for your return loop.) Now you head steeply uphill on the fire road, and all hope of shade vanishes in the hot, unforgiving sun. This is lizard country, plain and simple, but that's good news for a few species of sun-loving flowers. In the spring months, the roadsides come alive with penstemon, purple nightshade, and lupine. In just a few minutes of walking, you come around a bend and get your first big-impact view of Eagle Rock. The rounded outcrop is much bigger than you would expect. It's so big, in fact, it brings to mind many of the granite domes in Yosemite, even though Eagle Rock is made of sandstone. The monolithic rock, which looks nothing like an eagle, is estimated to be about 15 million years old.

The trail runs right alongside Eagle Rock, where you'll find a couple trash cans and a bench with a sign that reads "Rest for the Soul." Of course, you'll want to climb on top of the rock and explore its many nooks and crannies. Several small caves are located on the southeast side. A few are marred by colorful graffiti, but at least the art is of a whimsical nature, not a threatening one. If it's a warm day, you'll surely want to climb into one of the caves for some much-needed shade, and to enjoy the views of the Santa Ynez Canyon below and the far-off ocean beyond. It's not hard at all to imagine this being a ceremonial site for the Native Americans who once lived here.

Now it's time to finish out your loop. Unlike the hikers-only Musch Trail, the rest of your trip is on fire roads, so, if you don't like sharing the trail with mountain bikers, you might opt to return the way you came. Otherwise, continue on the fire road past Eagle Rock for 0.8 mile to Hub Junction, another major junction of dirt roads. Turn sharply right and hike gently downhill for

A hiker surveys the scene from on top of Eagle Rock.

1.3 miles to Eagle Junction. Just before you reach it, a spur trail on the right leads a few yards to Eagle Spring, where water dribbles (or pours, in winter) from an oak- and sycamore-shaded spring. It's a lovely spot, but exercise caution: poison oak is rampant here. At Eagle Junction, bear left on Eagle Springs Fire Road to return to Trippet Ranch. Remember, if you are desperately seeking relief from the baking sun (or the ubiquitous cyclists), you can always cut over to Musch Trail at Eagle Junction and hike back the way you came. This will only add one more mile to your day.

Options

You can easily lengthen this trip by turning the loop into a figure eight. About 50 yards beyond Eagle Rock, take the left turnoff for Garapito Trail and follow it 2.6 miles to Fire Road 30. Turn left and hike south on the fire road for 1.4 miles to Hub Junction, then finish out the loop as above. Garapito Trail is all single-track and densely vegetated. It descends steeply and then crosses Garapito Creek numerous times in its second mile. This figure-eight extension will add 3.2 miles to the loop described above.

Directions

From Highway 1/Pacific Coast Highway at Topanga Beach, turn north on Topanga Canyon Boulevard and drive 4.7 miles to Entrada Road. Turn right and drive 1.2 miles to Trippet Ranch.

Information and Contact

A $5 day-use fee is charged per vehicle at Trippet Ranch. Dogs are not allowed. A trail map of Topanga State Park is available for a fee at the Trippet Ranch Visitor Center, or from Tom Harrison Maps, 800/265-9090, www.tomharrisonmaps.com, or from National Geographic/Trails Illustrated, 800/962-1643, www.trailsillustrated.com. For more information, contact Topanga State Park, 20825 Entrada Road, Topanga, CA 90290, 310/455-4196 or 310/455-2465.

21 CABALLERO CANYON TRAIL
Topanga State Park

Level: Easy/Moderate

Total Distance: 3.5 miles round-trip

Hiking Time: 1.5 hours

Elevation Gain: 750 feet

Summary: A San Fernando Valley hike that provides access to Topanga State Park and multiple hiking options along the unpaved portion of Mulholland Drive.

Looking for a quick escape from suburbia? Caballero Canyon Trail is a lesser-used gateway to Topanga State Park that starts within a golf swing of a Tarzana country club.

The journey into the mountains begins almost as soon as you start driving south on Reseda Boulevard, away from the madness that is Ventura Boulevard. In two miles, you'll see a sign for Braemar Country Club. The trailhead is directly across the street and marked by a sign for the Santa Monica Mountains Conservancy. The trail immediately starts its descent into the canyon. You're heading south, hiking parallel to and slightly below Reseda Boulevard.

You'll be walking along burbling Caballero Creek, a seasonal stream that provides some welcome moisture on this northern, drier side of the Santa Monicas. In the springtime during years of heavy rainfall, the trail is muddy and puddles often teem with tadpoles.

Caballero Canyon is popular with wildflower seekers. Huge bushes of California lilac (ceanothus) burst with sprays of blooms starting in late winter. Yellow sunflowers blanket the canyon hillsides. The usual array of Santa Monica Mountains trees and shrubs can be seen here, including oaks, laurel sumac, black walnut, and various sages, along with more colorful plants like wild peony, larkspur, and the yellow-flowered stalks of black mustard.

About a half mile in, you'll boulder-hop across the creek and reach a trail fork. Take the left fork, away from the creek, and start to ascend. You'll gain most of this hike's elevation on this stretch. The canyon here is serene, with views of densely carpeted chaparral hillsides topped by subdivision mini-mansions clinging to the ridge top. Less than a half mile after the creek crossing is the entrance sign for Topanga State Park. Now the power lines of Mulholland Drive come into view straight ahead.

When you've climbed out of the canyon, look to the right for impressive views north across the San Fernando Valley. After feasting your

Sunflowers are a cheerful sight along the Caballero Canyon Trail in the spring and early summer months.

eyes, go right on Mulholland Drive. You're likely to see mountain bikers and trail runners, who access this popular stretch of "dirt" Mulholland from several points in the Valley. Roughly nine miles of Mulholland remain unpaved, stretching from just east of Topanga Canyon Boulevard west to Encino Hills Drive. In the mid-1990s, there was talk of paving the famed road that runs along the spine of the Santa Monicas, but protests from residents, including celebrities such as Jack Nicholson and Don Henley, put a halt to the plan. For now, this portion of road remains dirt and open only to hikers, dogs, and mountain bikers.

You can make a loop back to your car by hiking 0.8 mile west on Mulholland to the turnoff on the right for Tarzana Fire Road 29, which goes back down to Reseda Boulevard. This junction is an even better viewpoint across the valley. From here it's only 0.2 mile to the top of Reseda and parking for Marvin Braude Mulholland Gateway Park, named for the former Los Angeles City Councilman who was a supporter of mountain parkland. Gateway Park's 1,500 acres are far more civilized than neighboring Topanga State Park. People practice putting golf balls on its manicured lawns.

Once you reach the park and the top of Reseda, it's about one mile back to your car at the Caballero trailhead. A faint trail to the east of Reseda runs through chaparral and parallels the street for a short while, but peters out as the canyon gets more rugged. Grit your teeth and endure the sidewalk on Reseda the rest of the way, which should take about 20 minutes.

Options
You can access a network of hikes once you reach the top of Caballero Canyon Trail. On dirt Mulholland Drive, turn left (east) and hike 2.7 miles to San Vicente Mountain Park and the Nike Missile Site. You can also do a short loop from the top of Caballero Canyon Trail by turning right on Mulholland and hiking 0.2 mile to the Bent Arrow Trail, which is on the left (south) side of Mulholland. Take Bent Arrow 0.4 mile to Fire Road 30/Temescal Ridge. At the Bent Arrow/Fire Road 30 junction, turn right on the fire road and hike 0.6 mile back to Mulholland; or you can continue south 1.4 miles on Fire Road 30 to Hub Junction, a popular jumping-off point in Topanga State Park that leads to Eagle Junction to the west and Temescal Peak to the south. To bag Temescal Peak, hike 0.5 mile past Hub Junction and then, in about 0.2 mile, go left onto a short trail leading to the 2,126-foot peak. Bring a map to help with navigation.

Directions
From U.S. 101 in Tarzana, exit at Reseda Boulevard and drive south for two miles. The trailhead is across the street from Braemar Country Club. There's street parking on both sides of the street.

Public transportation: Metro Bus 150 and Metro Rapid Bus 750 stop on Ventura Boulevard at the Reseda Boulevard intersection. From there, it's a two-mile uphill walk south on Reseda to the trailhead.

Information and Contact
There is no fee. Dogs are allowed on the first part of the trail (up to and including the dirt Mulholland stretch), but not once you enter Topanga State Park. A trail map of Topanga State Park, which includes Caballero Canyon, is available for a fee from Tom Harrison Maps, 800/265-9090, www.tomharrisonmaps.com, or from National Geographic/Trails Illustrated, 303/670-3457 or 800/962-1643, www.trailsillustrated.com. For more information, contact Topanga State Park, 310/455-2465, or Santa Monica Mountains Conservancy, 310/589-3200 or 310/858-7272, www.lamountains.com.

22 LOS LIONES TRAIL TO PARKER MESA OVERLOOK BEST 🄲
Topanga State Park

Level: Moderate

Total Distance: 7.0 miles round-trip

Hiking Time: 3.5 hours

Elevation Gain: 1,305 feet

Summary: A hike high above one of L.A.'s wealthiest neighborhoods to a popular overlook with an unbeatable coastal view.

This is a hike best done on a clear day to take full advantage of sweeping ocean vistas. Given the star-studded neighborhood, you may even get a peek at a celebrity or two.

The trailhead is one of the lesser-used entrances to Topanga State Park and is located a few minutes from Sunset Boulevard in Pacific Palisades. The sign for Los Liones Drive isn't easy to see, so watch for a plant nursery and turn there. The parking lot is at the end of the street. Although hikers are often seen here accompanied by their dogs, keep in mind that dogs are not allowed on trails in Topanga State Park. Park rangers do ticket, and the fine is hefty—about $150.

The hike begins near the wealthy Palisades enclave of Castellammare, just east of the old J. Paul Getty Museum. You'll pass sprawling Mediterranean-style mega-mansions while negotiating the steep 1.5-mile climb up switchbacks through dense chaparral. After winter rains, a stunning white canopy of big-pod ceanothus blossoms umbrellas the trail. This is one of the many species of California lilac found in the state and one of the main members of the chaparral community in the Santa Monica Mountains.

If the steep climb doesn't get your heart pumping, the ocean vistas soon will. After the switchbacks, you'll take a sharp left onto East Topanga Fire Road. The ascent doesn't stop here, and you'll have plentiful Santa Monica Bay views on the left, along with views of lush Santa Ynez Canyon to your

© ANN MARIE BROWN

Sweet-smelling ceanothus, or California lilac, is one of the first flowers to bloom each spring along the Los Liones Trail.

right. The fire road continues for about two miles and an additional 720 feet of gain to the Parker Mesa Overlook turnoff. As the elevation levels off, you'll head farther away from the traffic noise way below on Highway 1 and become enveloped in the quiet canyon.

Just when you start wondering if the turnoff will ever appear, a sign shows up, and then it's a left turn and a half-mile walk on level trail to your bluff-top mesa destination. At this point, you'll see hikers on the fire road arriving from the other direction. They're coming from Trippet Ranch, the park's main headquarters. It's a slightly easier hike to the overlook from Trippet—6.4 miles round-trip and a mere 330-foot elevation gain.

Parker Mesa Overlook is a glorious spot to stay put for awhile. There's a bench from which to gaze at 360-degree views of Santa Monica Bay, stretching from the Palos Verdes Peninsula to Malibu. Sailboats can be seen bobbing in the waves below, and, on a clear day, Catalina Island is plainly visible. After having your fill of the view, return the way you came.

Options

Add mileage by continuing on East Topanga Fire Road past the Parker Mesa Overlook turnoff; it's another 2.6 miles, mostly level, to Trippet Ranch Visitor Center. You can also make this a shuttle hike by leaving one car at Trippet Ranch ($6 to park) and one at the Los Liones trailhead. It's about a 15 to 20 minute drive between the two.

Directions

From Highway 1/Pacific Coast Highway in Pacific Palisades, turn north on Sunset Boulevard. Drive 0.3 mile and turn left on Los Liones Drive (by The Outdoor Room plant nursery). Follow Los Liones Drive to its end in about a half mile and park in the lot across from a church.

Public transportation: From UCLA in Westwood, take the Metro Bus 2 line from the southwest corner of Hilgard Avenue and Westholme Avenue south to Sunset Boulevard and Los Liones Drive. Walk up Los Liones Drive to the trailhead.

Information and Contact

There is no fee at the Los Liones trailhead. Dogs are not allowed. A trail map of Topanga State Park is available for a fee at the Trippet Ranch Visitor Center, or from Tom Harrison Maps, 800/265-9090, www.tomharrisonmaps.com, or from National Geographic/Trails Illustrated, 800/962-1643, www.trailsillustrated.com. For more information, contact Topanga State Park, 20825 Entrada Road, Topanga, CA 90290, 310/455-4196 or 310/455-2465.

23 TEMESCAL CANYON, SKULL ROCK, AND BEYOND

Temescal Gateway Park/Topanga State Park

Level: Moderate

Total Distance: 5.4 miles round-trip

Hiking Time: 2.5 hours

Elevation Gain: 1,450 feet

Summary: One of the most scenic loop trails in the Santa Monica Mountains travels up Temescal Canyon, takes a detour to aptly named Skull Rock, and then returns on Temescal Ridge.

Here's an urban-edge hike—smack in the middle of Pacific Palisades—that will make you forget all about the proximity of the urban edge. Temescal Gateway Park and neighboring Topanga State Park offer myriad charms—a waterfall, wildflowers, ocean views, fascinating rock outcrops—in the backyards of millions. This is a place for the time-strapped nature lover, where it is possible to get away when you don't have time to get away.

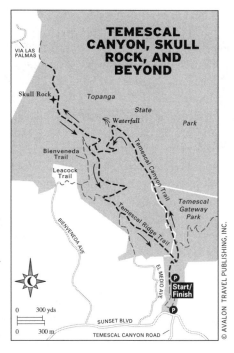

Sure, it's crowded here, especially on weekends, but deservedly so. For its scenic beauty alone, this loop hike in Temescal Canyon is one of the best hikes in the Santa Monica Mountains. If you want to get away from everybody, it's simple enough to follow Temescal Ridge Trail above and beyond Skull Rock, where you will leave most of the crowds behind. Or time your trip for a weekday, when the trails are mostly empty.

Begin your trip at the parking area just below the camp store in Temescal Gateway Park. Walk up the asphalt past the store, then bear left and follow the fence line to the trailhead. A signed path directs you up and around the park's youth camp, and in about 50 feet you come to a fork and the start of your loop: Temescal Canyon Trail to the right, Temescal Ridge Trail to the left. Go right.

Following Temescal Canyon Trail, you'll climb very gently uphill. In 0.5 mile, at a boardwalk over the wide wash of Temescal Creek, you reach a Topanga State Park boundary sign (no dogs past this point). Now the trail starts to ascend more seriously, but still on a very manageable grade. The path is lined with small rounded pebbles embedded in conglomerate rock. Bunnies and lizards scurry by as you parallel the stream, hiking underneath a canopy of big-leaf maples and sycamores. A few interesting rock formations add to the mix.

© ANN MARIE BROWN

the distinctive profile of Skull Rock in Topanga State Park

Shortly you'll hear the waterfall, which you cross over on a footbridge, one mile from the start. If you choose, you can follow a steep spur trail, a few yards before the bridge, to the fall's base, where you get a close-up view of the waterfall's three separate drops (not visible from the trail). Big boulders, clearly volcanic in origin, form the falls. The rocks look like they are made of cobblestones embedded in concrete.

Continuing uphill, the trail steepens and passes an impressive landslide. The dense foliage and shade in this canyon, combined with the smooth single-track footpath, well worn by multitudes of hikers, makes this a perfect place for trail running. At a junction with Temescal Ridge Trail, you climb for a few hundred feet more and then the trail levels out, offering stupendous views of the coast and Santa Monica Bay. You glimpse a small section of the city below, but the vista contains mostly a huge expanse of blue ocean, interrupted by Catalina Island on clear days. In spring, this high ridge is lined with wildflowers—mariposa lilies, purple nightshade, California poppies, and monkeyflower, to name a few. The combination of flowers and coastal views gives this hike a five-star rating, even without the bonus of a small waterfall and the strange rock formation known as Skull Rock, which lies ahead.

There is no mistaking Skull Rock when it appears in the distance. It looks distinctly like a human skull, with eye holes and a large forehead. Right next to it is another odd-looking outcrop, bearing a resemblance to some kind of animal, although what kind of animal is subject to debate. Side trails lead a few feet off the trail to the formations, where you can climb on top and enjoy more high views of the coast, or clamber inside one of their Swiss cheese–like caves and make like a caveman. The romantic might consider this to be a good spot for a marriage proposal, or at least a first kiss.

From here, it is simple enough to continue up the ridge trail for more high views, and a greater chance at solitude. As you climb, the ocean vistas only get better. The trail continues steeply up for another half mile to a high point at 1,700 feet, then makes a quarter-mile descent to another trailhead on Via Las Palmas. Might as well make the high point your turnaround. The trip back down Temescal Ridge Trail is a pleasure, with plenty more coastal-view eye candy. Too soon, you find yourself back down at the loop's start in Temescal Canyon, where you turn right and walk out the final short distance to your car.

Options

There are several other access points from which you can start this hike. The Temescal Ridge trailhead is located at the end of Via Las Palmas, off Chastain Parkway at the end of Palisades Drive. You can do this trip in reverse from there. Another trailhead is found at the end of Bienveneda Avenue, off Sunset Boulevard; a trail leads from there to join Temescal Ridge Trail. Another popular option is to start at the trailhead by the entrance kiosk at Will Rogers State Historic Park, then hike in 2.1 miles on Rivas Canyon Trail to join the trail in Temescal Canyon, near the youth camp.

Directions

From Highway 1/Pacific Coast Highway in Pacific Palisades, turn north on Temescal Canyon Road. Drive one mile to Sunset Boulevard, then cross it to enter Temescal Gateway Park. Drive up the park road for 0.5 mile to the parking lot just before the camp store.

Information and Contact

A $5 day-use fee is charged per vehicle. Dogs are not allowed beyond the first half mile of trail. A park map is available at the camp store. A map of Topanga State Park, which includes Temescal Gateway Park, is available for a fee from Tom Harrison Maps, 800/265-9090, www.tomharrisonmaps.com. For more information, contact Temescal Gateway Park, 15601 Sunset Boulevard, Pacific Palisades, CA 90272, 310/454-1395, www.lamountains.com.

24 INSPIRATION POINT AND RUSTIC CANYON LOOP
Will Rogers State Historic Park

Level: Moderate

Hiking Time: 3 hours

Total Distance: 5.8 miles round-trip

Elevation Gain: 850 feet

Summary: A perennial stream flows through Rustic Canyon, inviting hikers to explore the wilder side of Will Rogers State Historic Park.

Most folks come to Will Rogers State Historic Park to visit the home of the cowboy philosopher and humorist Will Rogers, have a picnic on the park's massive lawn, or go for a short walk. Rogers's humble abode was a gigantic 31-room ranch, built in the 1930s and done up in cowboy decorating style. His well-rounded life included stints as a steer roper, vaudeville lariat artist, Ziegfield Follies humorist, radio celebrity, and film star, but he was most famous for his common-sense philosophy and humorous observations. The ranch buildings are currently undergoing a major restoration project that should be completed in early 2006.

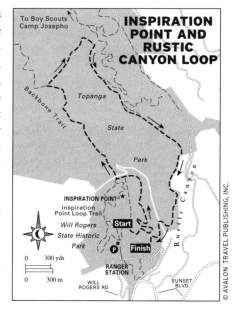

The park is centrally located in Pacific Palisades, so it sees a predictable amount of dog walkers, joggers, and casual weekend walkers. But with a little effort, you can leave the crowds behind and take an adventurous loop hike in Will Rogers Park and its neighbor, Topanga State Park. The contrast between the casual frivolity at the ranch and the rugged wildness of Rustic Canyon, especially in the winter and spring months when the stream runs high, will surprise you.

There are several trailheads at the park. Start at the one near the nature center and horse-riding arena, on the east side and in back of the main ranch house (not the trailhead nearest the entrance kiosk). It is marked by a large signboard; the wide dirt road is dually signed as Rogers Road Trail and Inspiration Point Trail. As you follow it, you'll see many single-track paths that lead off the main trail, but just stay on the wide fire road.

A very easy climb of 0.9 mile brings you to a junction of trails and the Inspiration Point turnoff on your left. Note the wide trail on your right; that's the next leg of your trip—the Backbone Trail heading into Topanga State Park. But first take a 100-yard detour to the summit of Inspiration Point, where the view includes the Pacific Ocean, the rugged Santa Monica Mountains, and downtown Los Angeles to the southeast. Considering the visual expanse, it's hard to believe you're only at 750 feet in elevation. On the clearest of days, you can see all the way to Catalina Island, 20-plus miles away. There's a horse-hitching post on the summit (this being a cowboy's park, of course) and a few picnic tables and benches. You'll leave most of the crowds behind here.

Head back down to the previous junction, then bear left at the sign that marks the entrance to Topanga State Park and the Backbone Trail. You'll continue uphill on Backbone, climbing for another 0.9 mile. The trail crosses over a bridge that spans Chicken Ridge, a narrow sandstone ridge that gives new meaning to the moniker "Backbone Trail." A high overlook with an even more commanding view than Inspiration Point is situated just above the bridged section. Pay close attention from here on because it is only a few hundred feet farther to the unsigned right turnoff for Rustic Canyon. The narrow trail is easy to miss; note that Backbone Trail descends slightly just before the turnoff appears.

© ANN MARIE BROWN

Hikers approach the bridge over Chicken Ridge above Inspiration Point.

After leaving Backbone Trail, you'll have a very steep 0.4-mile descent through tree-sized, tunnel-like chaparral to Rustic Canyon's stream crossing. Rock-hop your way across (the stream flow varies greatly from season to season), and you'll emerge—surprise—at an old boarded-up house surrounded by a chain-link fence. This cabin, and several others in the canyon, belonged to Will Rogers and his friends. Pick up the single-track trail between the house and the creek and follow it to your right, downstream. You are traveling on the old Rustic Canyon roadbed; occasionally you see remaining bits and pieces of concrete and blacktop. The canyon has had a strange history; the woodsy retreat was used at various times as an "old boys club," an artist colony, and, strangest of all, a Nazi camp in the 1930s (much to the chagrin of neighboring landowners). In the last half decade, Rustic Canyon has been ravaged by fire and flood. Several more abandoned structures can be seen, many of which have been defiled by graffiti.

Your trail, which is well defined for the first half mile in the canyon, soon more or less vanishes into the creek. The canyon becomes wilder, narrower, and steeper. In high water, you'll do a fair amount of trail-less slogging alongside, and through, the streambed. In extremely high water, the canyon can be impassable. In low water, you can follow an informal footpath alongside the stream, keeping your feet dry most of the time. Just keep heading downstream, crossing and recrossing the creek when necessary, and, at 1.5 miles from your first steps in Rustic Canyon, you'll spot a well-defined trail heading out of the streambed on the right. Suddenly what seemed wild becomes tame again. You'll head gently uphill on easy switchbacks, following a prototypical state park wooden fence. A quarter mile from the streambed, you come out at the far end of the polo fields at Will Rogers State Historic Park, once again amid the gaiety of picnickers and dog walkers.

Options

When you reach the initial stream crossing in Rustic Canyon, you can cross the creek and then walk left, upstream, instead of downstream. The trail continues for 0.5 mile to the Boy Scout Camp Josepho (private property). The upper reaches of Rustic Canyon can be explored from a trailhead off Mulholland Drive, near Caballero Canyon.

Directions

From Highway 1/Pacific Coast Highway in Pacific Palisades, turn north on Temescal Canyon Road. Drive one mile to Sunset Boulevard. Turn right and drive 1.4 miles to Will Rogers State Park Road, then turn left and drive one mile to the park entrance. The trail begins behind, and just east of, the Rogers's ranch house, near the nature center and horse arena.

Information and Contact

A $7 day-use fee is charged per vehicle. Dogs are not allowed except for on the first mile of trail to Inspiration Point. A map of Topanga State Park, which includes Will Rogers State Historic Park, is available for a fee at the park entrance kiosk, or from Tom Harrison Maps, 800/265-9090, www.tomharrisonmaps.com. For more information, contact Will Rogers State Historic Park, 1501 Will Rogers State Park Road, Pacific Palisades, CA 90272, 310/454-8212 or 818/880-0350, www.parks.ca.gov.

25 WEST MANDEVILLE FIRE ROAD TO SAN VICENTE MOUNTAIN PARK   BEST ☾

Westridge–Canyon Back Wilderness Park

🚶 🚴 ♿ 🐕 ⛺

Level: Moderate   **Total Distance:** 7.2 miles round-trip

Hiking Time: 3.5 hours   **Elevation Gain:** 700 feet

Summary: A lush, peaceful canyon trail in the Santa Monica Mountains that starts with ocean views and ends at a Cold War–era missile installation with views of the San Fernando Valley.

History buffs and "destination" hikers who relish treks with a reward at the top will love this easy-to-reach hike on the Westside. You can even meet your Valley friends hiking in from Encino or Tarzana for a picnic at the top.

Sandwiched between Rustic and Sullivan Canyons on the west side and Mandeville Canyon to the east, West Mandeville Fire Road runs through 1,500-acre Westridge–Canyon Back Wilderness Park. This land is a critical link in a proposed 20,000-acre urban wilderness area known as the "Big Wild"—an ambitious plan by the Santa Monica Mountains Conservancy to create a huge contiguous expanse of parkland and protected habitat for wildlife. The "Big Wild" would extend from the Nike missile site visited on this hike almost all the way to the Pacific Ocean.

radar towers at the Nike Missile Site, with a view of Encino beyond

West Mandeville is open to dogs without leashes, so be prepared to share the trail with a healthy population of man's best friend. If hiking with your pet, bring plenty of water. Despite its ocean views, the trail is not shaded and there is no water until the top, 3.6 moderately steep miles away. The park is also a favorite of mountain bikers, so pay attention when rounding the bends and keep your head up when walking past the trail's many spurs, which cyclists like to climb up and race back down.

After parking on the street (you'll have to park a block away from the trailhead if you arrive between 7 A.M. and 3 P.M. on weekends), go around the gate at the trailhead. It's all uphill from here. Look to the left soon after the fire road begins its ascent. On days without haze, Santa Monica Bay quickly comes into view. You'll notice Sullivan Ridge Fire Road to the west, amidst steep slopes of dense chaparral, parallelling your trail. Redtailed hawks ride the thermals and ravens prowl the hillsides. To the east lie a scattering of homes in the far-flung cul-de-sacs of Mandeville Canyon, and, way off in the distance, downtown L.A.'s buildings can be spotted on clear days.

The trail eventually flattens out as the missile site's tower comes into view. After a final climb to the summit, you'll go around a gate, with the Nike site just ahead and to the right. You are now in San Vicente Mountain

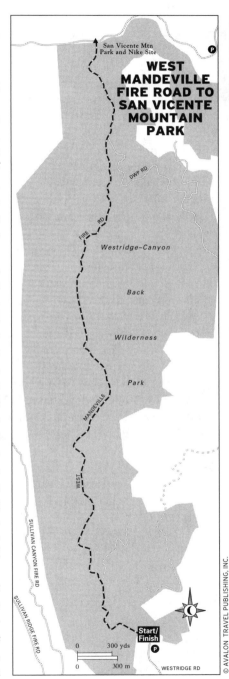

WEST MANDEVILLE FIRE ROAD TO SAN VICENTE MOUNTAIN PARK

Park, which can also be hiked or driven to via an unpaved section of Mulholland Drive in the hills above Encino. (Your less-ambitious friends can take the driving route and meet you here.) The park has picnic tables and dog bowls under the shade of oak trees, a bike rack, bathrooms, and a public phone. A telescope that costs a quarter to operate is pointed east, providing a view of downtown L.A.

Plenty of signage explains the site's former life as one of 16 Los Angeles–area Nike-Ajax supersonic antiaircraft missile launch sites. At 1,950 feet above sea level and with views in all directions, San Vicente Peak was considered an ideal spot for detecting enemy aircraft. From 1956 until 1968, radar at the site could detect an enemy plane and activate a computer that would launch a Nike missile from nearby Sepulveda Basin, targeting the hostile aircraft before it could bomb L.A. By the late 1960s, Nike missiles were rendered obsolete by the development of intercontinental ballistic missiles, which could travel faster, higher, and farther. Today, you can take advantage of the Nike site location to obtain far-reaching views of the L.A. basin. Climb the missile tower's three short flights of stairs to a deck at the top. Directly north is Encino Reservoir and beyond that the flat expanse of the Valley.

Land in Westridge–Canyon Back Wilderness Park was at one time under private ownership, with plans for the development of more than 500 homes. After several decades, it was finally purchased through funding from a 1996 park and open space ballot measure. The park was dedicated in 1999.

From this high point, you can easily wander to the east or west on the dirt stretch of Mulholland. If it's late in the day, hike back while enjoying the lengthening shadows on the surrounding hillsides. Not surprisingly, this is a great spot to catch an L.A. sunset.

Options

After reaching the missile site, you can continue hiking west 2.7 miles on dirt Mulholland Drive to Caballero Canyon Trail, which can then be hiked north (right) through Marvin Braude Mulholland Gateway Park for 1.4 miles until it ends at Reseda Boulevard. Return the way you came.

Directions

From Highway 1/Pacific Coast Highway in Pacific Palisades, turn north on Sunset Boulevard. Drive 5.8 miles to Mandeville Canyon Drive and turn left. At the first stop sign, which is Westridge Road, turn left and drive uphill through a neighborhood until the road dead-ends in 2.1 miles. Street parking on the block is available all day on weekdays but is not allowed from 7 A.M. to 3 P.M. on weekends (you can park farther down the street).

Alternatively, from I-405 in Brentwood, exit at Sunset Boulevard and drive two miles to Mandeville Canyon Drive. Turn north (right) and follow the directions above.

Information and Contact

There is no fee. Dogs are allowed. A trail map of Topanga State Park, which includes Westridge–Canyon Back Wilderness Park, is available for a fee from Tom Harrison Maps, 800/265-9090, www.tomharrisonmaps.com, or from National Geographic/Trails Illustrated, 800/962-1643, www.trailsillustrated.com. For more information, contact the Santa Monica Mountains Conservancy, 5750 Ramirez Canyon Road, Malibu, CA 90265, 310/589-3200 or 310/858-7272, www.lamountains.com.

26 TOWSLEY AND WILEY CANYONS   BEST ◖

Santa Clarita Woodlands Park

Level: Easy/Moderate

Total Distance: 5.0 miles round-trip

Hiking Time: 2 hours

Elevation Gain: 1,100 feet

Summary: Just off I-5, a dramatic section of sandstone narrows and a bird-filled canyon await hikers.

Towsley and Wiley Canyons are part of a conglomeration of parklands known as Santa Clarita Woodlands Park, owned and managed by the Santa Monica Mountains Conservancy. The canyons are one of the small miracles of open space in and around Los Angeles that was preserved by forward-thinking individuals. Despite being bordered by the I-5 freeway and closely encroached by the suburban sprawl of Santa Clarita, this is a pocket of wild land that is home to birds and wildlife. For an hour or two, as you hike this loop, you can largely forget the presence of so much civilization so close at hand.

The park is full of surprises. First, there is some remarkable geology, including a short stretch of canyon in which the walls have been folded, faulted, and eroded by water to such a degree that they pinch in to narrow proportions,

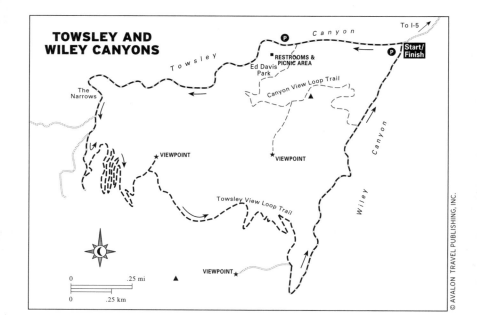

Death Valley style. Then there is the presence of tar seeps, once used for basket making by the Tataviam Indians who lived here and later by Darius Towsley and the San Fernando Petroleum District, who drilled productive oil wells that were eventually sold to Standard Oil. Lastly, there is the wildlife, including an abundance of mountain quail, many types of raptors, and various songbirds. Mule deer, bobcat, coyote, and brush rabbits are often spotted here. For the best experience, visit in winter or spring, when the water is running in the canyon. Summer can be unpleasantly hot except in the early mornings, so time your trip carefully.

© ANN MARIE BROWN

The sandstone walls pinch in tight at the Narrows at Towsley Canyon.

Begin at the park gates or the first parking lot inside the gates. Hike in on the park road and note a trail coming in from the left; this will be the return of your loop. For now, stay straight and walk past a second parking lot on your right and the park ranger station and picnic area on your left. The road surface turns to gravel and starts to parallel Towsley Canyon's creek. You quickly leave behind the unpleasant sound of the I-5 freeway as you walk westward. Signs of a recent wildfire are clearly evident, but new foliage is fast overtaking the burned areas. Particularly abundant are blue-purple lupine flowers in spring; this is a plant that thrives in disturbed areas, especially after a fire.

The trail narrows significantly, and, in only one mile from your car, the canyon walls squeeze in as well. If there is water in the stream, you'll be crossing and recrossing it on what now seems like only a makeshift path, not a trail at all. Slow down and enjoy the fascinating, water-worn geology here in the Towsley Canyon "Narrows."

After this fun stretch, your experience changes abruptly as you leave the canyon bottom and begin a well-graded but ambitious ascent, switchbacking uphill over the next 1.4 miles to gain 800 feet. You'll notice a few tar seeps coming out of the ground and may smell the accompanying rotten-egg smell of sulphur. The higher you climb, the more dramatic the views looking down into the rock formations of the Narrows. From this bird's-eye perspective, it is easy to visualize this gorge being carved out by the force of fast-moving water millions of years ago.

Where the trail tops out along a ridgeline, you also gain views of the burgeoning Santa Clarita Valley, with freeways and development as far as the eye can see. From this high perch, you can enjoy the pleasantly superior feeling of being above all the madness. At one 2,400-foot high point, take your pick from views of two vastly different worlds: the tranquillity of Towsley and Wiley Canyons in one direction, or the hustle and bustle of the sprawling city in the other.

Your loop makes its return through neighboring Wiley Canyon, which is more lush and overgrown than Towsley Canyon—it was untouched by the fire—with fine stands of canyon live oak and interior live oak. It's downhill all the way back to your car.

Options

Nearby Pico Canyon is also part of Santa Clarita Woodlands Park. The canyon was the site of Mentryville, an oil boom town in the late 19th century. A few historic buildings remain to be seen, plus a pleasant hike through the canyon. To reach Pico Canyon, take I-5 north to the Lyons Avenue exit in Santa Clarita. Cross over the freeway and follow Pico Canyon Road west. Bear left at the fork and follow the signs to Mentryville at the end of the road.

Directions

From the junction of I-5 and Highway 14, drive north on I-5 for five miles to Santa Clarita. Take the Calgrove exit, turn left (west), and drive 0.4 mile to the park entrance on the right. Park in the first parking lot ($5 fee charged), or park outside the gate for free.

Information and Contact

A $5 day-use fee is charged if you park inside the gate, or you can park for free outside the gate. Dogs on leash are allowed. A trail map is available at the ranger station/nature center. For more information, contact the Santa Monica Mountains Conservancy, 5750 Ramirez Canyon Road, Malibu, CA 90265, 310/589-3200 or 310/858-7272, www.lamountains.com. Or contact the rangers at Towsley Canyon, 661/255-2974.

27 CHUMASH TRAIL TO ROCKY PEAK

Rocky Peak Park

🏛 🌿 🦌

Level: Moderate   **Total Distance:** 7.4 miles round-trip

Hiking Time: 3.5 hours   **Elevation Gain:** 1,400 feet

Summary: A hike to a high summit in the Santa Susana Mountains with wild-flowers and sandstone outcrops lining the path.

Drive along Highway 118 and you'll see some wild-looking rock formations. Spectacular sandstone boulders and outcroppings line both sides of the freeway. A distinct feature of this part of the Santa Susana Mountains is 2,714-foot Rocky Peak, a high point covered with fractured rocks along a boulder-ridden ridgeline. The peak makes a great exercise-hike destination, offering high views of sprawling Simi Valley and Chatsworth below.

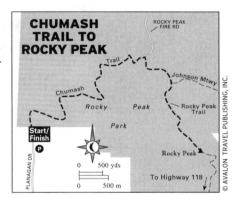

In the spring, it's not just the vistas and the pockmarked rocks that will wow you, but the wildflowers as well.

Bring lots of water on this hike, even on cool days, and especially if you are hiking with your dog. There isn't a lick of shade to be found anywhere. If you must hike in the hot summer months, get an early morning start. And one more caveat: Because this trail is popular with mountain bikers on weekends, you might want to confine your visits here to weekdays.

Several trails lead to Rocky Peak, but a favorite is the Chumash Trail, a wide single-track that is well graded and easy to follow. It heads gently uphill through an initial stretch of grasslands, which rapidly transitions into coastal sage scrub. The usual assortment of "soft chaparral" plants are represented: black and white sage, California sagebrush, California buckwheat, giant rye, purple needlegrass, mustard, and so on.

What stands out among the greenery, at least from late February to late May, is the colorful array of flowers: fiddlenecks, lupine, yellow bush monkeyflower, purple nightshade, golden yarrow, larkspur, and woolly blue curls, among others. Three different species of mariposa lily can be found along the trail: yellow, Plummer's, and the more rare Catalina mariposa lily. Flower

A trail runner pounds out the miles on the fire road to Rocky Peak.

treasure hunters should keep their eyes peeled for the rare Santa Susana tarplant. Look for it in the top half mile of Chumash Trail before it junctions with Rocky Peak Fire Road.

The trail gains elevation gradually, first tracing alongside a trickling creek, then moving away from it into a moonscape of odd rock formations. Mile markers are placed along the trail every 0.5 mile so you can keep track of your progress. In about 20 minutes, you've walked far enough to have distanced yourself from all evidence of Simi Valley's surrounding suburban sprawl. It's just you and the lizards and bunnies now. As you climb higher, the slopes are covered with prickly chaparral. A fire burned through these hills in the fall of 2003, but, if it weren't for the nude, blackened branches of manzanita and mountain mahogany, you wouldn't know. Chaparral plants thrive on fire and recover quickly.

Where the trail tops out at Rocky Peak Fire Road (2.5 miles from the start), head south (right) for Rocky Peak, 1.2 miles away. Your ascent is mostly completed; this last stretch is a mellow ridgeline walk along a wide fire road, passing by more sculpted outcrops. Rocky Peak is just what its name implies; a high point covered with boulders. On clear days, not only are the Simi and San Fernando Valleys laid out before you, but also the Santa Monica Mountains to the south and the high peaks of Los Padres National Forest to the northwest.

If you aren't in a hurry to head back downhill, backtrack to the Chumash

Trail junction and, instead of turning left, hike in the opposite direction along Rocky Peak Fire Road. The trail leads to a surprisingly large and shady oak grove in about 1.5 miles.

Options

You can also hike to Rocky Peak from the Rocky Peak trailhead (take the Rocky Peak Road exit off Highway 118; the trail begins right at the off-ramp). This trail is fire road all the way and steeper than the Chumash Trail. You can also use the Rocky Peak trailhead to access the single-track Hummingbird Trail (a left turnoff about 0.5 mile up the fire road). This is a popular option in winter and spring when water flows down the Hummingbird Trail's sandstone cliffs and boulders.

Directions

From Highway 118 in Simi Valley, exit at Yosemite Avenue and turn north. Drive 0.4 mile and turn right on Flanagan Drive. Drive 0.75 mile to the road's end at the Chumash trailhead. Park along the street.

Information and Contact

There is no fee. Dogs on leash are allowed. Download a trail map at www.lamountains.com (click on Hiking Trails and scroll down to Rocky Peak Park). For more information, contact the Santa Monica Mountains Conservancy, 5750 Ramirez Canyon Road, Malibu, CA 90265, 310/589-3200 or 310/858-7272, www.lamountains.com.

28 DEVIL'S CANYON AND YBARRA CANYON

Santa Monica Mountains Conservancy Lands

Level: Easy/Moderate   **Total Distance:** 5.0 miles round-trip

Hiking Time: 2.5 hours   **Elevation Gain:** 500 feet

Summary: A hidden canyon tucked amid burgeoning development offers surprising tranquillity in a wildlife-rich riparian corridor.

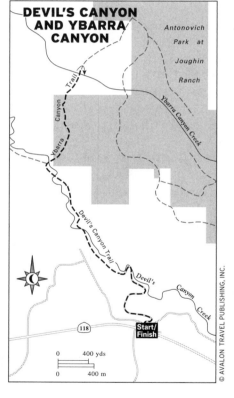

Not long ago, Chatsworth, Simi Valley, and the Santa Susana Mountains above them were cowboy country. But as the city of Los Angeles spread out into the surrounding countryside, large open spaces all but disappeared. Ranches were subdivided. Zoning changes turned residential properties into big-box store shopping centers. Huge housing developments like Porter Ranch were constructed, then a few years later, enlarged.

Fortunately, forward-thinking individuals like the people at the Santa Monica Mountains Conservancy have preserved small pockets of land in between freeways and apartment complexes, strip malls and shopping centers. Magnets for wildlife and nature lovers alike, these small islands of wild land perched on the urban edge may be our most important legacy for future generations. The build-out of Los Angeles will probably go on until there is no place left to build, but at least a few special places will be left as they were meant to be.

Devil's and Ybarra Canyons are such places. There is no formal "park" here, no official trailhead, and no trail signs. The trail is just a few feet off the 118 freeway, where Topanga Canyon Boulevard meets its northern terminus—not a promising-looking place to go hiking. You begin your trip by following a paved road uphill along the edge of a condominium complex for 50 yards, then connect to a dirt road heading downhill, on your right. The situation still doesn't look good, but, in only five minutes from your car, you descend into Devil's Canyon, and the first thing you notice is the birdsong. The canyons contain extensive oak and sycamore woodlands and riparian corridors with year-round water, creating a haven for wildlife.

In the 1940s, a road traveled through the canyon, but Mother Nature's one-two punch of fire and flood took care of that. The wide dirt trail you've been following quickly narrows to a footpath. You may come across a few pieces of scrap metal and concrete as you follow the old roadbed upstream. There are several

The willow-lined creek in Devil's Canyon is a haven for birds and wildlife.

stream crossings to negotiate, but even in the wet season the water is only a few feet wide and a few inches deep. The canyon is a sandy wash, choked with willows, alders, and live oaks, and the streambed is full of small rounded pebbles. Sandstone walls riddled with small caves, nooks, and crannies keep the stream, and you, hemmed in to a fairly narrow corridor. With the sandy streambed underfoot, hiking here is more like walking on the beach than hiking on a trail.

The going is slow but easy, and the elevation gain is negligible. You will quickly discern that this trip isn't about exercise, it's about meandering. About 0.6 mile in, you pass a major rockslide on the right, and a half mile farther, go through a metal gate. Shortly beyond the gate is where Ybarra Canyon comes in from the right to join Devil's Canyon. A large concrete check dam is located on the latter; bear right to follow Ybarra Canyon upstream. The trail climbs slightly and travels above, instead of in, the streambed, in order to bypass a series of small check dams. The streamside vegetation changes here; the trail passes through a densely shaded oak savannah occasionally interrupted by small grassy meadows. This pleasant stretch ends abruptly at a stream crossing with a dirt road on the far side, where a sign clearly states "private nature preserve." Equestrians are allowed to pass through, but hikers and bikers are not. Well, fine. We'll just have to pick a spot somewhere beneath a spreading oak, pull a snack out of our day pack, and listen to the birds sing.

Options

On your return trip, you might want to explore up Devil's Canyon past the large check dam where you turned off for Ybarra Canyon. A trail leads another mile past the dam into the upper reaches of Devil's Canyon, then ends at a gate marking private property.

Directions

From Highway 118 in Chatsworth, exit at Topanga Canyon Boulevard (Highway 27) and go north 20 yards. Park along the frontage road, Poema Place. Walk uphill on the unsigned paved road that runs just east of the condominium complex.

Information and Contact

There is no fee. Dogs are allowed. Download a trail map at www.lamountains.com (click on Hiking Trails and scroll down to Michael D. Antonovich Regional Park at Joughin Ranch). For more information, contact the Santa Monica Mountains Conservancy, 5750 Ramirez Canyon Road, Malibu, CA 90265, 310/589-3200 or 310/858-7272, www.lamountains.com.

SAN GABRIEL AND VERDUGO MOUNTAINS

© LONNIE DECLOEDT

BEST HIKES

This region contains what many would argue is the

best hiking country in all of Southern California. From the front country of the San Gabriel Mountains – the canyons and ridges that are accessed from the backyards of Pasadena, Altadena, Monrovia, Sierra Madre, and the like – to the Sierralike high country along the upper reaches of the Angeles Crest Highway, this area has a tremendous amount to offer for the time-strapped nature lover. The San Gabriels, which geologists claim is the most fractured and unstable mountain range in California (rock slides are an everyday occurrence), form a high, impenetrable shield that, unfortunately, prevents the Los Angeles smog from dissipating. But in the high reaches, the air is sweet and cool, the conifers grow to gargantuan proportions, and mountain streams run clear and cold. Snow falls in the winter – enough to close the Angeles Crest Highway each year from November until about May, and to open a handful of small ski resorts. And every spring, as the snow melts in the high country and rainwater swells the many watersheds of the San Gabriels, the mountain's multiple waterfalls come to life.

Most of the 60-mile-long range is contained in the 700,000-acre Angeles National Forest. This federally managed parkland sustains a network of more than 700 miles of hiking trails and three separate wilderness areas – the Cucamonga, Sheep Mountain, and San Gabriel. In these specially designated lands, no mechanization of any kind is permitted, including mountain bikes. Campsites are primitive at best; all land is left in its natural state except for the occasional trail cutting through. One of California's most striking emblems of wild nature resides within these mountains and is the namesake of the Sheep Mountain Wilderness – the magnificent Nelson bighorn sheep. Although there are only about 500 remaining in the range, they are frequently spotted on the high mountain trails near Mount Waterman and Mount Baldy.

It's not just the high elevation of the mountain country of the San Gabriel Range that makes it so appealing, but also the fact that the mountains are so easily accessed from the freeways and valleys below. Sick of the rat race? Head for the trails that grace the slopes of one of the San Gabriel's 8,000- to 10,000-foot-high peaks. You can hike all day and be back in L.A. in time for dinner.

Another, smaller mountain range also is found in this region – the Verdugo Mountains. This petite, steep range is clearly visible in the background of Burbank and Glendale, and yet is much less visited than either the San Gabriel Mountains to the east or the Santa Monica Mountains to the west. Although the entire range is only 13 miles long and its highest point barely tops 3,000 feet, its crest is remarkably vertical, making it difficult to explore without a challenging ascent. This steepness has also kept the developers away, leaving untouched slopes of coastal sage scrub and grasslands that bloom with wildflowers in spring.

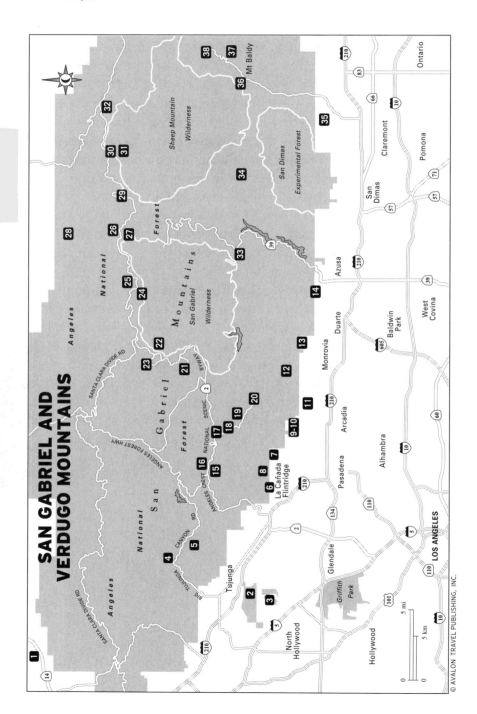

SAN GABRIEL AND
VERDUGO MOUNTAINS

© AVALON TRAVEL PUBLISHING, INC.

San Gabriel and Verdugo Mountains Hikes

1 GEOLOGY TRAIL AND FOOT TRAIL BEST ☾
Vasquez Rocks Natural Area

🌿 ⚙ 🐕

Level: Easy   **Total Distance:** 3.0 miles round-trip

Hiking Time: 1.5 hours   **Elevation Gain:** 500 feet

Summary: Get a close-up look at the bizarre tilted rock slabs that have made Vasquez Rocks famous in television and film productions, including the movie *The Flintstones* and several old Westerns.

It's worth the long drive way out to Agua Dulce to see Vasquez Rocks, an L.A. County Park like no other. The crazy geologic formations at Vasquez Rocks were formed around 20 million years ago by earthquake activity on the Elkhorn Fault, an offshoot of the more famous San Andreas Fault. Ancient sedimentary layers were folded, compressed, and tilted upward by the powerful forces of the earth's movement. The result of all this geologic upheaval is exhibited in Vasquez

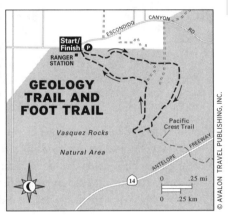

Rocks' broken, angular landscape. Massive rock slabs jut out at various angles from earth to sky, the largest slab towering nearly 150 feet high. Most are yellow and gray in color, but some are striated with deep hues of reddish brown. This park is a delight for photographers, particularly at sunset and sunrise.

Hiking here is a very casual affair. Although there are established trails, it's almost guaranteed that you will stray from the path. Each of the hundreds of slanted outcrops invites you to climb to its summit and explore its nooks and crannies. Who can resist such temptation?

A good place to start exploring is the small parking lot nearest the ranger's office, which is currently just a mobile home but soon will be replaced by a new, state-of-the-art visitor center. Begin following the signed Geology Trail, which is also a section of the Pacific Crest Trail and parallels the park road. The trail wanders amid sagebrush, juniper, and intriguing rock outcrops for 0.8 mile, passing the easternmost parking lot and a large open field that is popular for picnicking. Here the trail becomes a dirt road and makes a sharp bend southwest (right), then roughly parallels Highway 14 for 0.7 mile. Loop

You can't help but leave the trail to explore the massive sandstone slabs at Vasquez Rocks.

back on the signed Foot Trail (not the Horse Trail), with a final left turn on the History Trail to return to your car.

Aside from the geological history of the park, human history is in evidence at Vasquez Rocks. The Tataviam Indians, a band of Serrano Indians, once lived here and used the large rock outcroppings for shelter and shade. They were in the area when the Spanish arrived in the late 1700s, but because they were not warriors, they were quickly overrun. Many were sent to local missions; others learned Spanish, intermarried, and adopted Spanish surnames. After only a few generations, the Tataviam language and culture disappeared. Today, archaeologists come to Vasquez Rocks to try to recreate that culture, or at least imagine it, by studying the remaining pictographs, middens, stone tools, and burial grounds.

The park gets its name from Tiburcio Vasquez, a mid-1800s bandit who used the area's caves and rocks as his personal hideaway. He rustled horses, robbed stagecoaches, and did other dastardly deeds, but was considered a local hero because he gave money to poor Mexican families. Legend has it that a major shoot-out occurred between Vasquez's gang and the local sheriff's posse near the tallest rock formation in the park.

The 20th and 21st centuries have added another chapter to the history of Vasquez Rocks. The park is frequently used as a backdrop for Hollywood productions, including television shows such as *Star Trek* and *Fear Factor* and movies like *The Flintstones* and *Planet of the Apes*. That might explain the strange feeling of déjà vu you experience as you wander through these dramatic rock formations.

Options

Placerita Canyon County Park (www.placerita.org) is located 12 miles southwest of Vasquez Rocks off Highway 14, on Placerita Canyon Road. Although the park was severely burned in the July 2004 Foothill wildfire, its landscape is quickly recovering. In the next few years, this will be a fascinating place to witness the process of fire ecology and regrowth. Try hiking the 5.5-mile round-trip Placerita Canyon Trail from the nature center to the park's small waterfall.

Directions

From the junction of I-5 and Highway 14, drive northeast on Highway 14 for 15 miles to Agua Dulce. Take the Agua Dulce Canyon Road exit and drive north for 2.2 miles to the park entrance. Turn right and park in the first parking lot, near the ranger station trailer.

Information and Contact

There is no fee. Dogs on leash are allowed. A free trail map is available at park headquarters. For more information, contact Vasquez Rocks Natural Area, 10700 W. Escondido Canyon Road, Agua Dulce, CA 91350, 661/268-0840, http://parks.co.la.ca.us.

② LA TUNA CANYON TRAIL
Verdugo Mountains

Level: Moderate

Total Distance: 8.0-11.2 miles round-trip

Hiking Time: 4-5.5 hours

Elevation Gain: 1,600 feet

Summary: A lesser-used trail leads up to the network of fire roads that runs along the spine of the Verdugo Mountains, offering far-reaching views.

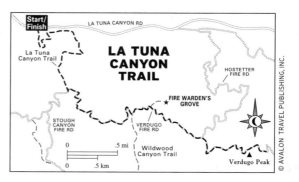

The Verdugo Mountains, sandwiched between the San Gabriel Range to the north and Griffith Park to the south, are popular with hikers in the northeast San Fernando Valley and La Crescenta Valley for good reason—they are rugged, easy to access, and offer a variety of trails.

The only problem is that the paths of the Verdugos are generally poorly signed. La Tuna Canyon Trail is a good example. It's not even easy to find the trailhead, tucked into the brush on La Tuna Canyon Road on the north side of the range. It's marked only by a Santa Monica Mountains Conservancy sign.

Nonetheless, La Tuna Canyon Trail is well worth the hunt. Once you park, you'll see two trails heading into the hills. Take the one on the left. In about a quarter of a mile, there is a creek and waterfall off a small path to the right, definitely worth a quick detour if the water is running full. Then head back to the main trail, which now starts switchbacking steeply up the chaparral-covered east side of the canyon. In the spring, the hillsides are colored with pale blue phacelia. Purple-stalked black sage and orange and yellow deerweed sprout in patches several feet high along the trail.

The trail swings back toward La Tuna Canyon Road, and in about 10 minutes you'll see and hear the I-210 freeway. As the trail leads south, you'll soon lose sight of the traffic. The trail starts to descend into the next canyon to the north and finally reaches a creek shaded by sycamores and oaks. Cross the creek, hike uphill, and then descend to another crossing. Now the real work begins. As you head uphill from the creek, look into the woods, where an old truck has come to rest at the canyon bottom.

The trail begins its final mile-long ascent out of the canyon, following the steepest grade of the day. A short distance from the top, you'll spot a flag perched on a hillock, but that's not the ridge's high point. A hiker sign with an arrow points the way. At 2.2 miles from the start, you'll reach Verdugo Fire Road (also known as Verdugo Motorway), which runs along the spine of the range.

Since you've climbed this far, you might as well continue along the ridge-line and enjoy the views you have already earned. Turn left (east) on Verdugo Fire Road and continue climbing, although thankfully more moderately now. Take a look around at the city spectacle far below: Burbank and its airport are directly south. To the north is the mouth of Tujunga Canyon, with Mount Lukens and its radio towers just to the east of it. The Glendale Freeway is prominent, as well as almost all of the San Fernando Valley.

Many hikers head for the 3,126-foot summit of Verdugo Peak, 3.4 miles from the top of La Tuna Canyon Trail. Follow Verdugo Fire Road all the way to a fork 0.3 mile beyond a junction with Hostetter Fire Road on the left. Head right and walk a final short stretch uphill to the antenna-covered summit (an 11.2-mile round-trip). If you aren't feeling that energetic, a good midpoint destination is the Fire Warden's Grove, a cluster of planted pines and cedars at 1.8 miles out along the fire road, accessible via a left turn and a quarter-mile walk, making it 8.0 miles round-trip. The grove was part of an experimental forest that was planted in the 1950s. No matter what you pick for your destination and turnaround point, the views along the

© JULIE SHEER

La Tuna Canyon Trail is lush with greenery and wildflowers in the spring.

Verdugos' high ridgeline will surely impress. And a bonus: The trek back to your car is all downhill.

Options

With two cars, you can do a 10-mile one-way shuttle hike between the La Tuna Canyon trailhead and Brand Park in Glendale. To get to Brand Park, take the Western Avenue exit off Highway 134 and follow Western Avenue northeast for 1.5 miles to Mountain Street and the park entrance.

Directions

From I-210 in Tujunga, exit at La Tuna Canyon Road and head west. In 1.5 miles, turn left into a pullout on the south side of the road (this requires making a U-turn, so exercise caution). The trail begins at the trailhead sign on the left.

Information and Contact

There is no fee. Dogs are allowed. A trail map of the Angeles Front Country, which includes the Verdugo Mountains, is available for a fee from Tom Harrison Maps, 800/265-9090, www.tomharrisonmaps.com. For more information, contact the Santa Monica Mountains Conservancy, 5750 Ramirez Canyon Road, Malibu, CA 90265, 310/589-3200 or 310/858-7272, www.la-mountains.com.

3 STOUGH CANYON TO VERDUGO FIRE ROAD   BEST ☾

Stough Canyon Park, Verdugo Mountains

🚶 🏕 🚌

Level: Easy

Hiking Time: 1 hour

Total Distance: 2.0 miles round-trip

Elevation Gain: 550 feet

Summary: The best views in the area can be had on an easy hike to the crest of the Verdugo Mountains, just minutes from downtown Burbank.

What is there to do in Burbank other than shop at Ikea and tour Warner Bros. Studios? Try a hike in the Verdugo Mountains, those velvety green peaks (in spring, at least) that form a scenic backdrop for this movie industry town.

The Verdugos are an island of wilderness—9,000 acres of open space wedged between the San Gabriel Mountains to the northeast and Griffith Park and the eastern Santa Monica Mountains to the south. They are considered a "significant ecological area" by Los Angeles County because they provide what remains of a link between plant and animal populations in the Santa Monica and San Gabriel Mountains. Although some housing developments have crept up the foothills on both sides of the range, the Verdugos are still primarily open space, offering great opportunities for hiking, biking, and horseback riding.

Stough Canyon is one of a series of canyons that run along the south end of the range. The canyon gives hikers the means (a fire road) to ascend to a network of trails centered around the Verdugo Fire Road, also known as the Verdugo Motorway (although cars are not permitted on it), which travels along the spine of the range. For this trip, a hike up Old Youth Campground Trail combines nicely with a visit to the Stough Canyon Nature Center, perhaps followed by a picnic at adjacent Stough Park and a nighttime performance at the Starlight Bowl outdoor amphitheatre.

Start out with a visit to the nature center, which is at the far end of the

Some of the best high views of Burbank are from the Old Youth Campground Trail in Stough Canyon.

parking lot at the end of Walnut Avenue. Here docents offer scheduled bird-watching, fitness, and full-moon hikes. You can pick up a trail map (for a small donation) and borrow a hiking stick if you wish. Begin hiking just behind the nature center. A fire road quickly ascends a steep hill above the parking lot. Pass a bench at the top, and the fire road continues to the right. Stay left for the Old Youth Campground Trail.

The trail continues to ascend steeply along chaparral-clad slopes. Look directly west for views of Burbank Airport and a constant parade of planes taking off and landing. Downtown L.A. can be seen straight to the south. In about a half mile are the ruins of what is believed to be a youth campground that burned down in the 1960s. All that is left is a concrete foundation and a still-intact pinkish stone fireplace.

Continue on the trail past the ruins to a small picnic area. Just beyond that is the top, Verdugo Fire Road. Make a loop by turning right on the fire road, walking about 100 yards, then turning right on Stough Canyon Fire Road, which travels 0.9 mile back to the nature center.

Options

Continue east or west on Verdugo Fire Road at the top of Stough Canyon Trail. To cross over to La Tuna Canyon, turn right (east) and hike 0.5 mile, then turn left on La Tuna Canyon Trail and head downhill 2.2 miles to the trailhead at La Tuna Canyon Road. You'll need to have a car shuttle waiting for you at the trailhead. Or, turn right on Verdugo Fire Road and hike east 2.7 miles (with another 1,000 feet of gain) to the Fire Warden's Grove, north of Wildwood Canyon.

Directions

From I-5 in Burbank, exit at Olive Avenue/Verdugo Avenue and head north. Drive 1.2 miles on Olive Avenue and turn left on Sunset Canyon Drive. Take

Sunset Canyon until it ends in about 0.75 mile and turn right (north) on Walnut Avenue, which turns into Stough Canyon Avenue. Take that until it ends in about one mile at the Stough Canyon Nature Center. If you park in the nature center lot, note that the parking lot closes promptly at 5 P.M. You can also park right outside the lot, on Walnut Avenue, just beyond De Bell Golf Course.

Public transportation: The Metro Bus 183 stops at the northwest corner of Bel Aire Drive and Magnolia Boulevard. From there, walk north on Magnolia one block, turn left on Sunset Canyon Drive and walk six blocks, then turn right on Walnut Avenue. Walk 1.25 miles to the Stough Canyon Nature Center.

Information and Contact

There is no fee. Dogs are allowed. A trail map is available for a donation at the Stough Canyon Nature Center. For more information, contact Stough Canyon Nature Center, 2300 Walnut Avenue, Burbank, 818/238-5440.

4 TRAIL CANYON TRAIL   BEST (

Angeles National Forest

Level: Moderate   **Total Distance:** 8.4 miles round-trip

Hiking Time: 4 hours   **Elevation Gain:** 2,000 feet

Summary: Visit one of the best wet-season waterfalls in the Angeles Front Country, then continue on a streamside ramble in the rugged canyon above the falls.

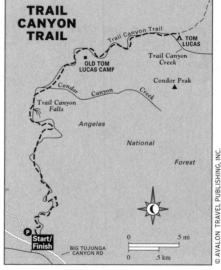

Tell your friends you want to go for a hike on the Trail Canyon Trail and they may accuse you of redundancy. But hey, that's what it's called. The "trail" in Trail Canyon doesn't refer to the path you walk but rather the remnants left behind from gold flakes in the creekbed. Placer miners worked this stream in the late 1800s and gave it its name.

During the wet season—and that is by far the most fun time to hike here—Trail Canyon Trail begins with a ford and has several more along the way, so make sure you wear waterproof boots or river shoes, or are willing to get your feet wet. Otherwise, Trail Canyon Trail is a breeze to follow and rewarding every step of the way. In spring, you'll see an abundance of wildflowers. During the wet months, you'll visit an impressive 40-foot-high waterfall. And any time of year, you'll enjoy treading this well-maintained footpath through a wild stream canyon.

After parking at the trailhead, follow the dirt road into a small community of 1930s-era cabins, then continue on the road past them, winding around the canyon. (Or follow the alternate hiker's trail, which meets up with the road again in short order.) At 0.7 mile, where the road makes a hairpin left turn, a single-track trail leads off to the right, crossing the stream. Follow it, and you'll leave the chaparral and enter a densely shaded riparian corridor lined with sycamores, alders, and oaks. Then, a mere half mile later, you'll leave the leafy

one of many stream crossings above the falls in Trail Canyon

shade and switchback gradually uphill across more sparsely vegetated slopes on the west canyon wall. You get a little bit of everything in Trail Canyon.

At 1.25 miles from the start, the trail curves left sharply, and suddenly Trail Canyon Falls appears up ahead, a quarter mile distant. At full flow, the falls make a stunning show of white as they thunder down the canyon. The water spills over a smooth granite precipice in a rectangular block shape as wide as 15 feet when the fall is flowing hard. By midsummer, of course, the waterfall is greatly diminished.

The trail, which ascends steadily up to this point, suddenly levels out for an easy stroll to the fall's crest. A few steps before you cross over the brink, a spur trail leads to its base and big pool. It is steep and often slippery, so tread carefully if you choose to descend.

After casting a few admiring glances at the falls from above or below, continue upcanyon, making your way through more stream crossings. Your destination is one of two Tom Lucas Trail Camps—the older camp, which is now nothing more than a single campfire ring, is found just to the right of the trail at 2.6 miles out (easy to miss). The rest of the camp was destroyed in a 1968 flood. The new camp, which is shaded by bay laurel and sycamore and has four tent sites, fire grills, and picnic tables, is 4.2 miles out on the lower edge of Big Cienaga meadow. You'll have to gain some elevation to get there, but the trail is moderately graded and a pleasant walk.

But in reality, you can call any point your destination. Just pick a suitable spot along the stream and make it your home for an hour or two. It's all about the journey here—the peace of this quiet canyon, a playful stream rushing over colorful granite rocks, and the leafy shade of sycamores and alders.

Options

If you choose to spend the night at the newer Tom Lucas Trail Camp, or if you don't mind a very long day hike, you can head for one of two summits—5,635-foot Iron Mountain or slighter shorter Condor Peak. Iron Mountain is three miles from the camp via Trail Canyon Trail and Mendenhall Ridge Fire Road. Condor Peak is 3.3 miles from the camp via Trail Canyon Trail and Condor Peak Trail.

Directions

From I-210 in Sunland, take the Sunland Boulevard exit. Cross Sunland Boulevard and head east on Foothill Boulevard for 1.2 miles to Mount Gleason Avenue. Turn left (north), drive 1.4 miles, then turn right on Big Tujunga Canyon Road. Drive 3.4 miles on Big Tujunga Canyon Road to a sign for Trail Canyon on the left. Bear left on a dirt road (Road 3N29), drive 0.25 mile to a fork, then bear right and drive 0.25 mile to a large parking lot. The trailhead is on the left side of the lot.

Information and Contact

There is no fee, but a national forest adventure pass is required; see page 297 for more information. Dogs are allowed. A trail map of the Angeles Front Country is available for a fee from Tom Harrison Maps, 800/265-9090, www.tomharrisonmaps.com. For more information, contact Angeles National Forest, Los Angeles River Ranger District, 12371 N. Little Tujunga Canyon Road, San Fernando, CA 91342, 818/899-1900, www.fs.fed.us/r5/angeles.

5 STONE CANYON TRAIL
TO MOUNT LUKENS
Angeles National Forest

BEST ☾

Level: Butt-kicker

Total Distance: 7.5 miles round-trip

Hiking Time: 4 hours

Elevation Gain: 3,300 feet

Summary: If you are itching to bag a peak but don't want to leave the city, here's a relentlessly steep hike to the highest peak within the boundaries of the city of L.A., with rewarding views at the summit.

Ask most Stone Canyon regulars why they hike the quadriceps-melting trail to 5,074-foot Mount Lukens, and they'll say it's good training for more grown-up Southern California peaks, such as 11,502-foot San Gorgonio.

Sure, there are higher practice peaks in the San Gabriels, but not many are as easy to access and allow you to tally up so much elevation in such a short distance as Stone Canyon Trail (3,300-plus feet in just under four miles). Several routes lead to Mount Lukens's summit, but the others tend to be long slogs on fire roads. Stone Canyon Trail is a footpath almost all the way, rocky in places, offering alpine-style views.

Because of its proximity to the northern San Fernando Valley, the area tends to bake in the summer and fall, so winter and spring are the best times to hike the trail. Make sure to bring plenty of water, even in winter. Keep an eye on the weather, too. Hikers here have been hit with rain, hail, and even snow en route to the summit.

After parking at Wildwood Picnic Area (last chance for a restroom), do some stretches and take a swig of water and a deep breath before setting out. The trail is not immediately obvious, but head to the far east end of the parking lot and you'll spot it. You'll hike about 100 yards before turning south and crossing Big Tujunga Creek. You can boulder-hop across it most of the year, but beware that during heavy rains, the creek becomes a raging torrent.

The trail starts out innocently enough, but once the ascent starts, it doesn't let up. There are a few shady spots, but the path is mostly exposed. As you follow the switchbacks steeply uphill, you'll be treated to views of Stone Canyon and surrounding peaks. During rest stops, in between huffing and puffing, note the gradual change in vegetation. It transitions from chaparral to big-cone Douglas fir on the northern slopes during the last 0.25 mile before cresting the ridge.

In about 3.5 miles, just when you are wondering if you'll ever reach the summit, there's a wooden sign pointing to misspelled "Mount Lukins" and Sister Elsie Peak, the peak's alternate name. Now you'll head east (left) 0.25 mile on a fire road to the top.

The summit itself is treeless and a bit unsightly with its array of transmission towers, but there are plenty of spots to sit and take in the views and a well-earned lunch. Geography fans will enjoy picking out landmarks. The deep green folds of the Verdugo Mountains are directly south, and downtown L.A. lies beyond. On a clear day you can spot Long Beach, along with the distinctive outline of the Palos Verdes Peninsula and Catalina Island shimmering in the distance.

Mount Lukens was named for Theodore P. Lukens, mayor of Pasadena in

The views continue on the hike back down from the summit of Mount Lukens.

the late 1800s and a pioneer forester who helped establish the experimental conifer forest at Henninger Flats, above Altadena. Lukens was a naturalist, a friend of John Muir, and an early land protection advocate who urged federal protection for Yosemite National Park. A lake in Yosemite, just off Tioga Pass Road, now bears his name.

On the way back down, you'll be breathing easier and will be more likely to catch the splendid views you missed trudging up. There's 5,440-foot Condor Peak due north, and Mount Baldy's snowy pate looming in the distance. Descending farther, you'll get a hawk's-eye view of Big Tujunga Canyon and the road below. If it's late in the day, the canyon will disappear into shadows as you make your way to the creek and the welcome comfort of your car.

Options
A much less strenuous hike is possible from the nearby trailhead at Stonyvale picnic area on Big Tujunga Canyon Road, 1.25 miles east of the turnoff for Wildwood picnic area. The trail to Grizzly Flat, a grove of planted pines, is seven miles round-trip with 1,500 feet of gain.

Directions
From I-210 in Sunland, take the Sunland Boulevard exit. Cross Sunland Boulevard and head east on Foothill Boulevard 0.75 mile. Turn left (north) on Oro Vista Avenue. In 0.8 mile, Oro Vista Avenue turns into Big Tujunga Canyon Road. Drive 5.25 miles on Big Tujunga Canyon Road to Doske Road. Turn right on Doske Road and park at Wildwood picnic area. (This lot is often closed from November through March; during these months you must park outside the Wildwood gate in pullouts along road. This adds 0.4 mile and about 100 feet of elevation gain on your return.)

Information and Contact
There is no fee, but a national forest adventure pass is required; see page 297 for more information. Dogs are allowed. A trail map of the Angeles Front Country is available for a fee from Tom Harrison Maps, 800/265-9090, www.tomharrisonmaps.com. For more information, contact the Los Angeles River Ranger District, 12371 North Little Tujunga Canyon Road, San Fernando, CA 91342, 818/899-1900, www.fs.fed.us/r5/angeles. After heavy rains, be sure to phone ahead to find out whether Big Tujunga Creek is crossable.

6 GABRIELINO TRAIL   BEST ◖

Angeles National Forest

Level: Easy/Moderate   **Total Distance:** 3.8-10.0 miles round-trip

Hiking Time: 2-5 hours   **Elevation Gain:** 250-700 feet

Summary: A leisurely ramble at the edge of Altadena along a sylvan creek in one of the Los Angeles area's most historic canyons.

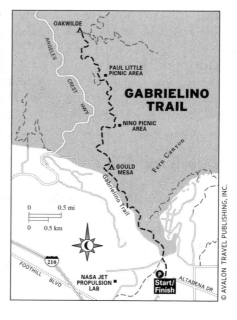

During the late 1800s and early 1900s, the canyon of the Arroyo Seco was lined with vacation cabins and resorts. Today, hikers will encounter ruins from those original structures, a washed-out bridge, and other remnants from that era. The Arroyo Seco is as popular today as it was in yesteryear. It is still one of the most heavily used outdoor recreation corridors in the Los Angeles area.

Arroyo Seco extends from its headwaters near Mount Wilson through Pasadena all the way to downtown Los Angeles, where it flows into the Los Angeles River. Its urban portions are encased in concrete, with the Pasadena Freeway running alongside it on the lower end. But its upper reaches still flow untamed in a densely wooded sylvan setting. The farther you are willing to hike, the wilder the Arroyo Seco becomes.

The hike is pretty most of the year, but it's worth a return trip in the late autumn when big-leaf maples and sycamores begin to show their colors. It's not exactly New England, but it's pretty close.

Park at the lot near the corner of Windsor Avenue and Ventura Street in Altadena and walk north on Windsor, which turns into Arroyo Avenue and eventually Gabrielino Trail. Stay to the right at the trailhead gate; the route left goes to NASA's Jet Propulsion Laboratory, which sits on the other side of the Arroyo Seco.

The first part of the hike is paved and decidedly not pristine, as it passes

The Gabrielino Trail runs alongside the Arroyo Seco, which swells during years of heavy rain.

various facilities owned by the Pasadena Water Department. The Arroyo Seco is an important water source for Pasadena. But be patient. A little over a half mile in, the forest closes in as the trail veers left after crossing a quaint stone bridge. Soon you pass a turnoff on the right to Lower Brown Mountain Road and El Prieto Trail. Stay to the left on the main trail, which now is an unpaved road bordering the creek. It's lush with vegetation, with much of the trail shaded by a maple and sycamore canopy.

At 1.9 miles in, you'll reach a picnic area set among oaks and pines called Teddy's Outpost, named for a small resort located here in the early 1900s. In wet years, the creek receives trout plants from the California Department of Fish and Game; the fish usually hang out in the bigger pools until some lucky angler finds them. In the really wet years, the creek can run so high that it's impassable.

For those hiking with small children, Teddy's Outpost is a good destination and turnaround point. For those who choose to continue, there are several more rest stops ahead. You'll boulder-hop across the creek to get to Gould Mesa Campground, which is 2.4 miles in and an easy destination for a day hike. The camp has picnic tables, grills, and restrooms.

The trail gets more woodsy as you forge ahead. You'll cross several bridges before reaching other popular picnic spots, including Nino, at three miles in, and Paul Little, at four miles. Beyond Paul Little, the trail climbs the canyon to avoid a debris dam, and then descends. In 0.8 mile is Oakwilde Campground, five miles in from the trailhead. Crumbling foundations remain from a resort that stood here in the early 1900s. This is also reportedly near one of the hangouts of famed bandit Tiburcio Vasquez, who spent the last several years of his bandido career in the 1870s in the mountains and desert of Southern California.

As Vasquez surely discovered, the trail gets gnarly after Oakwilde, so this is a good place to turn back. Herein lies the beauty of the Gabrielino Trail—you can hike in as far you want for an easy few miles or make it a long day by going all the way to Switzer picnic area, eight miles away.

Options

One popular shuttle hike is to leave a car at the Windsor/Ventura parking lot and start the hike at Switzer picnic area on Highway 2 (Angeles Crest Highway). It's eight miles downhill from there to the Gabrielino Trail start in Altadena.

Directions

From I-210 in Pasadena, exit at Arroyo Boulevard/Windsor Avenue north, heading into Altadena. Go north on Windsor Avenue for 0.7 mile, and at the intersection of Mountain View Road, just before Ventura Street, turn left into the parking area.

Public transportation: Metro Bus 267 line stops on Lincoln Avenue at Ventura Street. From the stop, walk west 0.5 mile (about four blocks) on Ventura Street. At Windsor Avenue, turn right (north) to the Gabrielino Trail trailhead. The Metro Bus 268 line stops on Oak Grove Drive at Windsor Avenue. From there, walk north on Windsor Avenue 0.75 mile to the trailhead. For more information, visit www.metro.net.

Information and Contact

There is no fee. This trail is wheelchair accessible and dogs are allowed. A trail map of the Mount Wilson area is available for a fee from Tom Harrison Maps, 800/265-9090, www.tomharrisonmaps.com. For more information, contact Angeles National Forest, Los Angeles River Ranger District, 12371 North Little Tujunga Canyon Road, San Fernando, CA 91342, 818/899-1900, www.fs.fed.us/r5/angeles.

7 SAM MERRILL TRAIL TO ECHO MOUNTAIN AND WHITE CITY BEST ◖

Angeles National Forest

🏕 🦌 🎿 ⚙ 🐎

Level: Moderate

Total Distance: 5.4 miles round-trip

Hiking Time: 2.5 hours

Elevation Gain: 1,400 feet

Summary: Climb to the summit of Echo Mountain to see the remains of a popular stop on the Mount Lowe Railway and enjoy sweeping city views.

As the late 19th century witnessed a huge surge in the popularity of outdoor tourism, Western ingenuity was frequently spent on inventions designed to increase travel to outdoor resorts and recreation sites. Automobiles weren't in common usage yet, so trains were the way to go. Two of the most famous tourist railways of this age were the "Crookedest Railway in the World" on Mount Tamalpais, near San Francisco, and the Mount Lowe "Railway to the Clouds" in the San Gabriel Mountains. The Sam Merrill Trail visits one of the most interesting stops on the Mount Lowe Railway, the great White City on Echo Mountain.

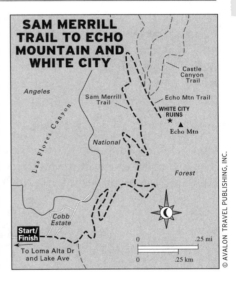

The railway was the brainchild of Professor Thaddeus Lowe and David McPherson. In the 1890s, they constructed not only the mountain-climbing rail line, but also the White City on Echo Mountain, the Alpine Tavern at Crystal Springs, and a pavilion in Rubio Canyon. The railway operated from 1898 to 1936, when it declined in popularity with the increase in automobile use and was eventually destroyed by fire and flood.

The Sam Merrill Trail begins on the right side of the stone pillars and driveway that mark the Cobb Estate, now a nature preserve that is managed by Angeles National Forest. In 50 yards the trail heads off to the right, departing the edge of the driveway. In short order it brings you to the lively stream in Los Flores Canyon. Trails go every which way along the creek, but you want to cross it above its large check dam and begin your climb to Echo Mountain.

The first couple miles of this hike are nothing more than a nature walk through some lovely chaparral-covered hillsides. Today it's difficult to imagine that a railway line and an entire city was built high up in these hills; it seems like this land could only be the tranquil home of bobcats and butterflies, lizards and wildflowers. The well-graded trail makes for a pleasant, albeit athletic, ascent. A few short sections in the first mile suffer from frequent washouts, but you can make your way around them.

Because this trail backs up on the neighborhoods of Altadena, you'll see plenty of hikers here; a weekday visit is advised for solitude-seekers. Many hikers wear tennis or running shoes, although the eroding treadway is much better suited for hiking boots. Poison oak is rampant, as are more well-liked chaparral plants such as yerba santa, sage, sticky monkeyflower, bush lupine, and ceanothus. Two miles up, as you near the top of the climb, you can look down and see the rows and rows of switchbacks you have climbed, cutting snaking swaths through the dense chaparral. On a clear day, views of the L.A. basin are spectacular. It's easy to pick out Catalina Island and the tall buildings of downtown L.A.

At a trail junction, Sam Merrill Trail ends and Echo Mountain Trail begins. Go right for Echo Mountain, and the grade suddenly levels out. In less than a quarter mile, you are at the White City ruins and a spectacular overlook atop Echo Mountain, elevation 3,200 feet. This spot was the top of the great

Hikers stand amid the ruins of the White City on Echo Mountain.

cable incline of the Mount Lowe Railway, which carried thrill-seeking guests uphill from Rubio Canyon, a steep 3,000 feet below.

First-timers will be surprised at the amount of ruins to be seen. Most obvious are the foundations for the city's power plant, old machine and cable workings from the incline railway, and the concrete steps and foundation of the Echo Mountain House. But in its heyday, the White City offered so much more: a hotel with a post office and dining room, an observatory with a resident astronomer, a dance hall, tennis courts, a pig pen, a casino, and more. Have a seat on the concrete foundation and enjoy the spectacular view of the valley below, and the feeling of history that resonates in the air.

Options

Castle Canyon Trail begins at Echo Mountain. You can follow it for two miles more to Inspiration Point, or 2.5 miles to Mount Lowe Campground. Either site is bound to have fewer visitors than the popular White City/Echo Mountain site.

Directions

From I-210 in Pasadena, take the Lake Avenue exit and drive north 3.5 miles to its end, where it junctions with Loma Alta Drive. Park along the street and begin walking on the trail to the right of the stone pillars of the Cobb Estate.

Information and Contact

There is no fee. Dogs are allowed. A trail map of the Mount Wilson area is available for a fee from Tom Harrison Maps, 800/265-9090, www.tomharrisonmaps.com. For more information, contact Angeles National Forest, Los Angeles River Ranger District, 12371 North Little Tujunga Canyon Road, San Fernando, CA 91342, 818/899-1900, www.fs.fed.us/r5/angeles.

8 DAWN MINE LOOP
Angeles National Forest

🏕 🦌 🌿 🚲 🐴

Level: Moderate   **Total Distance:** 5.8 miles round-trip

Hiking Time: 3 hours   **Elevation Gain:** 1,600 feet

Summary: A few scattered ruins of L.A.'s gold mining history can be seen in water-filled Millard Canyon.

This rugged canyon hike in the backyards of Pasadena and Altadena gives you a glimpse into Southern California's gold mining history. In the winter and spring months, you'll get your feet wet here; the rest of the year, Millard Creek is small and gentle enough for easy rock-hopping.

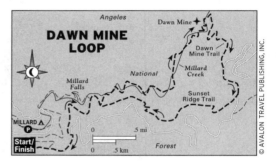

From the paved fire road where you begin walking, you'll quickly spot a trail to Millard Campground on your left and a sign interpreting the Mount Lowe Railway on your right. (For more on the railway, see previous listing, the Sam Merrill Trail to Echo Mountain and White City.) One hundred yards farther is the signed Sunset Ridge Trail. Leave the paved road and follow the dirt trail, and you'll soon be permitted a glimpse of Millard Falls across the canyon (see Options, below). Your surroundings change quite suddenly from dry and hot to damp and shady as you leave the chaparral and enter a fern-filled bay laurel forest.

At a fork 0.3 mile in, head left and downhill (the right fork is the return of this loop). You'll pass a small cabin and then start making your way up the streambed. Most of the travel is fairly easy, but in the rainy months you will have to do some slogging and scrambling. Just keep following the stream, heading gradually uphill. Where the canyon makes an obvious hairpin turn to the north, you'll find the mine ruins. Gold was discovered here in 1895, and the Dawn Mine was worked on and off for the next 50 years. The miners had big aspirations, but no one got rich.

Several informal paths head straight uphill from the mine ruins to join the Dawn Mine Trail, but it is far better to stay off the eroding canyon walls and instead backtrack about 100 yards downstream to a better trail that switchbacks uphill. Once you meet up with Dawn Mine Trail, go right. You now face a steep and narrow uphill tromp over 1.3 miles. It may not surprise you to learn that this cliff-hugging, eroded trail is the remains of an old mule pathway. It was used by two burros named Jack and Jill to carry partially processed ore from Dawn Mine to the railroad line on the ridge above.

The trail tops out at Stop 4 on the Mount Lowe Railway, where you have a chance to finally catch your breath and enjoy fine views of the canyon you just departed. The views continue, spreading out over much of Pasadena and its environs, as you head right on the dirt road to the Cape of Good Hope, a rocky overlook point. There, continue on a paved road until you see the signed Sunset Ridge Trail on your right. Follow Sunset Ridge Trail back down to the start of the loop, then bear left and walk the final short distance back to your car.

Options

From the same trailhead, follow the trail on the left to the parking area for Millard Campground. Walk through the campground and then continue hiking and rock-hopping upstream along the creek. In less than a half mile, you'll be holding court with Millard Canyon Falls, a 50-foot waterfall that runs with enthusiasm in the winter and spring months, less so in the summer and fall.

© ANN MARIE BROWN

A few bits and pieces remain from the hope-filled days of the Dawn Mine.

Directions

From I-210 in Pasadena, take the Lake Avenue exit and drive north 3.5 miles to the end of Lake Avenue. Turn left on Loma Alta Drive. Drive one mile and turn right on Chaney Trail. Drive 1.1 miles to the top of Sunset Ridge. Bear right at the junction and park alongside the road, near the white gate. Start walking on the paved fire road.

Information and Contact

A national forest adventure pass is required; see page 297 for more information. Dogs are allowed. A trail map of the Mount Wilson area is available for a fee from Tom Harrison Maps, 800/265-9090, www.tomharrisonmaps.com. For more information, contact Angeles National Forest, Los Angeles River Ranger District, 12371 North Little Tujunga Canyon Road, San Fernando, CA 91342, 818/899-1900, www.fs.fed.us/r5/angeles.

9 HENNINGER FLATS
Angeles National Forest

Level: Moderate

Total Distance: 6.0 miles round-trip

Hiking Time: 3 hours

Elevation Gain: 1,540 feet

Summary: With easy access from the San Gabriel Valley, Henninger Flats is a popular front country hike that offers a solid workout, big views on a clear day, and loads of history.

Where in L.A. can you catch a quick hike or backpack after work and still hit the office the next morning? On the Mount Wilson Toll Road to Henninger Flats, a fire road once used by early settlers to transport crops to Pasadena. The trek is very popular with local hiking groups because its steepness makes it a good warm-up for higher-elevation climbs. Some hikers even haul up grocery bags with dinner fixin's for an after-work meal under the pines.

Be prepared to break a sweat. It's not a long hike, but there is no letup to the climb, and little or no shade. This hike is perfect in the cooler months but should be avoided during the heat of day in summer.

A popular place to start is at Eaton Canyon Natural Area, a favorite spot for families and hikers escaping the surrounding suburban sprawl. From the parking lot, go to the north end of the nature center and follow the fire road past a gate and then down to and across Eaton Wash, which is usually dry or barely a trickle, but can be raging after winter rains (see the next listing, Eaton Canyon Falls). After crossing the creek, turn left (north) onto Eaton Canyon Trail. Enjoy the shade of the towering oaks and the gentle climb, because it won't last long.

This lovely stretch continues for about a mile toward the white-railed bridge over the wash. Instead of turning left and crossing the bridge, turn right onto the fire road that begins climbing severely uphill. This is the Mount Wilson

© JULIE SHEER

A grove of pines marks the top of the Mount Wilson Toll Road hike to Henninger Flats.

Toll Road and the start of your trek to the flats. While trudging along, try to think positive thoughts about what a great workout you're getting, and refrain from cursing the negative-body-fat trail runners jogging past you while gabbing on their cell phones.

You'll know you're at the last switchback when you get a birds-eye view of Santa Anita Racetrack, where the famous steed Seabiscuit once ruled. Just ahead, you'll spot Henninger's conspicuous grove of pine trees rising above the thick chaparral that dominates the terrain. Take a rest and enjoy a shady picnic beneath the towering pines. There are tables, grills, water, restrooms, a visitor center, and an old fire tower moved from Castro Peak in the Santa Monica Mountains. Stroll over to the tree nursery, which is maintained by the L.A. County Fire Department. An experimental conifer forest here in the early 1900s helped researchers determine which trees were best suited to Southern California's Mediterranean climate. After being raised in the mountains, trees were planted along roadsides throughout L.A. County, and seeds and seedlings were shipped to foresters around the world.

A visit to the visitor center will teach you that William Henninger was a gold miner, farmer, and politician who first settled the flats in 1880. In the center's small museum, you can get a glimpse of what life was like long before there were drive-through Starbucks. There are historic photos of the Mount Lowe Railroad, display cases with mining gear, and a diorama of a pioneer cabin room, complete with a stuffed raccoon warming its paws at a wood stove.

If you decide to spend the night, there is no fee at the 17 campsites at Henninger Flats, and firewood is free. If camping is not on the agenda, the return trip to Eaton Canyon will be a quick downhill jaunt. Unfortunately, at this book's press time, the trail to Henniger Flats was blocked by a landslide and is expected to reopen by summer 2006.

Options
Continue on Mount Wilson Toll Road from Henninger Flats for another 1.5 miles and 490 feet of gain to the turnoff (left) for the Idlehour Trail. Hike Idlehour another 1.5 miles and you'll reach a U.S. Forest Service backcountry campground. You can continue another three miles past Idlehour Camp to Mount Lowe. To get to Mount Wilson from Henninger Flats, it's an additional 7.5 miles and another 3,000 feet of gain—a genuine butt-kicker.

Directions
From eastbound I-210 in Pasadena, exit at Altadena Drive/Sierra Madre Boulevard and go north for 1.6 miles. Turn right into Eaton Canyon Natural Area.

From westbound I-210 in Pasadena, exit at Sierra Madre Boulevard/San Marino, which turns into Maple Street. Cross Sierra Madre Boulevard and turn right at Altadena Drive. Drive 1.6 miles and turn right into Eaton Canyon Natural Area.

Public transportation: Take the Gold Line light rail from Union Station in downtown Los Angeles to the last stop on the line, Sierra Madre Villa. At Foothill Boulevard next to the station, board the MTA's 264 bus, which can drop you at the intersection of Altadena Drive and New York Drive, a short walk from the park entrance. For more information, visit www.mta.net.

Information and Contact
There is no fee. Dogs are allowed. A trail map of the Mount Wilson area is available for a fee from Tom Harrison Maps, 800/265-9090, www.tomharrisonmaps.com. Mount Wilson Toll Road is closed to the public during extreme fire hazard periods and after heavy rains. For more information, contact the L.A. County Fire Department's Henninger Flats forestry unit, 626/794-0675, or Eaton Canyon Natural Area, 1750 N. Altadena Drive, Pasadena, CA 91107, 626/398-5420. Or contact Angeles National Forest, Los Angeles River Ranger District, 12371 North Little Tujunga Canyon Road, San Fernando, CA 91342, 818/899-1900, www.fs.fed.us/r5/angeles.

🔟 EATON CANYON FALLS

Eaton Canyon Natural Area

Level: Easy/Moderate

Total Distance: 3.0 miles round-trip

Hiking Time: 1.5 hours

Elevation Gain: 300 feet

Summary: An easy family hike in summer or a challenging wet slog in winter leads to one of L.A.'s most popular waterfalls.

How hard this hike is depends entirely on when you go. In the summer, when Eaton Canyon's stream level subsides, this trip is ridiculously easy. In late winter and spring, it can take well over an hour to go the short 1.5 miles to the falls. You will certainly get your feet wet (and maybe other body parts too), given the umpteen rock-hops that must be accomplished as you crisscross back and forth across the stream. Although this is a great walk for families in the summer and fall months, it is too rugged for children when the water flows hard, with wet boulders to scramble over and deep, cold stream crossings.

Keep in mind that Eaton Canyon is much more like a desert wash than many other L.A. streams. The predominant foliage is of the xeric variety—chaparral, willows, and low-growing oaks, plus a few chollas and cactus thrown in to keep you on your toes. Wear your sun hat, even in winter, and don't expect to find much shade.

Start hiking at the yellow metal gate at the far end of the parking lot. The trail drops down to the wide wash and travels about 70 yards to a place where you can comfortably cross the stream. On the far side, pick up the wide, level trail and head upstream (left). Some hikers choose not to cross here but instead follow one of several informal paths on the west side of the stream. Sooner or later, though, everyone is forced to cross.

At one mile out, just before the crumbling remains of a white bridge over the wash, the trail splits. A sign points upstream (toward the bridge) to Eaton Canyon Falls; another trail leads right and uphill. Stay low along the stream and continue up the wash, now on a considerably more rugged trail. The wide, straight wash you've been following becomes more chan-neled, more curvaceous, more wild. You'll see several old check dams and evidence of an aqueduct system—this canyon's water was once tamed for ir-rigating ranchlands. As the stream's curves get tighter, the canyon walls start to pinch in.

Crossing Eaton Canyon's stream in the spring months can be an adventure.

Soon you're in the stream more often than on the trail, crossing it several times as you work your way upcanyon. The route is different each time you hike it, depending on how much water is flowing. Finally, 0.5 mile from the bridge, the canyon makes a sharp left turn, and suddenly you're facing the waterfall. It's a great surprise.

Eaton Canyon Falls pours over a rock wall that has eroded into a low, jag-ged V shape. A large rounded boulder lies perched in its notch. The falls are about 40 feet high, with exceptional flow in springtime. This special spot is marred slightly by old graffiti marks; they are slowly wearing off with time. The great naturalist John Muir, who visited Eaton Falls in 1877, would surely roll over in his grave. Still, on a winter or early spring day, when the falls are flowing with exuberance, nothing could spoil this special place.

Options

At the junction one mile up Eaton Canyon Wash, you can take the right fork that leads uphill and out of the canyon, heading to Henninger Flats in two miles, or, for the very ambitious, Mount Wilson in seven miles (see the previ-ous listing, Henninger Flats).

Directions

From eastbound I-210 in Pasadena, exit at Altadena Drive/Sierra Madre Boulevard and go north for 1.6 miles. Turn right into Eaton Canyon Natural Area.

From westbound I-210 in Pasadena, exit at Sierra Madre Boulevard/San Marino, which turns into Maple Street. Cross Sierra Madre Boulevard and turn right at Altadena Drive. Drive 1.6 miles and turn right into Eaton Canyon Natural Area.

Public transportation: Take the Gold Line light rail from Union Station in downtown Los Angeles to the last stop on the line, Sierra Madre Villa. At Foothill Boulevard next to the station, board the MTA's 264 bus, which can drop you at the intersection of Altadena Drive and New York Drive, a short walk from the park entrance. For more information, visit www.mta.net.

Information and Contact

There is no fee. Dogs on leash are allowed. A park map is available at the nature center. For more information, contact Eaton Canyon Natural Area, 1750 N. Altadena Drive, Pasadena, CA 91107, 626/398-5420, http://parks.co.la.ca.us or www.ecnca.org.

11 BAILEY CANYON TRAIL
Angeles National Forest

Level: Moderate

Total Distance: 4.4 miles round-trip

Hiking Time: 2 hours

Elevation Gain: 1,500 feet

Summary: A front country hike leads to a historic site in a bucolic setting, just minutes from the quaint foothill community of Sierra Madre.

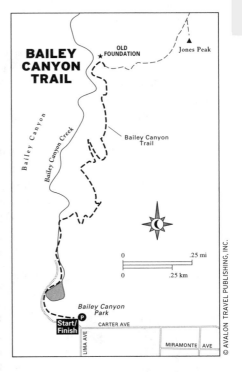

Many hikers drive right by San Gabriel Mountains foothill communities like Sierra Madre, en route to adventures off the Angeles Crest Highway or the high country of Mount Baldy, thinking they won't find a worthwhile trek so close to a shop-laden, small-town main street. But a few minutes from the coffee shops and California Craftsman homes in downtown Sierra Madre lies Bailey Canyon Wilderness Park, which offers something for everyone: a park with picnic tables, short nature trails for the kiddies, and a butt-busting 2,300-foot-gain hike to Jones Peak.

Don't let the nearby gentility fool you—Bailey Canyon is wilderness, and prone to washouts. The picnic area in the park is dedicated to John Henderson and his son Matthew, who were killed in a flash flood in the canyon in 1994. Huge floods in 1938 and 1969 also did considerable damage to an amphitheatre built by the Works Progress Administration, which was situated above the present debris basin adjacent to the park. Needless to say, don't hike here during heavy rain, or when the weather is threatening.

If you don't feel like grinding up to Jones Peak, a reasonable day hike in Bailey Canyon is the first 2.2 miles on Bailey Canyon Trail to the ruins of an early 1900s cabin, referred to as the "Old Foundation" on a sign at the trailhead. The hike starts from the west end of the park. To get there, walk to the left from the parking lot across the park's lawn, heading past the picnic tables. You'll pass through a turnstile leading out of the park and turn right, heading up a paved road. The debris basin is on the right. All of this may seem like a bit too much concrete for a nature experience, but the hike quickly improves once the pavement ends at a wheelchair-accessible parking area that marks the start of the Bailey Canyon Trail.

Bailey Canyon Creek rushes alongside the trail, and in 0.3 mile there is a signed turnoff to the right over a bridge to the Live Oak Nature Trail. This and the next nature trail, Canyon View, 100 yards farther, are good options if hiking with small children. A small waterfall is only 0.25 mile away on Canyon View. You can easily see why early Rose Parade floats were often bedecked with ferns and other vegetation plucked from this lush canyon.

To reach the cabin ruins, stay on the main trail, a single-track footpath that ascends steeply for the next two miles. The trail is lined with spring-blooming wildflowers. Several types of sage dominate, with bright red Indian paintbrush, purple canterbury bells, and blue lupine providing bursts of color. Below the trail you can see the buildings of a monastery, and off in the distance, downtown Los Angeles. Farther up the trail are clear views of Pasadena and neighboring Arcadia. On a clear day, the Palos Verdes Peninsula is visible.

The trail heads deeper up the east slope of the canyon, and in rainy years, a ribbonlike waterfall streams down the far canyon wall. The path continues its switchbacking ascent, with little or no shade. Once you enter a wooded area,

© JULIE SHEER

a bird's-eye view of Sierra Madre from Bailey Canyon Trail

you are close to your destination. It's not marked, but the turnoff to the left is obvious. A few bits and pieces of a stone foundation can be seen—the ruins of two cabins built in 1910 by three students from Cal Tech (called Throop Polytechnic back then), who carted in supplies using burros. The cabins were used by the students and their friends and family until 1942. The structures were eventually vandalized and destroyed.

Just beyond and below the cabin site, the creek reappears and offers a cool, shady respite. Follow a brief path to the water's edge, where you'll find large pools lined with big mossy boulders and massive oaks. Then scramble back up to the main trail and turn left to continue on the hardcore trek to Jones Peak (see Options, below), or turn right to return to your car.

Options

For a much more challenging hike, you can continue past the cabin ruins to 3,375-foot Jones Peak, which adds only another 1.1 miles but a tough 800 feet of gain, a brutal grade by any standard. Still have energy to burn? You can continue another 0.9 mile to a junction with the Mount Wilson Trail, then turn right to make a 7.6-mile loop back to Bailey Canyon Park. It's downhill all the way. You'll have to walk the final half mile back to the park on Miramonte and Carter Avenues.

Directions

From I-210 in Pasadena, take the Rosemead Boulevard/Michillinda Avenue exit and head north. Drive 1.3 miles and turn right on Grandview Avenue. Go 0.3 mile and turn left on Grove Street. Take Grove Street until it ends in 0.2 mile at Carter Avenue. Drive straight into the parking lot for Bailey Canyon Wilderness Park at 451 W. Carter Avenue.

Public transportation: Metro Bus 268 stops at the southeast corner of Sierra Madre Boulevard and Michillinda Avenue. From there, walk north on Michillinda four blocks to Grandview Avenue, then turn right (east) and walk six blocks to Grove Street. Turn left (north) and walk four blocks to the park entrance, at Grove Street and Carter Avenue.

Information and Contact

There is no fee. Dogs are allowed. A trail map of the Mount Wilson area is available for a fee from Tom Harrison Maps, 800/265-9090, www.tomharrisonmaps.com. For more information, contact the City of Sierra Madre, 232 W. Sierra Madre Boulevard, Sierra Madre, CA 91024, 626/355-5278, www.ci.sierra-madre.ca.us.

12 STURTEVANT FALLS AND BIG SANTA ANITA CANYON LOOP   BEST ☾

Angeles National Forest

🏕 🎣 🚲 🐕

Level: Moderate

Total Distance: 8.9 miles round-trip

Hiking Time: 4.5 hours

Elevation Gain: 1,800 feet

Summary: This loop visits one of Pasadena's most historic canyons and its graceful, free-leaping waterfall.

Sturtevant Falls is the crown jewel of Big Santa Anita Canyon, a lushly forested, almost magical gulch just a handful of miles from the Pasadena Freeway. Canyon hikers can't help but covet its cluster of summer cabins, set in the same beautiful ravine where Sturtevant Falls drops. This is a place filled with ferns and wildflowers, leafy trees, and mossy rocks.

STURTEVANT FALLS AND BIG SANTA ANITA CANYON LOOP

© AVALON TRAVEL PUBLISHING, INC.

The epic winter storms of 2005 took a toll on Big Santa Anita Canyon's main trailhead at Chantry Flat. After several landslides occurred due to excessive water runoff, the Chantry Flat access road was closed for most of a year as the four public agencies who manage it—the city of Sierra Madre, the city of Arcadia, Los Angeles County, and the U.S. Forest Service—tried to pull together the money and the manpower to fix it. Although L.A. hikers are accustomed to intermittent road closures at Chantry Flat, including an epic eight-month closure due to fire- and weather-related damage in 2000, none ever lasted as long as this one.

Assuming the road is open and in good repair when you visit, this loop hike around Santa Anita Canyon is well signed and easy to follow. Leave your car at the large Chantry Flat parking lot and hike downhill into the canyon on the Gabrielino National Recreation Trail. The first 0.7 mile follows a paved road, but once you reach the canyon bottom, the trail crosses Roberts Footbridge over Winter Creek, then turns right and becomes a wide dirt path. The trail to the left, Lower Winter Creek Trail, will be the return of your loop.

A sign near the footbridge details the period from 1912 to 1936 when the confluence of Winter and Big Santa Anita creeks was the home of Roberts Camp, a popular weekend resort. A stone lodge, dining area, and numerous cabins and tents once stood here—enough buildings to accommodate 180 guests at a time. Some of those cabins are still standing today.

Gabrielino Trail meanders under the shade of bay laurel, oak, and alder, heading upstream along Big Santa Anita Creek. The lively stream

© ANN MARIE BROWN

Sturtevant Falls is just one of many highlights along this loop in Santa Anita Canyon.

is tamed somewhat by a series of small check dams, forming oddly pretty artificial waterfalls and glassy pools. At a junction at 1.3 miles, Gabrielino Trail forks left and heads uphill, but you continue straight along the creek for another 0.3 mile to Sturtevant Falls. You cross the creek, the canyon bends to the left, then you cross again. Sturtevant Falls suddenly reveals itself, dropping 50 feet over a granite cliff into a perfectly shaped rock bowl. It is gracefully framed by alders and has a large pool at its base.

After visiting Sturtevant Falls, backtrack to the junction where Gabrielino Trail heads uphill. There are two trail options here; they rejoin in a little over a mile. Take the more interesting middle trail, which climbs above the waterfall's lip and sticks close to the stream's beguiling cascades and pools. Shortly after the paths meet up again, you come to Cascade picnic area, a shady spot near the creek and a good spot to catch your breath. Then it's one mile farther uphill to Spruce Grove Trail Camp, elevation 3,100 feet, with picnic tables and fire grills set among giant big-cone Douglas firs. These trees were once called big-cone spruce; hence the camp's name.

From Spruce Grove, you soon begin the return leg of your loop. At a junction of trails 0.3 mile beyond the camp, bear left; then at the entrance to

Sturtevant Camp (a church camp), go left again on Mount Zion Trail. In a little more than a mile you can take a 0.25-mile detour to the summit of 3,575-foot Mount Zion.

Then it's a remarkably steep and exposed descent to Hoegee's Camp, where you will be grateful for the shade of big-cone Douglas firs. Just downstream from the camp are a few remains from the original Hoegee's trail resort of the early 20th century. The resort serviced hikers making their way along the long trek to Mount Wilson. Pick up Lower Winter Creek Trail near the camp and head east (left) to return to the footbridge in Santa Anita Canyon. The 1.5-mile stretch on Lower Winter Creek Trail offers much of the same sylvan scenery as what you experienced on the way to Sturtevant Falls: a crystalline stream, a canopy of oak and alder, historic cabins and cabin remains, and more of those odd-looking concrete check dams.

Options
You can alter this loop by returning on Upper Winter Creek Trail instead of Lower Winter Creek Trail. The upper trail departs from just west of Hoegee's Camp. It contours over chaparral-clad slopes and offers good views of Sierra Madre and Arcadia, then returns to the Chantry Flat parking area. The loop mileage remains about the same.

Directions
From I-210 in Pasadena, drive seven miles east to Arcadia. Exit on Santa Anita Avenue and drive six miles north to the road's end at Chantry Flat. The trail begins across the road from the first parking area as you drive in.

Information and Contact
There is no fee, but a national forest adventure pass is required; see page 297 for more information. Dogs are allowed. A trail map of the Mount Wilson area is available for a fee from Tom Harrison Maps, 800/265-9090, www.tomharrisonmaps.com. For more information, contact the Los Angeles River Ranger District, 12371 North Little Tujunga Canyon Road, San Fernando, CA 91342, 818/899-1900, www.fs.fed.us/r5/angeles.

13 BEN OVERTURFF TRAIL
Monrovia Canyon Park

Level: Easy/Moderate   **Total Distance:** 6.4 miles round-trip

Hiking Time: 2.5 hours   **Elevation Gain:** 1,000 feet

Summary: A woodsy hike leads through Sawpit Canyon to the remains of Deer Park Lodge.

Of all the city-owned parks in the Los Angeles area, Monrovia Canyon County Park ranks as one of the best. It's clean, well managed, and has beautiful hiking trails. The only thing to complain about is if you try to visit it on a Tuesday. That's when the local police use the park for target practice, and they lock the gates and close the whole place down for the day.

If you want to hike the Ben Overturff Trail, it's not just Tuesdays that are

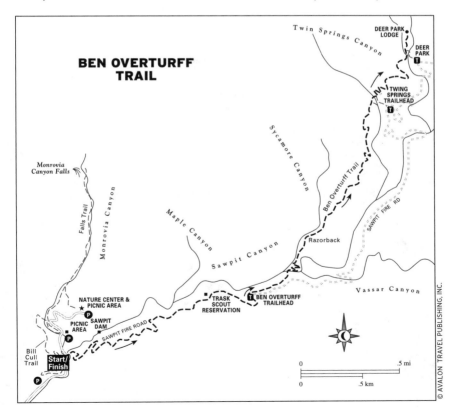

© AVALON TRAVEL PUBLISHING, INC.

off-limits. The trail is closed on Wednesdays also, although the rest of the park is open, due to more activities at the firing range. And figure in one more scheduling issue—the park gates close at 5 P.M. daily, so start this hike early in the day. You'll want a morning start anyway; it gets hot in this canyon in the afternoon.

Once you get the schedule right, the hike is simple. From the lower parking lot by the entrance station, walk up the park road about 50 yards to the right turnoff for the Trask Boy Scout Camp. Turn right and walk 1.25 miles along this mostly paved access road. You'll pass the massive, 157-foot-high Sawpit Dam, which was built for flood control in 1927. It's the only interesting sight on this rather unpleasant stint on pavement. The road is shadeless and carves a few steep switchbacks uphill, then turns to dirt and continues its monotonous climb. But the trail that follows is so sweet, it's worth the bother.

You'll leave the heat and the mountain bikers behind when you reach Overturff junction and the turnoff for the single-track, hikers-only Ben Overturff Trail. Bear left, and you'll quickly descend into a lovely sylvan area, soon crossing Sawpit Creek. This is a very woodsy stretch, filled with big woodwardia ferns, oaks and bay laurel, and various spring-blooming flowers including bleeding heart, purple nightshade, and miner's lettuce. On the creek's far side, you climb back uphill into the sunshine and onto a narrow, backbone ridge that separates Sycamore and Sawpit Canyons. A well-meaning trail sign warns that this stretch is "narrow." Yes, indeed.

After more up and down, occasionally in exposed chaparral but mostly in

© ANN MARIE BROWN

The stone ruins of Deer Park Lodge are being slowly overtaken by nature.

the pleasant shade of bay laurel and oaks, you reach what appears to be a sink-hole, where Twin Springs Creek goes underground and then comes out on the other side of the trail. Just beyond it, 2.5 miles from your start, is the first of two junctions; bear left for the Deer Park Lodge site. Ten minutes later is a second junction with the right fork leading to Twin Springs; bear left again.

In about an hour from the trailhead, you're at the Deer Park Lodge site, marked by old stone steps to the entrance, a few crumbling foundations, bits and pieces of stone walls, plus a few mattress springs and rusted pipes. The lodge was built by Monrovia building contractor Ben Overturff in 1907. It was a popular tourist resort through the 1920s and 1930s but declined in popularity shortly thereafter. Overturff and his family continued to use the retreat until 1948.

Loop lovers can make their return by following either of the two trail junctions to Sawpit Canyon Fire Road, then taking the fire road back to the paved road and trailhead. But a far better choice is to retrace your steps on Ben Overturff Trail, enjoying this woodsy scenery all over again.

Options

From the same parking lot, you can hike the Bill Cull Trail to Monrovia Canyon Falls, a lovely 30-foot waterfall that is spring fed and flows year-round (3.4 miles round-trip). Or, if you'd like to see the waterfall via a shorter route, drive uphill on the park road for another half mile to the upper parking lot by the nature center. Walk through the picnic area and follow the trail only 0.6 mile to Monrovia Canyon Falls.

Directions

From I-210 in Monrovia, take the Myrtle Avenue exit and drive north for one mile. Turn right on Foothill Boulevard and drive 0.2 mile to Canyon Boulevard. Turn left and drive 1.6 miles to the park (bear right where the road forks). Park in the lot just before the entrance station.

Information and Contact

A $5 day-use fee is charged per vehicle. Dogs on leash are allowed. A free park map is available at the entrance station. For more information, contact Monrovia Canyon Park, 1200 North Canyon Boulevard, Monrovia, CA 91016, 626/256-8282, www.ci.monrovia.ca.us.

Special note: The entire park is closed on Tuesdays, and this trail is also closed on Wednesdays. Park gates close at 5 p.m. each day.

14 FISH CANYON FALLS   BEST C
Angeles National Forest

Level: Butt-kicker   **Total Distance:** 9.4 miles round-trip

Hiking Time: 6 hours   **Elevation Gain:** 3,000 feet

Summary: For the sake of a beautiful waterfall, hikers endure a supremely challenging ridge climb and descent before entering the enchanted canyon of Fish Canyon Falls.

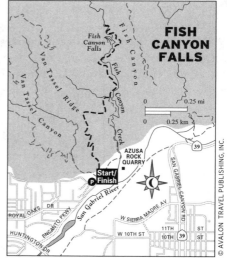

There's no getting around it. If you want to see Fish Canyon Falls, you have to sign up for a difficult hike. Sure, there is a trail that leads all the way to the falls—no off-trail scrambling is required—but it has a grade that will leave you begging for mercy.

Public access to the trail to Fish Canyon Falls was closed for most of the 1980s and 1990s. Even though the waterfall is on the lands of Angeles National Forest, the popular trail to reach it had been blocked off by the expansion plans of a private quarry, Azusa Rock Company. This caused a fair amount of outrage among local hikers, who for decades had been hiking to the falls via an easy, five-mile round-trip trail. To quell the hoopla, Azusa Rock Company and the cities of Duarte and Azusa obtained a grant to build a three-mile-long bypass trail around the quarry. The trail opened in 1998, and Los Angeles-area hikers once again have access to one of the most beautiful waterfalls in Angeles National Forest.

Except that this applies to only the hardiest of hikers. It is now a 9.4-mile commitment to reach Fish Canyon Falls, with a 3,000-foot elevation gain. Not only that, the trail was poorly constructed, so it is steep, loose, too narrow, riddled with poison oak, and doesn't have nearly enough switchbacks. Oh yes, and it offers unattractive views of the aforementioned quarry. Yikes.

If you decide to go see Fish Canyon Falls, bring your hiking poles and wear your best-gripping boots. They aren't luxury items here, they are necessities. Also, pick up the Fish Canyon Trail Guide from the signboard near the trail's start; its map will be useful to you as you trudge up (and down) this merciless trail. And start hiking early in the morning. You are ascending south-facing slopes for the first couple miles, so unless it is a gray day, the sun will bake you.

The trail begins at a parking lot just outside the quarry entrance, then climbs steeply up to Van Tassel Ridge via the canyon's west wall. The first part of the ascent doesn't seem too bad, but it quickly gets worse. Spring hikers have the good fortune of passing a spectacular display of wildflowers (lupine, campanula, poppies, larkspur, brodiaea) on this sunny canyon wall, but that is its only redeeming feature. When you stop to catch your breath, you'll see ugly views of the concrete-channeled San Gabriel River basin below and various industrial enterprises, plus hear the annoying pow-pow-pow from the San Gabriel Valley Gun Club. Boy, this is some fun.

At the ridge top, 1.4 heart-pumping miles later, you join a dirt road and continue the unpleasant ascent for another half mile. You get a short breather as the trail mellows a bit along the quarry's fence line. Then the trail

drops abruptly down the other side of the ridge, losing 1,000 feet in one mile. Thankfully, there are plenty of switchbacks, as well as a bumper crop of poison oak. This brutal up and down on Van Tassel Ridge must be accomplished in both directions of your hike—out and back—and is responsible for almost all of the trail's 3,000-foot elevation gain.

At 3.2 miles from the start, the trail finally joins the old, pleasant Fish Canyon Trail in the canyon bottom. Your world is suddenly transformed, and your legs won't believe the contrast. This sylvan path meanders gently uphill, sticking closely to Fish Creek, for 1.5 miles. Stone foundations, walkways, and walls of old cabin sites from the early 1900s can be seen, including one belonging to a family made famous by having

The triple stair-stepped tiers of Fish Canyon Falls are hard to get to, but worth the effort.

the only two-seater outhouse. The cabins were destroyed in a fire and flood in the late 1950s.

But after your shadeless climb and descent, it's the greenery that impresses most. The canyon is blessed with an abundance of leafy trees. Big-leaf maples, California bays, alders, and live oaks line the streambanks, and non-native ivy and vinca have covered the ground near the cabin sites. This is one of the most charming canyons in all of the San Gabriel Mountains. Thank goodness you made it.

Less than a half mile before you reach the waterfall you'll cross over Fish Creek, then shortly find yourself in a high box canyon, where the waterfall drops. Even at low water, it is an impressive sight: Fish Canyon Falls drops 90 feet in three stair-stepped tiers, finally sliding its way into a large and clear pool.

So, is it worth it? For hikers in good physical condition, definitely yes. You may not choose to hike this trail regularly, but you should see this waterfall at least once in your life.

Options

If you aren't up for the rather brutal hike to Fish Canyon Falls, Los Angeles has many more waterfalls that are much easier to access. Try Eaton Canyon Falls, Millard Falls, Sturtevant Falls, or Monrovia Canyon Falls instead. All are described in this chapter.

Directions

From I-210 in Duarte, take the Mount Olive Drive exit (one exit east of I-605), drive 0.25 mile, and turn right (east) on Huntington Drive. Drive 0.6 mile and turn left on Encanto Parkway. Drive 1.4 miles to the parking area just before the quarry entrance, on your left.

Alternatively, from the I-605 and I-210 split, take I-605 north to its end, then turn right on Huntington Drive and follow it to Encanto Parkway, as above.

Information and Contact

There is no fee. Dogs are allowed. A Fish Canyon trail guide, with a topo map, is available from the city of Duarte (and is sometimes available at a signboard by the trail's start). For more information, contact City of Duarte Parks and Recreation Department, 1600 Huntington Drive, Duarte, CA 91010, 626/357-7931, www.accessduarte.com.

15 SWITZER FALLS AND BEAR CANYON
Angeles National Forest

Level: Moderate

Total Distance: 8.0 miles round-trip

Hiking Time: 4 hours

Elevation Gain: 1,100 feet

Summary: A charming waterfall and two historic trail camps are visited on this sylvan streamside walk.

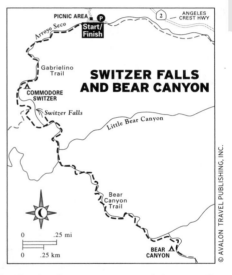

This is a walk for when you want to get lost for a few hours. And if a few hours isn't long enough, bring your backpack and spend the night at Bear Canyon Campground. Then you can enjoy getting lost for a night or two. The waterslides, mini-cascades, and limpid pools of spectacular Bear Canyon are always waiting for those who choose to get lost.

From the often-crowded Switzer Falls Picnic Area, follow the paved trail that heads gently downhill along the stream. Soon the pavement becomes more sporadic and gives way to a smooth dirt path. It crosses the stream a half dozen times in the first half mile, forcing you to rock-hop in all but the driest months of the year. The route is pleasantly shaded by willows, alders, oaks, and maples. Less than a mile of trail brings you to Commodore Switzer Trail Camp, a few primitive campsites near the creek. You can't tell from here, but you're perched above 50-foot Switzer Falls.

Cross the creek by the camp and head uphill, climbing above the canyon, following the Gabrielino National Recreation Trail. As you ascend, you'll leave the cool canyon shade and break out into the sunshine. The drop-offs are so steep that a chain-link fence is in place to prevent potential mishaps. Views of the narrow and steep gorge below the trail are impressive, to say the least. The surrounding foliage is of a vastly different ilk from that of the leafy stream canyon. Interspersed among an array of aromatic chaparral are tall oaks, occasional big-cone Douglas fir, and delicate ferns growing out of the cliff sides.

From your vantage point on the trail, Switzer Falls appears through the brushy foliage as a tempting tease, about 50 yards away and impossible to reach because of the steep, deep canyon that separates you from it. The big upper pool above its lip and first 20 feet of its drop are clearly visible, but that is all. The rest is up to your imagination.

© ANN MARIE BROWN

The stone building ruins to the right of the falls are the remains of the chapel at Switzer's Camp, a popular trail resort in the early 1900s. Perry Switzer was called "Commodore" because of his talents in maneuvering his fleet of burros in rocky Arroyo Seco Canyon. Visitors would ride a half day on mules from Pasadena, traveling through eight miles of wild terrain and more than 60 stream crossings, to reach the camp. They were treated to a cozy bed, three meals, and plenty of mountain air, all for $1.50 per day. On Sundays, Switzer's guests attended services at the chapel, accompanied by the background music of the waterfall. The scenery probably attracted even the not-so-devout.

Lined with dense alder trees that block out much of the light, Bear Canyon is always a cool and shady retreat.

A few steps beyond the falls viewpoint is a junction where the Gabrielino Trail heads right and uphill, and the Bear Canyon Trail heads left and downhill. Enjoy the lofty view of Arroyo Seco Canyon from this high point, then take the left fork for Bear Canyon and descend steeply for 0.25 mile through a couple of switchbacks. When you reach the canyon bottom and a smattering of trail signs, take a 0.3-mile detour upstream (left) to see the lower cascades of Switzer Falls. Resist the temptation to climb over the lower, smaller falls to reach the large drop. There have been too many accidents here.

After you've seen enough, return to the main junction and follow the Bear Canyon Trail downstream. Most signs of human intervention are now left behind, as few casual hikers proceed much farther than Switzer Falls. The canyon becomes increasingly narrow, bounded by 50-foot-high granite walls that bear a pinkish cast. The dense canopy of sycamore, bay laurel, and alders allows in very little light. This is wild and rugged country by any standards.

One mile from the junction below Switzer Falls, you reach a fork in the stream. You'll head upstream on a fork of Bear Creek, following the old Tom Sloan Trail. More waterslides and small falls await on this historic trail, which is in varying states of disrepair, with many washouts and rock slides. Orange tape is wrapped around trees to mark the route. The path crosses and recrosses the creek dozens of times, and in high water you'll be rock-hopping and scrambling over boulders to try to keep your feet dry. The continual roar and splash of mini-cascades will keep you entertained.

The camp finally shows up on your right, 2.2 miles from where you first joined the Bear Canyon Trail. A prominent sign marks the spot where there are three tent sites with picnic tables, stoves, and fire grills. The camp is shaded by a copse of oaks and bay laurel. Pull out a sandwich if you are here for the day, or your sleeping bag if you are here for the night, and enjoy this special spot, so close to the city but so far away. Chances are good, by the time you get back to your car, you'll be planning the next time you can get lost in Bear Canyon.

Options

With a car shuttle, you could continue hiking from Bear Canyon Trail Camp another 1.8 miles to Tom Sloan Saddle, then take the right fork and continue downhill through Millard Canyon for another 3.5 miles, past Dawn Mine, to the trailhead near Millard Campground (see the Dawn Mine Loop listing in this chapter).

Directions

From I-210 in La Cañada, take Highway 2/Angeles Crest Highway northeast for 9.8 miles to the Switzer picnic area. It is on the south side of the road, 0.5 mile past Clear Creek Information Station. Turn right, drive down the access road 0.3 mile, and park in the main lot.

Information and Contact

There is no fee, but a national forest adventure pass is required; see page 297 for more information. Dogs are allowed. A trail map of the Mount Wilson area is available for a fee from Tom Harrison Maps, 800/265-9090, www.tomharrisonmaps.com. For more information, contact Angeles National Forest, Los Angeles River Ranger District, 12371 N. Little Tujunga Canyon Road, San Fernando, CA 91342, 818/899-1900, www.fs.fed.us/r5/angeles.

16 COLBY CANYON TRAIL TO JOSEPHINE PEAK
Angeles National Forest

🚶 🐴

Level: Strenuous

Hiking Time: 4 hours

Total Distance: 8.4 miles round-trip

Elevation Gain: 2,000 feet

Summary: A cool-weather hike with inspiring views of high country peaks in the San Gabriel Mountains, which can be combined with scaling another popular front country peak.

Josephine Peak is kind of like the dweeb in high school who didn't get as many dates as the handsome school jock. Many San Gabriel Mountains peak-baggers bypass Josephine for its popular neighbor, Strawberry Peak, located due east and some 600 feet higher than Josephine. Sometimes Angeles National Forest rangers even advise hikers to skip Josephine for the more "interesting" rock scramble up Strawberry.

But, like anyone who has given a dweeb a chance knows, it can be just as much fun, and often more rewarding, to break from the crowd. Josephine is a perfectly respectable peak in its own right and offers its own unique summit vista.

The hike from Colby Canyon to Josephine Saddle is a water-lover's delight, particularly in winter and spring. The trail skirts a creek for the first 0.25 mile. You'll boulder-hop across the water three times, at which point the trail begins to climb. Shortly after beginning the ascent, go right at an unmarked junction (although it's no disaster if you go left—the fork meets up with the main trail after a few hundred feet). As you ascend, you are constantly serenaded by the sound of running water, although the creek is sometimes far below the trail. You'll hear several small waterfalls and could easily miss seeing them if you don't keep your eyes peeled for their cascading sprays.

About a mile in, the trail again descends to the creek, requiring another boulder-hop. This crossing is one of the only shady areas on the trail and makes a nice creekside picnic spot. Fuel up on some trail mix, because it's nothing but "up" from here to the saddle.

a view of Strawberry Peak from just west of Josephine Saddle, en route to Josephine Peak

The trail switchbacks up and away from the creek as the canyon narrows. As you ascend, turn around and admire the view, which includes the curling ribbon of trail you've just conquered. The trail ascends 2.2 scenic miles through the chaparral-covered canyon to Josephine Saddle, where it's a good idea to take a well-deserved rest near the water tank. To continue on to Josephine Peak, turn left at the saddle and take the connector trail 0.5 mile to the fire road leading to the peak. (The trail on the right leads to neighboring Strawberry Peak; see Options, below.)

There's a marked change in terrain once you drop over the saddle. Scrubby chaparral is replaced by oaks, pines, and sweeping views of distant peaks that remain snow-capped well into the spring months. The trail from the saddle is initially level and shaded, but don't let that mislead you. You still have two miles and 700 feet of gradual elevation gain to the summit. The views will make you forget your trail-weary quadriceps.

The trail winds around to Josephine's 5,558-foot summit, which has a small building with a wind gauge atop that spins fast and furious in the constant gusts. If it's not too cold and breezy, you can have lunch at a flat area where a stone foundation remains from an old fire lookout tower. The tower was in service on the peak from 1937 to 1976. The peak is named for Josephine Lippencott, wife of USGS surveyor Joseph Barlow Lippencott, who used the summit as a survey station in 1894.

From your high vantage point, you'll have an expansive view of the L.A.

basin to the south, with downtown L.A. and Silverlake Reservoir in sight if it's a clear day. Straight east is Strawberry Peak, and beyond it, massive Mount Baden-Powell. You can't miss the white dome of the Mount Wilson Observatory to the southeast. To the west, the Big Tujunga drainage lies before you, with Mount Lukens easy to spot. Way off in the distance is the Palos Verdes Peninsula, and on a clear day, Catalina Island beyond. Not too shabby for a peak that gets no respect.

Options

From Josephine Saddle, you can hike to Strawberry Peak. Once at the saddle, go right and head east 3.1 miles to Strawberry Peak Trail. The turnoff to the peak is not signed, but spray-painted arrows on the ground point the way up the west side of the mountain. Some hands-and-feet scrambling is required to reach the summit from this direction.

Directions

From I-210 in La Cañada, take Highway 2/Angeles Crest Highway northeast for 10.5 miles to the trailhead, which is one mile past the Clear Creek ranger station. Turn left into one of two parking lots; Colby Canyon trailhead is in the first (westernmost) lot.

Information and Contact

A national forest adventure pass is required; see page 297 for more information. Dogs are allowed. A trail map of the Mount Wilson area, including Josephine Peak, is available for a fee from Tom Harrison Maps, 800/265-9090, www.tomharrisonmaps.com. For more information, contact Angeles National Forest, Los Angeles River Ranger District, 12371 North Little Tujunga Canyon Road, San Fernando, CA 91342, 818/899-1900, www.fs.fed.us/r5/angeles. Or contact the Clear Creek ranger station, 626/821-6764.

17 STRAWBERRY PEAK
Angeles National Forest

Level: Moderate

Total Distance: 7.2 miles round-trip

Hiking Time: 3.5 hours

Elevation Gain: 1,500 feet

Summary: The easier of two popular routes to Strawberry Peak, this trail provides a good workout to a summit rich with views of surrounding peaks.

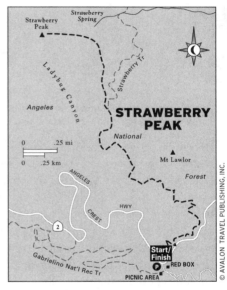

At 6,164 feet, Strawberry Peak is a San Gabriel Mountains summit that is worth attaining. It's the highest peak in the front range of the San Gabriels, a mere three feet higher than nearby San Gabriel Peak. Granted, its elevation pales when compared to the much higher mountains that you'll find farther east on the Angeles Crest Highway, but, for a backyard peak, it's pretty impressive. And even better, Strawberry Peak gets only an occasional dusting of snow, so it is accessible almost year-round. When you are hankering for a peak to bag and higher summits are buried in the white stuff, Strawberry fills the bill. In summer, on the other hand, you could easily fry an egg on its summit.

With only a 1,500-foot elevation change, the hike is not overly strenuous, although the last steep mile to the top certainly provides a workout. Two popular routes lead to the summit; one from Colby Canyon (see Options, below) and the other from Red Box. The Red Box route, described here, is longer mileage, but easier.

The trail starts out just east of, and across the road from, the Red Box parking lot. What was once a wide fire road has narrowed to a comfortable pathway that makes a mellow ascent through oaks and chapparal. The trail carves a neat lateral path across the side of Mount Lawlor on a grade so gradual that you hardly feel like you're climbing. You'll marvel at the trail builders who managed to contruct this pathway on such steep slopes—the drop-offs are often nearly vertical. At 2.3 miles out, the path makes a surprising dip downhill to

Spectacular views of snow-capped Mount Baldy and its neighbors can be had along the ridgeline of Strawberry Peak.

the saddle between Lawlor and Strawberry. The trail continues due north, but you will head northwest (left) on an old firebreak to the summit.

Leaving the gently graded trail behind you, make your way up the ridgeline on an obvious sandy path. This is serious chaparral country and not the place you want to be at midday in summer. The route is now a steep "up," gaining 900 feet in a mile, but the worst part is that it dips twice more, causing you to lose a few feet of hard-won elevation.

As you huff and puff your way to the summit, you'll spot a few wind-sculpted coulter pines and big-cone Douglas firs facing to the north. There's a clear dividing line to the vegetation, with the conifers preferring the shadier side of the peak. You might want to make a beeline for their limited cover, but first, check out the summit view. On a clear day, Strawberry Peak rewards you with a superlative vista of many other peaks and ridges of the San Gabriel Mountains. In the winter months, snow-capped Mount Baldy to the northeast is of course the standout (and you get even better views of it on your way back down the ridge). To the north, you'll spot the winding ribbon of Big Tujunga Road and its surrounding rugged watershed. You won't see much of the L.A. basin from this summit, but, hey, maybe that's a good thing.

Options

You can also climb Strawberry Peak from the Colby Canyon trailhead (six miles round-trip). Note that this western route is somewhat more challenging than the one described above; it involves some scrambling over boulders, using both hands and feet, to reach the summit. Or, if you can arrange a car shuttle from the Colby Canyon trailhead to the Red Box trailhead, you can make the trip as a 7.2-mile one-way hike. The Colby Canyon trailhead is located on Angeles Crest Highway, 3.5 miles west of Red Box.

Directions

From I-210 in La Cañada, take Highway 2/Angeles Crest Highway northeast for 14.2 miles to Red Box Station on the right. Park on the east side of the parking lot, then cross the Angeles Crest Highway and walk east for about 20 yards to the start of the trail.

Information and Contact

A national forest adventure pass is required; see page 297 for more information. Dogs are allowed. A trail map of the Mount Wilson area, including Strawberry Peak, is available for a fee from Tom Harrison Maps, 800/265-9090, www.tom-harrisonmaps.com. For more information, contact Angeles National Forest, Los Angeles River Ranger District, 12371 North Little Tujunga Canyon Road, San Fernando, CA 91342, 818/899-1900, www.fs.fed.us/r5/angeles.

18 SAN GABRIEL PEAK

Angeles National Forest

Level: Moderate

Total Distance: 6.0 miles round-trip

Hiking Time: 3 hours

Elevation Gain: 1,400 feet

Summary: Get some perspective on the L.A. basin on this heart-pumping summit hike just minutes from the city.

The summit of 6,161-foot San Gabriel Peak offers a front-country view that brings most of the L.A. basin into perspective. Pick a clear winter or spring day and get an early morning start for the best chance at good visibility. By noon, the haze and fog takes over, even in winter. Days just before or after a storm are often ideal for this hike—that's when you can watch the waves of clouds come in off the coast, then be pushed upward and rolled back.

The trail offers a good workout as well. The mileage is short, but the grade is steep. After a mellow 0.3-mile walk on the Mount Wilson Road to the start of the trail, the next 1.8 miles consist of multiple dozen switchbacks going up, up, and up some more through an enclave of oaks and manzanita, which provide welcome shade. (This trail used to be shorter, but it was reworked and lengthened by adding more switchbacks.) There is no rest in this initial stretch. The trail is quite narrow—only 12 inches wide in places—and has steep drop-offs along the leaf-strewn slope. Watch your footing.

You know you've gained some elevation when you start seeing big-cone Douglas fir alongside the trail. As you rise higher, you catch glimpses through the trees of an upside-down ice-cream-cone-shaped peak over your left shoulder. That's your destination, San Gabriel Peak.

At 2.1 miles from your car, the trail tops out at an old paved road that leads to the transmitter towers atop San Gabriel Peak's neighbor, Mount Disappointment. Turn left on this paved road, which is blissfully level (or at least bears a much gentler grade). You are treated to views of surrounding San Gabriel peaks, including Mount Baldy to the east. After 100 yards on the paved road, a sharp switchback to the right leads uphill to the antenna-covered summit of Mount Disappointment. You go straight instead, coming to a series of old concrete foundations in a wide clearing punctuated by Coulter pine trees. Look on the left side of this clearing for the continuation of the San Gabriel Peak Trail. The path descends a bit, tunneling through a canopy of oaks, then begins a steep ascent to the summit. This is the steepest pitch of the entire hike, gaining 400 feet in less than a half mile.

© ANN MARIE BROWN

This yucca on the summit trail to San Gabriel Peak couldn't decide which way it wanted to grow.

Once on the summit, catch your breath by taking a seat on its large steel bench, which bears an odd spray-painted comment that it is "only 20 miles up to space." The view takes in the close-in peaks of Mount Wilson (obvious because of the white golf ball of its observatory) and antenna-covered Mount Disappointment, plus the larger San Gabriel peaks to the northeast: Mount Williamson, Mount Baldy, and Cucamonga Peak. Beyond those snow-capped giants lie two even bigger peaks: 11,502-foot Mount San Gorgonio and 10,834-foot Mount Jacinto. To the west, of course, is the Pacific Ocean, with Catalina Island and a smattering of other Channel Islands poking out of the sea. In the foreground are more pedestrian landmarks: the city of Glendale, the campus of Jet Propulsion Laboratories, and the high-rises of downtown Los Angeles.

Options

San Gabriel Peak can also be reached via a shorter route by hiking from the trailhead at Eaton Saddle, two miles from Red Box on Mount Wilson Road. The trail travels 0.5 mile west to Markham Saddle, then turns north (right) for 0.7 mile to join up with the final summit trail described above. The mileage for this route is 3.2 miles round-trip.

Directions

From I-210 in La Cañada, take Highway 2/Angeles Crest Highway northeast for 14.2 miles to Red Box Station on the right. Park in the large parking lot, then walk 0.3 mile down the Mount Wilson Road to an unsigned paved road on the right. The trail (unsigned) begins on the left side of this paved road.

Information and Contact

A national forest adventure pass is required; see page 297 for more information. Dogs are allowed. A trail map of the Mount Wilson area is available for a fee from Tom Harrison Maps, 800/265-9090, www.tomharrisonmaps.com. For more information, contact Angeles National Forest, Los Angeles River Ranger District, 12371 North Little Tujunga Canyon Road, San Fernando, CA 91342, 818/899-1900, www.fs.fed.us/r5/angeles.

19 EATON SADDLE TO MOUNT LOWE

BEST C

Angeles National Forest

Level: Easy

Total Distance: 5.5 miles round-trip

Hiking Time: 2.5 hours

Elevation Gain: 500 feet

Summary: This front-country peak offers sweeping mountain-to-ocean views, from 10,064-foot Mount Baldy to Catalina Island.

The San Gabriel Mountains rise like a vertical wall behind Pasadena. This short, rewarding hike begins by driving behind the wall and then climbing up, up, and up to the trailhead at Eaton Saddle, along Mount Wilson Road. Unlike some trails, the scenery on this one is literally outstanding from the outset. You step behind the locked Forest Service gate and find yourself looking straight down into

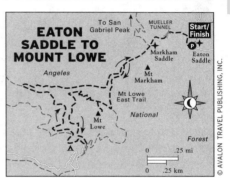

the chasm that is Eaton Canyon. Follow the line of that long and narrow valley, and the canyon opens onto Altadena.

The initial part of the hike follows an old fire road that the Forest Service chiseled out of the canyon walls in the 1930s and '40s. At 0.3 mile, hikers arrive at the Mueller Tunnel, which was finished in 1942. It's short enough that you don't need a flashlight, but still sufficiently cold and clammy in the middle. Shortly beyond the tunnel, you arrive at Markham Saddle and a confusing intersection (a classic trademark of the Angeles National Forest hiking network). Watch for an obvious footpath on the left, marked by a small metal post and stand, on which someone has scratched "Mount Lowe/East Trail." Go in the direction that points to Mount Lowe.

The trail begins climbing and parallels the fire road below it for a while. Finally, the trail reaches another saddle. To the left is another tributary to Eaton Canyon. To the right is the utterly empty and undeveloped Bear Canyon, a tributary to the Arroyo Seco. Soldier on, as you are now on the east flank of Mount Lowe. After 0.25 mile, look for an unsigned trail on the right that goes uphill. Turn right on the signless trail, which happens to be the East Trail, and follow its moderate-to-steep ascent. In short order, the path bends

heading into Mueller Tunnel en route to Mount Lowe

around to the left, plunges through a forest of oaks, and then emerges on the summit of Mount Lowe, elevation 5,603 feet.

You'll soon see why it is critical to visit in the winter on a clear day, soon after a storm blows through and visibility is at its best. To the south is Pasadena, downtown Los Angeles, Palos Verdes, and Catalina Island. You can also see the coast, the Santa Monica Mountains, and the San Fernando Valley. To the north and the east are the higher peaks of the San Gabriels, with often-snowcapped Mount Baldy dominating the view. Metal viewing tubes placed on the summit long ago allow visitors to peer at various peaks.

A small exhibit on the mountain pays tribute to the old Mount Lowe Railway. In the early 1900s, tourists could ride an incline railway from Pasadena to the top of Echo Mountain. From there, they boarded a trolley that wound up the mountains to a hotel located just 1,000 feet below Mount Lowe's summit.

For the return trip, you can head back down the way you came on the East Trail, or, if you still have energy to spare for some more up and down, try the signed West Trail instead. For 1.5 miles the trail descends, often steeply, over rocky switchbacks and through dense oak and pine groves, occasionally crossing tiny seasonal springs. More viewing tubes along the way help you pick out various L.A. landmarks.

Finally, the trail deposits you on a fire road. Immediately to your left will be another footpath climbing up from the fire road. Don't take it; that's the East Trail going back up to the summit. Instead, turn right on the fire road.

The view soon opens up to reveal the so-called "Grand Canyon of the San Gabriels," which holds another tributary to the Arroyo Seco. After one mile, you're at another junction. Don't follow your intuition and go straight, but instead follow the fire road as it makes a hard right and begins a gradual one-mile climb back up to the saddle where you originally turned onto the Mount Lowe East Trail. Continue straight on the trail, go back through the tunnel, and it's a short walk back to the car.

Options

To add some mileage, you can visit San Gabriel Peak on the same trip. Start at the same trailhead and go through Mueller Tunnel. At Markham Saddle, instead of heading toward Mount Lowe, take a right on an unmarked trail just past the water tank and follow it 0.7 mile toward Mount Disappointment. Then head right to 6,161-foot San Gabriel Peak. This option adds 3.2 miles and 1,000 feet of gain to the Mount Lowe hike.

Directions

From I-210 in La Cañada, take Highway 2/Angeles Crest Highway northeast for 14.2 miles to Red Box Station on the right. Turn right at Red Box on Mount Wilson Road. Drive two miles to the Eaton Saddle parking areas on both sides of road. The trail begins behind the locked gate on the right.

Information and Contact

There is no fee, but a national forest adventure pass is required; see page 297 for more information. Dogs are allowed. A trail map of the Mount Wilson area is available for a fee from Tom Harrison Maps, 800/265-9090, www.tomharrisonmaps.com. For more information, contact Angeles National Forest, Los Angeles River Ranger District, 12371 North Little Tujunga Canyon Road, San Fernando, CA 91342, 818/899-1900, www.fs.fed.us/r5/angeles.

20 KENYON DEVORE TRAIL

Angeles National Forest

Level: Strenuous

Hiking Time: 4 hours

Total Distance: 8.6 miles round-trip

Elevation Gain: 2,700 feet

Summary: This upside-down hike assures blissful shade and the most solitude en route to the West Fork San Gabriel River.

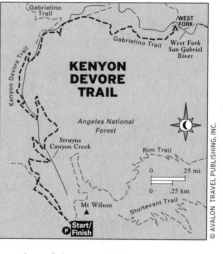

Sometimes you just get sick and tired of chaparral. You long to hike in a real forest with real trees, not an elfin forest of manzanita and scrub oak. You want to feel pine needles underfoot and the cool shade of conifer branches overhead. But since the best forest country in Angeles National Forest is buried under snow for six months of the year, what can you do in midwinter when you hanker for a real forest?

Hike the Kenyon Devore Trail. The trailhead is just below the summit of Mount Wilson, so you can depend on the road being open almost every day of the year. With a short drive up to Red Box Station and along the Mount Wilson Road, you're ready to hike. There's only one catch: the trail is downhill on the way in, and uphill on the way back. You'll need to save your energy for the return trip, which has a 2,700-foot elevation gain.

This historic pathway was previously known as the Rattlesnake Trail, although the terrain doesn't look especially like rattlesnake territory. It was renamed in 1996 for Kenyon Devore, a devoted Angeles National Forest volunteer, whose parents once owned a trail camp at the present site of West Fork Campground, this trail's destination. The path traverses Mount Wilson's cool and shady northwest slopes, which are covered with big-cone Douglas fir, incense cedar, Jeffrey and sugar pines, leafy oaks, bay laurel, and ferns. Just so you don't forget that you are still in Southern California, there are occasional spiny yucca whipplei, too.

Winter and early spring are the best times to hike here, not just to get your forest fix, but also because that's when Strayns Canyon fills with water, with one pool-and-drop cascade after another dancing over myriad granite boulders. Waterfall lovers will enjoy the many small falls to be seen here. The smooth, well-maintained trail crosses the creek three times and parallels it for a mile or more. As it nears the canyon bottom, the forest changes from dense conifers to tall, leafy trees—mostly alders and cottonwoods. The first trail junction shows up at 2.8 miles, where the Gabrielino National Recreation Trail heads left to Valley Forge Camp. You stay straight on Kenyon Devore, still paralleling Strayns Canyon, for another half mile to a second junction. There you turn right on the Gabrielino Trail toward West Fork Campground.

You'll reach the camp in just one mile, following a nearly level grade through a drier forest of Coulter pines and oaks. In the wet season, you'll cross over the top of yet another cascade along the way. The camp is set at a junction of trails alongside a pretty stretch of the West Fork San Gabriel River. Old-timers can remember the days when you could just drive your car to West Fork Campground, but the Red Box–Rincon Road has been closed to cars since the early 1990s. Walk across this dirt road and pick out an empty picnic table at the campground, or, better yet, a spot alongside the river. Pull up a rock and rest your legs before the long tromp back uphill. Remember, whatever praise you heaped on this trail on the way down, you are bound to be more critical on the way back up. FYI: The top and bottom miles are the easiest; the middle two are the steepest.

© ANN MARIE BROWN

Shaded by big-cone Douglas firs, the Kenyon Devore Trail is easy going on the way down, and a workout on the way back up.

Options

From West Fork Campground, you can continue another 1.1 miles east on Gabrielino Trail to Devore Campground. You can also access West Fork Campground via another all-downhill hike on the Silver Moccasin Trail through Shortcut Canyon (3.3 miles one-way). This trail is less steep than the Kenyon Devore Trail, but it tends to have more users, including mountain bikers.

Directions

From I-210 in La Cañada, take Highway 2/Angeles Crest Highway northeast for 14.2 miles to Red Box Station on the right. Turn right at Red Box on Mount Wilson Road. Drive 4.3 miles (the road becomes one-way) to a small parking turnout near the summit. Walk back downhill to the start of the one-way stretch. The trail begins next to the Do Not Enter/Wrong Way signs on the north side of Mount Wilson Road.

Information and Contact

There is no fee, but a national forest adventure pass is required; see page 297 for more information. Dogs are allowed. A trail map of the Mount Wilson area is available for a fee from Tom Harrison Maps, 800/265-9090, www.tomharrisonmaps.com. For more information, contact the Los Angeles River Ranger District, 12371 North Little Tujunga Canyon Road, San Fernando, CA 91342, 818/899-1900, www.fs.fed.us/r5/angeles.

21 VETTER MOUNTAIN LOOKOUT   BEST ◖

Angeles National Forest

🏕 🔭 🐕

Level: Easy

Hiking Time: 1.5 hours

Total Distance: 3.0 miles round-trip

Elevation Gain: 500 feet

Summary: Vetter Mountain's fire lookout provides a fascinating history lesson as well as far-reaching views.

Vetter Mountain is a San Gabriel Mountains summit that even small children can reach, via a trail that's only 1.5 miles long and gains just 500 feet in elevation. The peak was named for Victor Vetter, who was a hardworking forest ranger during the 1920s and 1930s. In the last century, Vetter Mountain's summit was used mostly as a fire lookout station, but

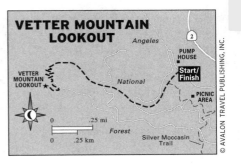

during World War II it served a brief stint as a lookout tower for spotting enemy aircraft. Today, its only function is for the enjoyment of hikers, who visit its peak for inspiring views of the San Gabriel Mountains.

The trail begins at a turnaround at the end of the Charlton Flat Picnic Area, on the left side of the road across from the start of the Wolf Tree Nature Trail. Look for an indistinct path between the two "No Parking Any Time" signs about 40 yards before the old pump house building. The path meanders uphill, following alongside a small ravine, then crosses a maintenance road in 0.4 mile. (If you can't decipher the proper start of this trail, you can always follow the pump house road a short distance to this junction, then pick up the trail.) In the winter and early spring months, water flows steadily through the ravine, creating sweet music to accompany your short hike.

The most notable feature of this landscape is a plethora of pine cones. The largest, egg-shaped ones are Coulter pine cones, the heaviest cones of all the world's pine species. You don't want to be underneath one when it drops from a tree; the heaviest cone ever found weighed in at seven-plus pounds. Four-pounders measuring almost a foot long are common along this trail. Sugar pine cones are longer—up to two feet—but Coulter pine cones can really throw their weight around.

The trail shortly leaves the forest and enters a more exposed area clad with

© ANN MARIE BROWN

The Vetter Mountain Lookout was used mostly for fire spotting, but was also used to detect enemy aircraft during World War II.

chaparral. It crosses the road again at 0.7 mile. The final half mile to the top is the steepest; after a bit of huffing and puffing, you'll come out at a dirt road. Turn left and walk the last 100 yards to the lookout tower at elevation 5,903 feet. A concrete walkway leads to the classic old-style lookout, a white wooden box on a stone foundation. On summer weekends, the tower building is open, and docents are available to answer questions and interpret the history of lookout towers in fighting fires. The square structure is surrounded on all sides by a perimeter deck, so, even if the tower isn't open, you can enjoy the deck's 360-degree views.

Vistas are extraordinary in all directions, with more than 20 named peaks visible, including Mount Baldy, Mount Williamson, Mount Waterman, Twin Peaks, and Mount Wilson. The latter is easy to spot; Mount Wilson is crowned with electronic equipment and the obvious "white golf ball" of its observatory. Pack along a good map so you can identify all the peaks and valleys in sight.

Options
You can hike to Vetter Mountain via a longer route from Little Pines Campground, located five miles farther east on Angeles Crest Highway near Chilao. Starting at Little Pines makes the hike 4.6 miles round-trip.

Directions
From I-210 in La Cañada, take Highway 2/Angeles Crest Highway northeast for 23.3 miles to Charlton Flat. Turn left on the road to Charlton Flat picnic

San Gabriel and Verdugo Mountains   **179**

area, then bear right at the fork. Continue through Charlton Flat for 0.5 mile to a closed gate just before the Forest Service pump house. The trail begins on the left side of the road, at the wide turnaround area before the gate between the two "No Parking Any Time" signs. Note: The picnic area is usually closed in the winter months, but you can park near the entrance and walk in, adding 0.6 mile round-trip to your hike.

Information and Contact

There is no fee, but a national forest adventure pass is required; see page 297 for more information. Dogs are allowed. A trail map of the Mount Wilson area, including Vetter Mountain, is available for a fee from Tom Harrison Maps, 800/265-9090, www.tomharrisonmaps.com. For more information, contact the Los Angeles River Ranger District, 12371 North Little Tujunga Canyon Road, San Fernando, CA 91342, 818/899-1900, www.fs.fed.us/r5/angeles.

22 DEVIL'S CANYON

Angeles National Forest/San Gabriel Wilderness

🚹 🏕 🕷 🐕

Level: Moderate   **Total Distance:** 7.0 miles round-trip

Hiking Time: 3.5 hours   **Elevation Gain:** 1,500 feet

Summary: This downhill hike into the San Gabriel Wilderness leads through a rugged canyon to a remote campground.

When you have tired of the front country, it's time to make a trip to the rugged San Gabriel Wilderness. Just be prepared to pay for your pleasure, because this is an upside-down hike—down on the way in and up, up, up on the way out. It's a trail of extremes. There's chaparral on some slopes, then tall pines and big-cone Douglas fir on others. There's sun, then shade, then sun again. The landscape is dry for the first two miles, then you reach a tributary creek and follow its meandering path downhill to Devil's Canyon.

It doesn't take long to hike the 2.5 miles down into the main canyon, less than an hour for most people, following well-graded switchbacks. The upper part of the trail provides many fine views into Devil's Canyon and the San Gabriel Wilderness; as you descend you lose the vistas but gain a shady oak canopy. The trail traces along a bench about 15 feet above the small tributary. Shaggy big-cone Douglas fir and clusters of shade-loving ferns make an appearance. When you reach the canyon bottom, you find that Devil's Creek is surrounded by sycamores and oaks—a much drier environment than what you'll find at nearby Bear Canyon 10 miles to the west, below Switzer Falls. This is xeric habitat, a landscape that thrives with only a small amount of moisture. The trail now meanders alongside Devil's Creek for about a mile. In one stretch, the trail travels right through the dry creekbed.

You'll reach the old Devil's Canyon Campground alongside the creek at 3.5 miles from the start. This area is very exposed, with little shade, making this a great place to camp in the winter months but not so great in the summer. Since this is a wilderness area, the camp is primitive: there are only a few fire rings and level sleeping spots, plus easy places to wade into the stream on warm days. For day hikers, it's a pleasant spot any time. The creek is not

© ANN MARIE BROWN

A shady canopy of oak, bay laurel, and big-cone Douglas fir eases the climb back uphill from Devil's Canyon.

deep enough for swimming, but at least you can take off your boots and cool your feet.

After a rest by the stream, it's time to head back up the trail. Just remember: the 3.5 miles back up to the trailhead seem twice as long as the trip down.

Options

From the camp, the trail continues downstream for another half mile, then peters out. If you want to see more of Devil's Canyon, be prepared for a boulder-hopping, wet-feet adventure. The stream is completely cloaked in alders and largely choked with willows; occasionally you must bushwhack your way through them. The canyon gets narrower as you go; it's slow travel but not particularly treacherous. The walls squeeze in tighter and steeper until you come to a series of small cascades, two to five feet high. Soon these increase to full-size waterfalls.

Directions

From I-210 in La Cañada, take Highway 2/Angeles Crest Highway northeast for 25.5 miles to the Chilao Campground turnoff on the left, then continue past it for 0.75 mile to a parking lot on the left side of the highway. (It is 0.25 mile west of the Chilao Visitor Center turnoff.) The signed Devil's Canyon trailhead is located across the road.

Information and Contact

There is no fee, but a national forest adventure pass is required; see page 297 for more information. Dogs are allowed. A trail map of the Angeles High Country is available for a fee from Tom Harrison Maps, 800/265-9090, www.tomharrisonmaps.com. For more information, contact Angeles National Forest, Los Angeles River Ranger District, 12371 N. Little Tujunga Canyon Road, San Fernando, CA 91342, 818/899-1900, www.fs.fed.us/r5/angeles.

23 MOUNT HILLYER
Angeles National Forest

Level: Easy/Moderate

Hiking Time: 3 hours

Total Distance: 6.0 miles round-trip

Elevation Gain: 1,000 feet

Summary: A gentle hike through a rocky wonderland dotted with pines and wildflowers.

The trip to Mount Hillyer is all about the journey, not the destination, which happens to be the mountain's 6,162-foot summit. Despite its fairly impressive elevation, Mount Hillyer is surrounded by a high, view-obscuring ridge, and its summit amounts to little more than a hill, or maybe a bump on a hill. But the trail to reach it is a rocky wonderland, dotted with odd-shaped granite outcrops that beg to be climbed. In between the rocks are marvelous stands of pines and incense cedars. Bring a good book or a picnic with you, and pick any inviting spot along the trail to pass a few hours. You'll enjoy the wind in the pines, spring wildflowers, and a relatively mellow hike in the mountains.

From the Chilao trailhead, the pathway begins by following a seasonal creek up a modest grade. In spring, you'll pass by multitudes of blooming yucca whipplei, its creamy white flowers a sharp contrast to its spiky foliage, and sweet-smelling ceanothus or mountain lilac. In 1.1 miles you reach a T intersection near Horse Flats Campground and go left. The path skirts around the camp, then climbs through a steep, rocky area, passing through scenery reminiscent of the southern Sierra, with sandy soil, Jeffrey and ponderosa pines, and big granite boulders.

The summit is fairly easy to miss, so pay close attention to the trail. If it

Lots of intriguing granite outcrops will tempt you to explore along the mellow trail to Mount Hillyer.

starts to descend, you walked right past Mount Hillyer, a boulder-strewn high spot a few yards off the trail. A summit register is buried amid a pile of rocks. If you want more of a view than you get from this "bump on a hill," leave the main trail and walk 0.25 mile southwest along the ridge to a point 35 feet higher than Hillyer's official summit. Here you'll find a pleasant view of Mount Pacifico (to your right at 7,124 feet in elevation) and the canyon of the Middle Fork of Alder Creek, a major tributary to Big Tujunga Creek. You can also see Round Top Peak and Iron Mountain to the west, and Vetter Mountain to the south.

Beyond the summit, the trail descends gently and in 0.5 mile reaches Santa Clara Divide Road. If you are enjoying this hike, you might as well wander a little farther, before you choose your private spot for reading, eating, or just enjoying the scenery.

Options

Start at Horse Flats Campground for an even shorter hike to the summit of Mount Hillyer—only 2.5 miles round-trip. The trail starts right across from the horse corral at the far end of the campground loop. Horse Flats Campground is located off the Santa Clara Divide Road, which junctions with Angeles Crest Highway 2.5 miles east of Chilao.

Directions

From I-210 in La Cañada, take Highway 2/Angeles Crest Highway northeast for 26.5 miles to the Chilao Visitor Center turnoff on the left (not the turnoff for Chilao Campgrounds). Drive 0.7 mile on the Chilao Visitor Center road to a small parking pullout where the Silver Moccasin Trail crosses the road. Park here and follow the trail that is signed for Horse Flats Campground.

Information and Contact

A national forest adventure pass is required; see page 297 for more information. Dogs are allowed. A trail map of the Angeles Front Country is available for a fee from Tom Harrison Maps, 800/265-9090, www.tomharrisonmaps.com. For more information, contact Angeles National Forest, Los Angeles River Ranger District, 12371 North Little Tujunga Canyon Road, San Fernando, CA 91342, 818/899-1900, www.fs.fed.us/r5/angeles.

24 MOUNT WATERMAN

Angeles National Forest/San Gabriel Wilderness

Level: Moderate

Total Distance: 5.4 miles round-trip

Hiking Time: 3 hours

Elevation Gain: 1,300 feet

Summary: Watch for bighorn sheep as you ramble uphill through Sierra-like scenery to the summit of 8,038-foot Mount Waterman.

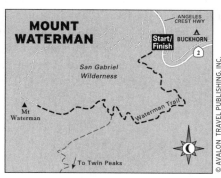

The path to Mount Waterman is one of the most well-graded mountain trails in the San Gabriels. Most of the time you barely notice you are climbing, even though you gain 1,300 feet from the trailhead to the top. That's largely due to the fact that the trail is pleasantly shaded by a conifer canopy of firs, incense cedars, and Jeffrey and sugar pines, keeping the trail comfortably cool even in the heat of summer. And the view from the top is a winner—on the clearest days you can see all the way to 10,834-foot Mount San Jacinto, standing sentinel above Palm Springs.

The first mile lacks any wide-angle views but has plenty of close-up looks at the mountain's big trees. With that completed, you reach a saddle on a ridge where the vista opens wide. From here on, your views continually expand, looking north toward the western Mojave Desert surrounding Lancaster and Palmdale, and south over the San Gabriel Wilderness. Once you've gained this ridge, there are plenty of spots where you can take a break to enjoy the view.

The trail continues to ascend over long, well-graded switchbacks to a junction at 2.1 miles, where you turn right for the summit. It's another 0.6 mile to the top, still on an easy grade. With a rapidly multiplying number of granite boulders peppering the conifer forest, it is easy to see why many L.A. hikers consider the San Gabriel High Country to be "the poor man's Sierra Nevada." Here at 8,000 feet, the landscape is much more Yosemite-like than you would expect.

Because of the openness of the forest on Waterman's slopes, early summer wildflowers make an appearance, usually best in mid- to late June. At any time of year, you have a fair chance at a prime wildlife sighting on Waterman's slopes, as magnificent Nelson bighorn sheep frequent the area. According to a California Department of Fish and Game monitoring study, there were 740 bighorns populating the San Gabriel Mountains in 1980, but in the last quarter century, their numbers have declined significantly. Seeing one, especially a bighorn ram with its great backward-curving horns, is a thrilling event.

When you reach the U-shaped top of 8,038-foot Mount Waterman, you have one small problem: Figuring out which summit is really the summit. Waterman's top is so wide that it has three summits, and informal use trails lead to all of them. Head left for 0.25 mile, toward the southwest, and you'll find the highest of the lot. Climb to the top of one of the big boulder piles and you'll see no signs of civilization for miles around, except for the distant towers on top of Mount Wilson. Pull out a map and name all the peaks in view—Twin Peaks, Strawberry Peak, and Mount Lawlor are only a few. Is there a big city called Los Angeles down there? You just can't believe it.

Options

If you can handle the mileage and elevation change, you can turn this easy hike into a butt-kicker by continuing from Mount Waterman to Twin Peaks. Return to the junction you passed at 2.1 miles from the trailhead and turn right. You'll begin a long, 1,400-foot descent over two miles to the saddle that lies in between Mount Waterman and Twin Peaks, then turn left at a

© LONNIE DECLOEDT

the highest summit of 8,038-foot Mount Waterman, a peak with three summits

junction and have to regain almost all of that elevation in the next 1.5 miles to the peaks. This section of trail is much more primitive than what you've been traveling on so far. All in all, you're looking at a nearly 12-mile day with some strenuous up and down (total 3,900 feet of elevation gain), but the trip is doable for most well-conditioned hikers.

Directions

From I-210 in La Cañada, take Highway 2/Angeles Crest Highway northeast for 34 miles to the signed trailhead for Mount Waterman Trail on the right side of the road, east of the Mount Waterman ski lift operation and west of Buckhorn Campground. Park in the pullout across the road from the trailhead sign.

Information and Contact

A national forest adventure pass is required; see page 297 for more information. Dogs are allowed. A trail map of the Angeles High Country is available for a fee from Tom Harrison Maps, 800/265-9090, www.tomharrisonmaps.com. For more information, contact Angeles National Forest, Los Angeles River Ranger District, 12371 North Little Tujunga Canyon Road, San Fernando, CA 91342, 818/899-1900, www.fs.fed.us/r5/angeles.

25 COOPER CANYON

Angeles National Forest

BEST ☾

Level: Easy/Moderate

Total Distance: 6.0 miles round-trip

Hiking Time: 3 hours

Elevation Gain: 1,000 feet

Summary: Big conifers and a glistening waterfall await hikers in this high-country canyon.

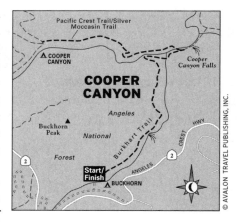

L.A. campers love Buckhorn Campground and L.A. hikers love neighboring Cooper Canyon, and it's all because the scenery makes you feel like you're in the southern Sierra Nevada, not a mere hour's drive from your house in Pasadena. Here, at 6,400 feet in elevation, the air is clean and the conifers are big. You have to experience it to believe it.

Start off from Buckhorn Campground at the trailhead for the Burkhart Trail. The first stretch of trail is often busy, with many campers heading out for short strolls and others seeking the perfect swimming hole in Buckhorn Creek. (There are plenty within a short distance of the campground.) Just keep hiking and soon you'll leave the crowds behind, as you wander through a dense forest of big firs, incense cedars, and Jeffrey and sugar pines. Almost no undergrowth thrives in these woods, only tall conifers and big rocks. The trees are so immense that they block out much of the light that would otherwise reach the forest floor.

Burkhart Trail laterals along the canyon slopes high above Buckhorn Creek. At 1.2 miles out, the route makes a left turn out of Buckhorn Canyon and into Cooper Canyon and traces a long switchback downhill. Look for a group of five young incense cedar trees, an unusual set of quintuplets, growing together near a tiny stream crossing.

At 1.6 miles, you'll reach a junction with the joint Pacific Crest Trail/Silver Moccasin Trail. A sign points left to Cooper Canyon Camp, your destination, but take a short detour first. Go right toward Burkhart Saddle and Eagle's Roost, and in 100 yards you come to Cooper Canyon Falls, which drops just below the trail's edge. From the top, the waterfall doesn't look like much, but continue another 30 yards to a spur trail that drops steeply to the fall's base. A rope is often in place near the bottom to help you get down (and up) the last few feet. At the canyon bottom, you can stand in the middle of the stream on an island of large boulders for a perfect view. The 35-foot-high fall spills into a steep rock bowl with a big pool at its base.

Having gotten your negative ion fix at the waterfall, return to the previous junction and head toward Cooper Canyon Camp, a little more than a mile away. This hike-in campground is well equipped for the Boy Scouts who come marching through on their ritual hike along the 53-mile Silver Moccasin Trail. The trail has been making Scouts out of boys since the 1940s. Enjoy a picnic here before retracing your steps back to Buckhorn Campground.

Extra-long sugar pine cones are a common sight in Cooper Canyon.

Options

With a short car shuttle, it is possible to hike a semiloop from Buckhorn Campground to Cooper Canyon Camp and then up to Cloudburst Summit, six miles total. Or, for a shorter hike in the same neighborhood, park at the gated road across the highway and slightly east of Mount Waterman Ski Area. Hike up the gated road to a saddle, then follow an informal use trail along the ridgeline to the obvious summit of Buckhorn Peak, elevation 7,283 feet. This hike is 1.4 miles round-trip.

Directions

From I-210 in La Cañada, take Highway 2/Angeles Crest Highway northeast for 35 miles to Buckhorn Campground on the left, shortly past Cloudburst Summit. The Burkhart Trail starts from the hikers' parking lot at the far end of the camp road.

Information and Contact

There is no fee, but a national forest adventure pass is required; see page 297 for more information. Dogs are allowed. A trail map of the Angeles High Country is available for a fee from Tom Harrison Maps, 800/265-9090, www.tomharrisonmaps.com. For more information, contact Angeles National Forest, Los Angeles River Ranger District, 12371 N. Little Tujunga Canyon Road, San Fernando, CA 91342, 818/899-1900, www.fs.fed.us/r5/angeles.

2 6 MOUNT WILLIAMSON   BEST C
Angeles National Forest

Level: Moderate   **Total Distance:** 5.0 miles round-trip

Hiking Time: 2.5 hours   **Elevation Gain:** 1,600 feet

Summary: Sweeping views of the Devil's Punchbowl and Mojave Desert are yours for the taking from this 8,214-foot summit.

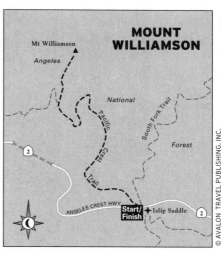

The summit of Mount Williamson has something that makes it unique from all the other high peaks of the San Gabriel Range. Perched above the Devil's Punchbowl, the San Andreas Rift Zone, and the Mojave Desert, 8,214-foot Mount Williamson offers a remarkable perspective on the desert terrain to the north—what appears to be a vast inland sea of tan and white nothingness. Hiking this trail is a study in contrasts. Although you walk through a high-elevation forest of big Jeffrey pines and white fir, you look down 5,000 feet below to a wide sweep of Mojave landscape.

Not surprisingly, the forest on this side of the San Gabriel crest is more sparse and exposed. Although the conifers are mighty in size, as they are throughout the high country, here they are more sporadic. What grows best are the hardiest and most rugged of species, including some wind-sculpted Jeffrey pines on the summit itself. Each tree, twisted and curved by the hand of Mother Nature, is a piece of artwork.

Start out from Islip Saddle and take the upper (left) trail by the restrooms, which is signed as Silver Moccasin Trail and Pacific Crest Trail. After a few switchbacks around the mountainside, you'll soon understand why this trail is famous for its steep drop-offs. This probably isn't a good trail for hiking with children.

At a saddle two miles out, the Pacific Crest Trail drops down to the west (left), and you'll head north (right) for the summit of Williamson. But first you'll want to linger here for a while and enjoy the south-facing views: A big

Wind-sculpted Jeffrey pines decorate the top of snow-dusted Mount Williamson.

chunk of the San Gabriel Mountains is spread out before you. Once you're on the summit trail, you have only a half mile remaining, but it's a memorably steep half mile. A few switchbacks would be welcome here, but, alas, there are none.

Although the views have been inspiring all along, nothing prepares you for the scene on top of Mount Williamson's narrow ridgeline, which delivers dizzying views on both sides. The San Gabriel Mountains are on your left, and on the clearest days you can see beyond them and the valley land mass farther beyond, to the Pacific Ocean and Catalina Island. On your right, of course, is the Mojave Desert to the north. Mount Williamson is the apex of Pleasant View Ridge, a sequence of peaks that runs from the desert floor to the Angeles Crest.

Don't call it quits at the first pointy summit you reach; follow the ridgeline trail a bit farther to a second and flatter summit, which is 30 feet higher. The view from here is even more extraordinary—you can look down directly into the jumbled rocks of the Devil's Punchbowl and the San Andreas Rift Zone.

Options

You can summit Mount Williamson via a shorter route, starting from the turnout 0.3 mile west of the westernmost tunnel on Angeles Crest Highway, 1.5 miles west of Islip Saddle. This is only a 3.4-mile round-trip, but with a much steeper grade than the hike above.

Directions

From I-210 in La Cañada, take Highway 2/Angeles Crest Highway northeast for 41 miles to the large parking area at Islip Saddle (one mile east of the tunnels). The trail begins on the north side of the road near the restrooms.

Alternatively, from the junction of Highway 138 and Highway 2 northeast of Wrightwood, head west on Highway 2 for 25 miles to the large parking area at Islip Saddle. The trail begins on the north side of the road near the restrooms.

Information and Contact

A national forest adventure pass is required; see page 297 for more information. Dogs are allowed. A trail map of the Angeles High Country is available for a fee from Tom Harrison Maps, 800/265-9090, www.tomharrisonmaps.com. For more information, contact Angeles National Forest, Los Angeles River Ranger District, 12371 North Little Tujunga Canyon Road, San Fernando, CA 91342, 818/899-1900, www.fs.fed.us/r5/angeles.

27 MOUNT ISLIP   BEST [(

Angeles National Forest

Level: Moderate   **Total Distance:** 6.6 miles round-trip

Hiking Time: 3 hours   **Elevation Gain:** 1,600 feet

Summary: A view-filled hike to an old fire lookout foundation on an easily reached 8,250-foot summit.

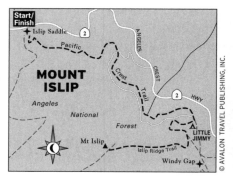

The finest views aren't always from the tallest summits. Mount Islip at 8,250 feet is not even in the Top 10 of highest San Gabriel Mountain peaks, but its 360-degree view is a winner.

As a bonus, the summit is easy to reach. The trail, which is both the Little Jimmy Trail and a segment of the Pacific Crest Trail, begins at Islip Saddle on the Angeles Crest Highway. From the large parking area, cross the highway carefully and pick up the trail on the south side. The first half mile climbs steadily and is completely exposed, but the reward for all your huffing and puffing is a wide view to the south over a panorama of San Gabriel peaks and ridges, which comes into sight just before you enter a forested stretch. Keep heading upward, now sheltered in the welcome shade of pine and fir trees, and cross a dirt service road one mile from the trailhead. The path parallels the road and levels out. With a glance over your left shoulder, you'll see the west Mojave Desert and the far-off, but rapidly expanding, suburbs of Palmdale.

At 2.3 miles out, you reach Little Jimmy Trail Camp, a large developed campground with dozens of sites, picnic tables, fire grills, and even a few vault toilets and garbage cans. With water available from a reliable spring only a quarter of a mile away, the camp is a popular stop for Pacific Crest Trail hikers and Boy Scouts. The camp and its nearby spring were named after Jimmy Swinnerton, creator of the popular "Little Jimmy" comic strip of the early 20th century, who spent a few summers camping near here.

Walk through the camp and pick up the signed Mount Islip Trail on the far side. In about 100 yards, you'll pass a few choice campsites perched on the edge of a cliff overlooking the desert. Make a mental note of these sites for a

The stone remains of an old fire lookout tower can be seen on top of Mount Islip—and a sublime mountain view as well.

future backpacking trip—one that is easy enough to take the kids on. Continue switchbacking uphill past the campsites for 0.4 mile to Mount Islip's high ridgeline, which offers more great views of the mountains and valleys to the south and west.

Turn right on Islip Ridge Trail, then enjoy a mellower stroll along the view-filled ridgeline. That tiny spot of blue far below is Crystal Lake, the only natural lake in the San Gabriel Mountains. The surrounding Crystal Lake Recreation Area was badly burned in the Curve Fire of 2002, and, as of 2005, is closed to public access while the vegetation recovers. The landscape you are traveling through was just on the edge of the conflagration and shows some burn evidence, but the signs of fire are becoming harder to distinguish with every passing year.

At a junction with the summit trail, bear right for the peak, now only 200 yards uphill. Once on the 8,250-foot summit, you'll find the remains of an old stone cabin, which was part of a complex of buildings that included an old fire lookout tower. The lookout stood sentinel here from 1927 to 1937, when it was moved to nearby South Mount Hawkins.

And of course you'll find the promised views. Islip's peak is very pointy and has little surface area, so when you're on top, you really know you're on top. Although its summit elevation isn't a record-breaker, there are no higher peaks close by, so all of the middle portion of the San Gabriel Mountains, and the hazy valley beyond, comes into view.

Options

From Little Jimmy Trail Camp, you can remain on the Pacific Crest Trail and follow it 2.3 miles east to the right turnoff for 8,850-foot Mount Hawkins, located just a few hundred feet off the trail. This 9.2-mile round-trip hike has a 2,100-foot elevation gain. Or, with a car shuttle, you could continue from Mount Hawkins for another 1.2 miles to Throop Peak, then follow the Dawson Saddle

Trail back downhill to Angeles Crest Highway and your waiting car shuttle. This makes a one-way hike of 7.8 miles.

Directions

From I-210 in La Cañada, take Highway 2/Angeles Crest Highway northeast for 41 miles to the large parking area at Islip Saddle (one mile east of the tunnels). The trail begins on the south side of the road.

Alternatively, from the junction of Highway 138 and Highway 2 northeast of Wrightwood, head west on Highway 2 for 25 miles to the large parking area at Islip Saddle. The trail begins on the south side of the road.

Information and Contact

A national forest adventure pass is required; see page 297 for more information. Dogs are allowed. A trail map of the Angeles High Country is available for a fee from Tom Harrison Maps, 800/265-9090, www.tomharrisonmaps.com. For more information, contact Angeles National Forest, Los Angeles River Ranger District, 12371 North Little Tujunga Canyon Road, San Fernando, CA 91342, 818/899-1900, www.fs.fed.us/r5/angeles.

28 BURKHART TRAIL TO THE DEVIL'S CHAIR

BEST ◖

Devil's Punchbowl Natural Area

Level: Moderate

Total Distance: 7.0 miles round-trip

Hiking Time: 3.5 hours

Elevation Gain: 1,000 feet

Summary: A visit to an otherworldly rock landscape created by movement along an earthquake fault.

The Devil's Punchbowl and the Devil's Chair are visual proof that you're in earthquake country, where faulting and erosion have made bizarre shapes out of ancient sedimentary rocks. The park's namesake Punchbowl is essentially a hole in the ground—a round-shaped gorge lined with slanted, strange-looking sandstone slabs. The Devil's Chair is just the opposite—a hogback ridge culminating

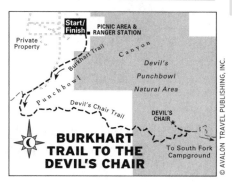

in a high promontory decorated with similarly bizarre rock formations. Get a look at both on this fascinating hike at Devil's Punchbowl Natural Area. But better do it soon, before these strange geological phenomena get swallowed up completely by the perpetual movement of the earth (or eroded away by the forces of entropy).

Sure, it's a long drive out here from almost anywhere in the Los Angeles area, but this park is worth it. Although it is located on the north slope of the San Gabriel Mountains, just below 8,214-foot Mount Williamson, this arid landscape is far different from the San Gabriel high country. Lying midway between mountains and desert in the pinyon pine and juniper transition zone, the ground might be snow-covered in winter, or, then again, the weather might be 75 degrees and balmy. Elevations in the park range from 4,000 to 6,000 feet. Although you drive through desertlike terrain to reach the trailhead, you'll soon be walking through a conifer forest, listening to the wind in the pines.

In the interest of full disclosure, the first 20 minutes or so of this hike leave much to be desired. At the parking lot, the Burkhart Trail starts out as a promising-looking single-track pathway. It passes a water tank and skirts

the fence-lined final steps to the Devil's Chair

the edge of the Devil's Punchbowl abyss (be sure to take a short detour to see the Punchbowl now or on your return hike). Then, disappointingly, the trail joins a dirt road, which travels uphill through a barren-looking landscape. Its only notable feature is an overabundance of manzanita. Just keep looking ahead to those pine-covered slopes—that's where you are heading. The dirt road splits into two forks, which rejoin a short distance farther near a storage building. Finally, after 0.9 mile of steady climbing on this uninspiring road/ trail, you reach a sign for the Devil's Chair Trail, a left turnoff. Take it, and in a matter of minutes you are out of the desert and into the pines, following a well-maintained, smoothly graded, and pleasant trail.

You'll cross Punchbowl Creek and follow an extremely mellow grade as you lateral across the slopes above the Devil's Punchbowl. The trail undulates gently up and down, crossing one small ravine after another. As you gradually gain elevation, you also gain views of the white rocks of the Devil's Punchbowl and the desert beyond. Two different rocky promontories, just off the trail, provide particularly imposing viewpoints. You'll know you are nearing your destination when on your right you spot a huge round sandstone boulder perched on the edge of yet another abyss. From here, you have about a half mile to go.

At a junction with a trail coming in from South Fork Campground, head left and begin the final leg of your journey. Surprisingly, the final jaunt to the Devil's Chair is downhill—10 short switchbacks downhill, to be exact. The last 50 yards of the path, which lead out on a narrow backbone ridge to the Chair itself, are so prone to erosion that the trail is encased in a tunnel of fencing. Have a seat on the Devil's Chair and enjoy this surreal scene for a while, before retracing your steps and heading back up those switchbacks.

Options

You can walk two other short trails at this park: the one-mile Devil's Punchbowl Loop and the 0.25-mile Piñon Pathway. Or, time your trip carefully so that you show up during a summer full moon, when park rangers lead night hikes around the Devil's Punchbowl. Also, make sure you stop in at the nature center, which always has a fascinating collection of live birds, usually owls and raptors.

Directions

From Highway 14 near Palmdale, take the Highway 138 exit east for 16 miles to Pearblossom. Turn right on County Road N-6 (signed as Longview Road) and drive south for 7.5 miles to the Devil's Punchbowl entrance. The road makes several turns and changes names along the way, but all junctions are signed for the park. You will end up on Devil's Punchbowl Road. From the park entrance, continue another 0.25 mile to the parking lot by the nature center. The Burkhart Trail begins on the south side of the parking lot.

Information and Contact

There is no fee. Dogs on leash are allowed. Free trail maps are available at the visitor center. For more information, contact Devil's Punchbowl Natural Area, 28000 Devil's Punchbowl Road, Pearblossom, CA 93553, 661/944-2743, http://parks.co.la.ca.us or www.devils-punchbowl.com.

29 THROOP PEAK FROM DAWSON SADDLE
Angeles National Forest

Level: Easy/Moderate

Hiking Time: 2 hours

Total Distance: 4.4 miles round-trip

Elevation Gain: 1,200 feet

Summary: A summit hike to a 9,138-foot peak named for the founder of Cal Tech.

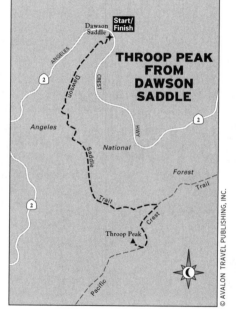

The highest point on the Angeles Crest Highway is Dawson Saddle at 7,901 feet, so what better place to start hiking? Your car has already delivered you to the high country. You begin from here with your feet planted firmly in the clouds.

A great destination from Dawson Saddle is 9,138-foot Throop Peak (pronounced "Troop"), named for Amos Gager Throop, the founder of Throop University, which later became the California Institute of Technology. The peak was named by a group of Cal Tech students who first climbed it in 1916. Although this summit hike is not as well known as Mount Baldy or Mount Baden-Powell, its rewards are of the same caliber. Because the trip is so short, many hikers make this an evening sunset walk or do it during a full moon. A few obvious campsites on the summit make it possible to spend the night, if you have obtained a campfire permit from Angeles National Forest.

The old Dawson Saddle Trail begins right across the highway from the parking lot; a new, improved trail starts 150 yards to the east. Walk down the highway carefully to pick up the newer trail, which was built by energetic Boy Scouts in the 1980s.

The trail climbs steadily through an open forest of pine and fir, passing a junction with the old trail in 0.25 mile. Expansive views are yours for the taking as you switchback uphill, heading generally southward. As you ascend, pause occasionally to catch your breath and look to the north for views of the western Mojave. Occasionally you gain a clear sight line to the west, where, if the horizon is haze free, you may catch a fleeting glimpse of the city of Los Angeles.

Two miles out, you reach a junction with the Pacific Crest Trail. Turn right (southwest) and walk an easy 0.25 mile to the summit spur trail. A few hundred yards farther uphill and you're on top of Throop Peak. A rectangular plaque embedded in the ground marks the spot and bears a dedication to Amos Throop. Now is the time to relax and enjoy the view, which includes the rugged canyons of the Sheep Mountain Wilderness and looming Mount Baldy to the southeast, plus a vast expanse of desert to the north. Although neighboring Mount Hawkins to the southwest was severely burned in the Curve Fire of 2002, fortunately Throop Peak was spared.

Before you head back downhill, look around for the summit register (usually buried in a small pile of rocks). Take a moment to read what others have penned before you, then add a few pithy words of your own.

Options

If you still have energy to burn after summiting Throop Peak, you can continue east along the Pacific Crest Trail to Mount Burnham (8,997 feet) and Mount Baden-Powell (9,399 feet). This will add 4.6 more miles (2.3 miles out and back) to your total mileage for the day.

© LONNIE DECLOEDT

a view of the vast Mojave Desert along the trail from Dawson Saddle to Throop Peak

Directions

From I-210 in La Cañada, take Highway 2/Angeles Crest Highway northeast for 47 miles to Dawson Saddle. Park on the north side of the highway. Cross to the south side and walk east about 150 yards to find the start of the Dawson Saddle Trail.

Alternatively, from the junction of Highway 138 and Highway 2 northeast of Wrightwood, head west on Highway 2 for 19 miles to Dawson Saddle. Park on the north side of the highway. Cross to the south side and walk east about 150 yards to find the start of the Dawson Saddle Trail.

Information and Contact

A national forest adventure pass is required; see page 297 for more information. Dogs are allowed. A trail map of the Angeles High Country is available for a fee from Tom Harrison Maps, 800/265-9090, www.tomharrisonmaps.com. For more information, contact Angeles National Forest, San Gabriel River Ranger District, 110 N. Wabash Avenue, Glendora, CA 91741, 626/335-1251, www.fs.fed.us/r5/angeles.

30 VINCENT GAP TO MOUNT BADEN-POWELL

BEST

Angeles National Forest

Level: Strenuous

Total Distance: 8.0 miles round-trip

Hiking Time: 4 hours

Elevation Gain: 2,800 feet

Summary: A challenging hike to the fifth-highest peak in the San Gabriel Mountains, named for the founder of the Boy Scouts.

Much like the ascent to the summit of Mount Baldy, the hike to the top of Mount Baden-Powell is something of a requirement for Los Angeles hikers. The good news is that this requirement is within the reach of most, because the trail is only four miles one-way with a 2,800-foot elevation gain. That makes this hike very popular, especially since the season to hike it is so short—usually June to early November, depending on snow levels and the dates of the winter road closure on the Angeles Crest Highway surrounding Vincent Gap. To avoid the perpetual summer crowds, visit on an autumn weekday if you can.

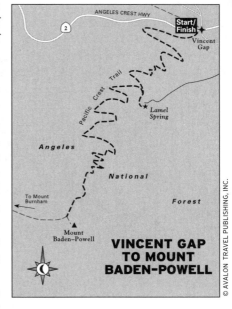

VINCENT GAP TO MOUNT BADEN-POWELL

© AVALON TRAVEL PUBLISHING, INC.

At 9,399 feet, Baden-Powell is no shirker in the elevation department. It is the fifth highest peak in the San Gabriels, after Mount Baldy (10,064 feet), Pine Mountain (9,648 feet), Dawson Peak (9,575 feet), and Mount Harwood (9,552 feet). It is also a botanist's delight: its upper slopes are home to gnarled, thousand-year-old limber pine trees, a species known for its extremely flexible twigs (you can tie one into a knot and it will not break). This tree is well adapted to living in high-elevation areas that are too windy and dry for other kinds of trees. If you've ever visited the Ancient Bristlecone Pine Forest in the White Mountains of eastern California, you'll remember that limber pines are the only trees that share those high desert slopes with ancient bristlecone pines, the oldest living things on earth.

Mount Baden-Powell has other reasons for its popularity: It is the terminus of the 52-mile Silver Moccasin Trail, a five-day backpacking trip that is a rite of passage for Southern California Boy Scouts. This leg of the Silver Moccasin Trail also coincides with a portion of the 2,600-mile Pacific Crest Trail.

From the southwest side of Vincent Gap, the trail (signed here as Pacific Crest Trail) leads through open forest on the northern slopes of Baden-Powell. Initially you are surrounded by oak, sugar pine, Jeffrey pine, white fir, and incense cedar, but, as you gain elevation, the landscape transitions to a more exposed forest comprised of lodgepole pine and occasional limber pines. The shade cover is spotty, so the trail can be quite hot in summer.

The Wally Waldron Tree on Mount Baden-Powell is estimated to be at least 1,500 years old.

On the other hand, the summit is often windy, so wear or carry layers.

The trail is well built, with 42 switchbacks zigzagging all the way to the top. They get steeper as they go, and, since the elevation is so high, you'll feel your cardiovascular system working hard. Still, while the "up" is nonstop, the grade is manageable enough that many repeat hikers make it a point to try to beat their personal-best records to the summit.

Halfway up the trail, a 200-yard side trip is possible to Lamel Spring, a trickle of water that is usually dry by late summer. A quarter mile from the top you leave the Pacific Crest Trail and head south (left) on the summit trail. Near this junction you'll find the signed Wally Waldron Tree, a limber pine that is about 1,500 years old, named for a dedicated Boy Scout volunteer.

When you reach the summit, you'll find a hikers' register and a tombstonelike monument to the British Lord Baden-Powell, who founded the Boy Scouts organization in 1907 and wrote the first scout manual, *Scouting for Boys*. The peak was dedicated in 1931 by Major Frederick Russell Burnham, whose name, coincidentally, is attached to a neighboring peak.

What about the view? The summit is directly across the East Fork San Gabriel River basin from, and slightly west of, Mount Baldy. As you might guess, the views are extraordinary. You can see more than a vertical mile below you into the canyon of the East Fork San Gabriel River and the Sheep Mountain Wilderness, across the canyon to Baldy, and north to the Mojave Desert and beyond. On clear days, it's not hard to pick out Catalina Island off the coast, Mount San Gorgonio and Mount San Jacinto way off in the distance beyond Baldy, and even some of the peaks and ridges of the southern Sierra Nevada, far to the north.

There's only one downer on this trail, and that's the amount of erosion that has been caused by hikers cutting the switchbacks on their descent. Please don't do this, and remind others if you catch them in the act.

Options
With a car shuttle, you can visit 9,138-foot Throop Peak and 8,997-foot Mount Burnham as well as Mount Baden-Powell via a 9.0-mile one-way trek. Leave one car at Vincent Gap and drive the other to the trailhead at Dawson Saddle, five miles farther west on the Angeles Crest Highway. Follow the Dawson Saddle Trail uphill to join the Pacific Crest Trail (PCT). Turn right on the PCT for 0.25 mile to bag the summit of Throop Peak. Then retrace your steps and head in the opposite direction on the PCT to go to Mount Burnham and finally Mount Baden-Powell.

Directions
From I-210 in La Cañada, take Highway 2/Angeles Crest Highway northeast for 53 miles to Vincent Gap. Follow the Pacific Crest Trail uphill from the parking lot.

Alternatively, from the junction of Highway 138 and Highway 2 northeast of Wrightwood, head west on Highway 2 for 13 miles to Vincent Gap. Follow the Pacific Crest Trail uphill from the parking lot.

Information and Contact
A national forest adventure pass is required; see page 297 for more information. Dogs are allowed. A trail map of the Angeles High Country is available for a fee from Tom Harrison Maps, 800/265-9090, www.tomharrisonmaps.com. For more information, contact Angeles National Forest, Santa Clara/Mojave Rivers Ranger District, 30800 Bouquet Canyon Road, Saugus, CA 91390, 661/296-9710, www.fs.fed.us/r5/angeles. Or contact the Big Pines Visitor Center, 760/249-3504.

31 BIG HORN MINE   BEST ◖

Angeles National Forest/Sheep Mountain Wilderness

🔭 ❖ 🐾

Level: Easy   **Total Distance:** 4.0 miles round-trip

Hiking Time: 2 hours   **Elevation Gain:** 700 feet

Summary: A fascinating historical hike to the ruins of an old gold mine.

Way up in the high country of the San Gabriel Mountains, the Big Horn Mine was founded in 1894 by Charles Tom Vincent. Vincent sold his mine to investors, who spent a fortune boring tunnels and developing the mine site. Although it is rumored that the mine produced as much as $50,000 in gold ore during its most productive years, nobody ever got rich. A big-game hunter and prospector with a shady past, Vincent built a rustic cabin near the mine on the east slope on Mount Baden-Powell, where he lived until his death in 1926. Today Vincent's name lives on at Vincent Gap, a major trailhead along the Angeles Crest Highway.

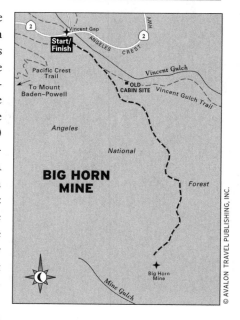

© AVALON TRAVEL PUBLISHING, INC.

You don't have to visualize much on this trip through history. An abundance of mine ruins are plainly visible, and even the trail itself is the mine's old wagon road. Considering its age, the road is in decent shape, although it is washed out in a few sections. It's hard to know which is better—the fascinating mine remains or the breathtaking views of Mount Baldy, Mount Baden-Powell, Pine Mountain, and Iron Mountain that you see from the trail and the mine site.

Follow the closed road from the Vincent Gap trailhead. After a mile's walk through pine and fir forest, you'll pass a water-filled shaft and some foundations and other debris left from the cabins that housed the miners. More mine shafts and bric-a-brac follow, but nothing prepares you for your sense of surprise when you round a bend and see the large stamp mill building, perched precariously on the hillside. It's tempting but ill-advised to explore inside

© LONNIE DECLOEDT

The old stamp mill at the Big Horn Mine clings precariously to a steep slope.

the ramshackle building—there is no guarantee that something won't come crashing down on your head. A better idea is to find a suitable spot outside the stamp mill for lunch, and enjoy the fine views across the gorge of the East Fork San Gabriel River to Mount Baldy and its sibling peaks.

Unfortunately, as with too many special places in Angeles National Forest, this wonderful piece of history has been degraded by graffiti and trash. You might want to bring along an extra bag to collect some of the junk that others have left behind.

Options

On your way back to the trailhead, take a side trip to see Vincent's cabin, which, through the efforts of Forest Service volunteers, was reroofed and reinforced to preserve its place in history. Just 150 yards from the trailhead is a Sheep Mountain Wilderness sign and the Vincent Gulch Trail. Follow it 0.5 mile to an unmarked junction; bear right and walk 100 yards to the cabin.

Directions

From I-210 in La Cañada, take Highway 2/Angeles Crest Highway northeast for 53 miles to Vincent Gap. Park on the south side and start hiking on the gated road (not the nearby trails).

Alternatively, from the junction of Highway 138 and Highway 2 northeast of Wrightwood, head west on Highway 2 for 13 miles to Vincent Gap. Park on the south side and start hiking on the gated road.

Information and Contact

A national forest adventure pass is required; see page 297 for more information. A free wilderness permit is also required; they are available at the trailhead. Dogs are allowed. A trail map of the Angeles High Country is available for a fee from Tom Harrison Maps, 800/265-9090, www.tomharrisonmaps.com. For more information, contact Angeles National Forest, Santa Clara/Mojave Rivers Ranger District, 30800 Bouquet Canyon Road, Saugus, CA 91390, 661/296-9710, www.fs.fed.us/r5/angeles. Or contact the Big Pines Visitor Center, 760/249-3504.

32 BLUE RIDGE
Angeles National Forest

Level: Easy

Total Distance: 4.4 miles round-trip

Hiking Time: 2 hours

Elevation Gain: 950 feet

Summary: A relatively easy climb leads to sweeping high country views on the far east side of the San Gabriel Mountains.

You don't necessarily have to climb a peak in order to relish sweeping mountain vistas in the Angeles High Country. The Blue Ridge Trail provides breathtaking views of Mount Baldy, Mount Baden-Powell, and other Angeles giants with only a mellow uphill walk to a ridgeline.

The trail neighbors Mountain High East Ski Resort and begins near the restrooms across from the Big Pines Information Station. It heads away from the highway and into the woods, crossing a footbridge over a seasonal stream at 0.2 mile. The climb is steady but gradual; if it weren't for the 7,000-foot elevation, it wouldn't feel like a workout at all. You'll switchback along a slope covered with oaks and Jeffrey pines, then notice the forest transition to white fir and lodgepole pine as you climb higher.

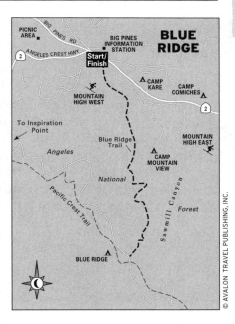

One mile out you cross a dirt road used for maintaining the ski lift at Mountain High, and suddenly your views open up to the north. You can easily pick out the white "golf ball" observatories on Table Mountain amid a sweeping expanse of Mojave Desert. Two miles out you're on top of often windy Blue Ridge, where your trail meets up with the Pacific Crest Trail and a road that services Blue Ridge Campground. A short walk of a few hundred yards in either direction provides more memorable views. Pick any high point, then have a seat and enjoy the show. From Blue Ridge, you can admire the highest peaks in the San Gabriel Mountains, plus the vast canyon of the East Fork San

Gabriel River, which bisects the Sheep Mountain Wilderness and separates massive Mount Baden-Powell from monolithic Mount Baldy.

Options

With a car shuttle, you can take a 4.2-mile one-way hike from Inspiration Point on Angeles Crest Highway (two miles farther up the road) downhill to the Blue Ridge trailhead. From Inspiration Point, follow the Pacific Crest Trail east for 2.2 miles to Blue Ridge Campground, then turn left on the Blue Ridge Trail and follow it two miles to its start. Another pleasant option is to hike the one-mile Lightning Ridge Nature Trail, which starts at Inspiration Point.

Directions

From I-210 in La Cañada, take Highway 2/Angeles Crest Highway northeast for 58 miles to the Blue Ridge trailhead on the right, just past the Big Pines Information Station, near the public restrooms. The trail begins 50 yards east of the restrooms, near a dirt road that parallels the highway. Park alongside the highway or in the restroom lot.

Alternatively, from the junction of Highway 138 and Highway 2 northeast of Wrightwood, head west on Highway 2 for 8.3 miles to the Blue Ridge trailhead on the left (south) side of the highway, about 100 yards before the Big Pines Information Station, near the public restrooms.

© ANN MARIE BROWN

9,399-foot Mount Baden-Powell is an impressive sight from the top of Blue Ridge.

Information and Contact

A national forest adventure pass is required; see page 297 for more information. Dogs are allowed. A trail map of the Angeles High Country is available for a fee from Tom Harrison Maps, 800/265-9090, www.tomharrisonmaps.com. For more information, contact Angeles National Forest, Santa Clara/Mojave Rivers Ranger District, 30800 Bouquet Canyon Road, Saugus, CA 91390, 661/296-9710, www.fs.fed.us/r5/angeles. Or contact the Big Pines Visitor Center, 760/249-3504.

🔢 WEST FORK NATIONAL RECREATION TRAIL

BEST 🄲

Angeles National Forest

🔣 🔣 🔣 🔣

Level: Easy/Moderate

Total Distance: 8.0 miles round-trip

Hiking Time: 4 hours

Elevation Gain: 240 feet

Summary: An easy walk along Southern California's premier angling river is the perfect trek for hikers who like to fish.

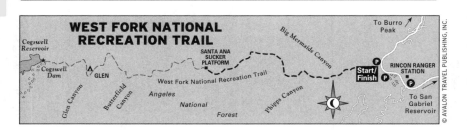

About 12 million people live within one to two hours of the West Fork of the San Gabriel River, and on summer weekends it feels like at least half of them are there.

You can't blame them. The West Fork is a great place to be, especially on a warm day, and especially for people who like to catch fish. The river's head-waters are at Red Box Gap, high in the San Gabriel Mountains northwest of Mount Wilson. The river flows east through a steep canyon until it reaches Cogswell Reservoir. Cogswell Dam, which was built in 1932 for flood control, cuts the 17-mile river roughly in half and regulates the West Fork's flows. During seasons of heavy rain, the dam prevents flooding. Year-round, the dam's water releases provide uninterrupted fishing opportunities.

A relatively flat, paved road runs alongside a 7.3-mile stretch of the river from Highway 39 to the dam. The ease of the trail, convenient fishing access, and a pleasant road from Azusa through the scenic San Gabriel Canyon make the West Fork extremely popular. Traveling the paved trail is a cinch for anglers who want to bicycle or walk to their favorite fishing hole.

The beauty of hiking the West Fork Trail is that you can walk in a few miles to get away from the crowds, and the farther you go, the better it gets. Keep that in mind as you negotiate the first mile, which is usually inundated with people.

After parking in the second and larger of the two lots just past the Rincon ranger station, walk to the lot's south end. Access the trailhead by turning right and walking along Highway 39, crossing the bridge, and making a right onto the trail by passing through a big metal turnstile.

From here on in you won't lose sight of the water. During the first mile, the array of trail users includes hikers, bikers, anglers on foot and bike, families hanging out at the river, and game wardens driving through checking for fishing licenses. After a few miles, you'll lose most of the families, but not the cyclists or anglers.

A map at the trailhead shows the location of four handicapped-accessible fishing platforms named for species of native fish, all still found in the river. The platforms and distances from the trailhead are: Rainbow Trout (3.1 miles in), Santa Ana Sucker (3.9 miles), Arroyo Chub (5.5 miles), and Speckled Dace (6.2 miles). These make useful landmarks for planning a day hike.

A little under one mile from the trailhead, you'll cross a bridge over the West Fork near its confluence with Bear Creek, which flows in from the north. This is a very popular fishing spot, accessible by a short footpath off the right of the road just before the bridge. If you boulder-hop across the West Fork, you'll find a trail along Bear Creek that leads north into the San Gabriel Wilderness and makes a good backpacking option. The wilderness, which harbors bighorn sheep, deer, and mountain lions, is mostly inaccessible, except for a few entry points such as Bear Creek.

Beyond the bridge, the river switches to the left side of the road and the path narrows and becomes more shaded. Steep rock walls now line the south side of the trail. A bridge crosses the river again about two miles in and delivers you back on the south bank. From this point upstream to the dam is the catch-and-release stretch of river for anglers. For the health of the fish population, only artificial lures with barbless hooks are allowed, and all fish must be released. With so many users—and abusers—at one time, the West Fork was in danger of being loved to death. In the 1970s, conservation groups such as California Trout and the Pasadena Casting Club began efforts to help the river, including periodic cleanups and the creation of this special-regulations stretch.

About three miles in, the trail gets progressively more wild, while gaining barely noticeable elevation. In spring during particularly rainy years, waterfalls tumble down the steep rocks that line the path, sweeping across spillways along the trail and into the river. Wildflowers abound during those times, with bunches of Indian paintbrush, baby blue-eyes, and canterbury bells sprouting from rock walls and amidst the grasses on the riverbanks.

You can stop and fish at any one of the many deep pools along West Fork.

looking upstream along the West Fork San Gabriel River during the first mile of the West Fork National Recreation Trail

Fly-fishing with nymphs such as Pheasant Tails drifted through the pools is an effective technique. You are most likely to catch a stocked rainbow, most in the six- to eight-inch range, although very lucky anglers will pull an occasional 12-inch-plus trout from the river.

To do an eight-mile day hike, turn around at the Santa Ana Sucker fishing platform and head back. If you caught fish, don't forget to fill out the angler survey on the way out, which helps state Fish and Game officials in their stocking efforts.

Options

For an easy overnight backpack, continue another 2.3 miles past the Santa Ana Sucker platform to Glen Trail Camp, where there are fire pits and picnic tables. Another mile beyond is Cogswell Dam and the end of the trail. In low water, another hiking option begins at the confluence of the West Fork and Bear Creek. If you boulder-hop or wade across, a trail follows Bear Creek north (the trail isn't on all maps, but it's there). Hike about one mile on the Bear Creek Trail to reach Lower Bear Creek Trail Camp. Upper Bear Creek Trail Camp is three miles farther. You can finish the entire Bear Creek Trail by hiking another six miles to Smith Saddle and then the Bear Creek trailhead on Highway 39, just south of Coldbrook Camp.

Directions

From I-210 in Azusa, exit at Highway 39 (Azusa Avenue) and head north. In 1.5 miles, Azusa Avenue becomes San Gabriel Canyon Road. Continue 13 miles and turn left into the trailhead parking lot, just past the Rincon ranger station. The first lot on the left is small, so keep going a few hundred yards, over a bridge, and turn left into the second, larger lot.

Information and Contact

A national forest adventure pass is required; see page 297 for more information. Dogs are allowed. A trail map of the Angeles High Country is available for a fee from Tom Harrison Maps, 800/265-9090, www.tomharrisonmaps.com. For more information, contact San Gabriel River Ranger District, 110 N. Wabash Avenue, Glendora, CA 91741, 626/335/1251, www.fs.fed.us/r5/angeles.

34 BRIDGE TO NOWHERE AND THE NARROWS

BEST (

Angeles National Forest/Sheep Mountain Wilderness

Level: Moderate

Total Distance: 9.4-12.0 miles round-trip

Hiking Time: 5-6 hours

Elevation Gain: 950-1,400 feet

Summary: An architectural marvel and a magnificent narrow canyon can be seen on the East Fork San Gabriel River.

It's not our style to endorse major brand names, but, just this once, we'll make an exception. Some type of Tevas or river shoes are an absolute necessity for this trip. Without them, you'll suffer from "soggy feet syndrome" all day long. With them, you'll slog through the East Fork San Gabriel River as happy as a golden retriever, enjoying one of the most wild and woolly stretches of moving water that Los Angeles has to offer.

It's all about the river level here. The difficulty of this hike varies greatly from month to month. A late springtime hike when the river is knee- or thigh-high could easily be rated strenuous, but an August hike when the river is mere-

The Bridge to Nowhere has withstood the test of time, but the road it was intended to bridge was not so stalwart.

ly a playful brook would be easy to moderate, especially considering the trail's elevation gain is spread out over several miles. You can forget about hiking here altogether in the midst of the rainy season, when the multiple river crossings are risky at best and a recipe for drowning at worst. During the record-setting rains of the winter of 2005, the water was chest-high for several months, rendering the trail impassable until May. It's not just deep; it's also cold and fast.

Late summer is when most hikers make the trip, even though the temperature often soars to an uncomfortable level. Don't be put off by the crowds; most people walk only a short distance, find a suitable swimming or wading hole, and settle in for the afternoon. The farther upstream you go, the fewer people you see.

The primary destination on this trail is an architectural oddity known as the Bridge to Nowhere. This 120-foot-high arched structure was built in the 1930s for the new highway that was intended to bisect the mountain front, connecting the San Gabriel Valley to Wrightwood and the desert beyond. The great rainy season of 1938 washed out most of the roadway

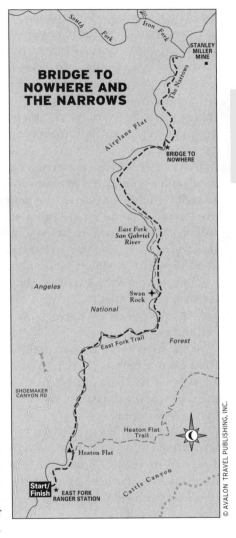

that had been completed (you'll see bits and pieces of it as you hike), but the stalwart bridge survived. Even though its appearance is grossly out of step with its natural surroundings, its graceful concrete ramparts make a strangely appealing place to have lunch.

The hike directions are simple enough. From the trailhead, you set out on the East Fork Trail, which begins as a dirt road and leads upstream along the east side of the East Fork San Gabriel River. Only a half mile out, you reach Heaton Flat Campground, and just beyond it the trail drops down to the river's edge. Here the multiple soggy crossings begin. At 2.4 miles out is distinctive Swan Rock, a soaring cliff, which, if you squint hard enough, appears to bear the outline of a swan. Where the trail climbs high above the tumbling waters of the North Fork and follows the old roadbed, you'll make some time, but where it dips down to the water's edge for its multiple crossings, you will be forced to slow down for careful boulder-hopping. The trail crosses through some private property; be sure to obey all signs and respect the owners' rights.

Just as the river canyon starts to narrow, you'll reach the infamous bridge at 4.7 miles. Its remarkably good condition after three-quarters of a century is a tribute to the engineers who designed it. Many hikers make this their turnaround point for a 9.4-mile round-trip, but it's a pity not to go at least a half mile farther. Cross the bridge and pick up a narrower trail on the far side that descends into a skinny, swimming-hole-laden stretch of canyon known as The Narrows. A rough use trail continues for about 1.3 miles upriver, squeezing and weaving its way through the constricted canyon walls. Recreational gold miners still occasionally work this stretch, but their return is not much to brag about. Anglers, however, can fare well here. The river pools are full of hungry trout.

At six miles from the start, you'll see the Iron Fork of the San Gabriel River coming in from the left. An old trail camp here is a good place to take a breather, call it a day, and head back down the canyon. You'll get to enjoy the soaring walls of The Narrows canyon and the rushing waters of the East Fork all over again.

Options
Those seeking more of an adventure can continue beyond the confluence of the Iron Fork and the East Fork. One mile farther, the Fish Fork joins the main river from the right. If you follow it upstream (you'll be scrambling now; there is no trail), you'll find myriad mini-waterfalls and swimming holes in one of the most remote and pristine areas of Angeles National Forest.

Directions
From I-210 in Azusa, exit at Highway 39 (Azusa Avenue) and head north. In 1.5 miles Azusa Avenue becomes San Gabriel Canyon Road. Continue 10 miles and then turn right on East Fork Road. Drive six miles and park in the large lot on the left, across from the East Fork ranger station. Fill out a free wilderness permit at the ranger station.

Information and Contact

A national forest adventure pass is required; see page 297 for more information. A free wilderness permit is also required; they are available at the ranger station near the trailhead. Dogs are allowed. A trail map of the Angeles High Country is available from Tom Harrison Maps, 800/265-9090, www.tomharrisonmaps.com. For more information contact San Gabriel River Ranger District, 110 N. Wabash Avenue, Glendora, CA 91741, 626/335/1251, www.fs.fed.us/r5/angeles.

35 COBAL CANYON LOOP
Claremont Hills Wilderness Park

🏕 🦌 🐕

Level: Easy

Total Distance: 5.0 miles round-trip

Hiking Time: 2.5 hours

Elevation Gain: 300 feet

Summary: A loop trail in an easy-to-reach wilderness park just minutes from downtown Claremont.

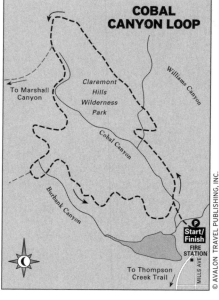

Claremont is one of the nicer of the 88 cities in Los Angeles County, with its seven college campuses and pleasant, and very walkable, downtown. It's not surprising that the city has also taken a progressive view of open space by protecting some of the San Gabriel Mountain foothills on the town's northern fringe.

Less than a decade old, Claremont Hills Wilderness Park is 1,440 acres of open space that borders Angeles National Forest. The park is home to 86 bird species, rattlesnakes and other reptiles, and a host of mammals, including coyotes and mule deer. Mountain lions, bobcats, and even bears have been spotted here. Intermittent streams flow out of the park's canyons. The park is a favorite playground for mountain bikers, who ride up to 3,360-foot Potato Mountain or drop into neighboring Marshall Canyon to the west of Cobal Canyon. The trails are also popular with trail runners from the nearby Claremont Colleges.

The scenery here is exceptional for a park so close to a city. Mount Baldy is, after all, just due north of the park. Sunsets are grand in scale and color.

The Cobal Canyon Loop starts on Cobal Canyon Trail and returns on Burbank Canyon Trail. Both are fire roads that when hiked counterclockwise make for a slightly less steep route. Mileage markers along the trail indicate, however, that the loop was set up to go clockwise.

Either way you choose to go, the trailhead is found just past the informa-

© JULIE SHEER

Stately oaks form a canopy near the start of the Cobal Canyon Trail in Claremont Hills Wilderness Park.

tion sign at the park entrance. Cross Thompson Creek and you're on your way. To hike counterclockwise, stay to the right, heading up Cobal Canyon Trail. Oaks and sycamores form a canopy as the trail rises above the creek. About a mile in, the trail opens up, becoming sunny and exposed. The surrounding peaks come into view, including Mount Baldy in the distance. At about 1.75 miles in (at trail marker 3.25), the trail begins to head west. In another half mile is the high point of the loop.

Follow the arrow on a post pointing to Johnson Pasture. At the 2.25 mile marker, there's another sign pointing to Johnson-Miller; ignore the road to the right and continue following the path you're on. The trail ascends again. Burned tree branches are evidence of the huge Grand Prix fire that ravaged the area to the east in 2003, destroying dozens of homes in the Claremont hills. The park's foothills marked the fire's westernmost boundary.

At a yellow post marked "Burbank," turn left. As the trail ascends, the views are still impressive. During the last mile, you'll spot Thompson Dam. After citrus farming and other industries in the 1800s overtaxed the water supply from Thompson Creek, a series of ditches and streambeds were developed to help harness mountain runoff in underground aquifers. That's how Claremont gets its water today, and it is what you'll see at the Thompson Creek Spreading Grounds, located at the trailhead.

Options

At 2.25 miles in (2.75 trail marker), take a right on Marshall Canyon Road, heading west into Marshall Canyon, where there is a network of trails to be explored.

Directions

From I-210 in Claremont, exit at Baseline Road and head west. Drive 0.7 mile and turn right (north) on Mills Avenue. In 1.1 miles Mills Avenue veers right and turns into Mount Baldy Road, stay on Mills Avenue and proceed north another 0.25 mile to the park entrance. Park in the lot just before the park entrance.

Information and Contact

There is no fee. Dogs are allowed. A trail map and more information is available by contacting the City of Claremont, 207 Harvard Avenue, Claremont, CA 91711, 909/399-5335 or 909/399-5490, www.ci.claremont.ca.us.

3 6 BEAR CANYON TRAIL

Angeles National Forest

🖼 🖼 🖼 🖼 🖼

Level: Easy/Moderate

Hiking Time: 2 hours

Total Distance: 3.6 miles round-trip

Elevation Gain: 1,300 feet

Summary: A historic, view-filled hike up the old trail to Mount Baldy.

It's hard to imagine that anyone would head for the summit of Mount Baldy on a trail as steep as this one. But that's what everyone did in the late 19th and early 20th century, before there was any other established trail to the summit. Considering that the Bear Canyon route to Baldy is a 6.4-mile one-way trek with 5,700 feet of elevation gain, it's not surprising that other routes have supplanted it in popularity. But in its lower reaches, Bear Canyon Trail offers myriad charms, from its casual first mile alongside spirited Bear Creek to its more secluded middle reaches on the slopes above Mount Baldy Village.

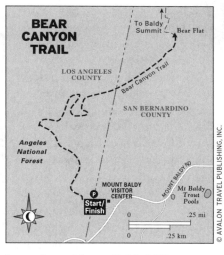

The trail begins as the paved Bear Canyon Road, which takes off from Mount Baldy Road just below the Mount Baldy Visitor Center. You can access the road/trail from the parking lot behind the visitor center, but you might not want to leave your car in the lot because the gates close at 4:30 P.M. each day. (Park in front of the visitor center, along Mount Baldy Road, if you plan to hike later in the day.)

Bear Canyon Road climbs vigorously from the start. You'll pass numerous private cabins, some of which can only be accessed by footbridges crossing the lively, cascading stream. These are private homes, not leased Forest Service cabins, so many of the inhabitants live here year-round. Watch for Old Glory, a massive big-cone Douglas fir growing a few inches from one of the lower cabins; a small sign states that its trunk diameter is seven feet, five inches. Where the pavement ends and the official Bear Canyon Trail begins, the remaining cabins have only walk-in access, and many have fallen into disrepair. You pass by the last of them at 0.8 mile from your car.

Soon after leaving the pavement and gaining the trail, the path splits; take the right fork to continue uphill in the most direct fashion. Note the left fork for an option on your return trip; it drops down to the stream and passes a few more cabins, then rejoins the right fork in 0.5 mile. You'll see a water pipe paralleling the trail; it travels to Mount Baldy Village from a wooden tank higher up along the stream.

The path gains elevation quickly and will soon leave the canopy of live oaks, bay laurel, and big-cone Douglas fir. Bright yellow wallflowers sprout from the sun-dappled slopes in the spring months. In short order, the trail comes out to an exposed, chaparral-covered slope with views of

A thumb-tack lettered sign marks fern-filled Bear Flat on the Bear Canyon Trail.

Mount Baldy's summit above and Mount Baldy Village below. Another half mile of more gradual ascent follows. The trail plunges back into the sylvan forest and follows within close range of Bear Creek, then comes out at tiny Bear Flat, a small sloping meadow at 5,580 feet in elevation. It is marked by a wooden sign lettered with thumbtacks. Occasionally backpackers will stop here to spend the night; the best campsite is about 25 yards before Bear Flat under the shade of an oak. The creek crossing just below the flat is the last water supply for hikers heading to the summit of Mount Baldy, 4.6 miles farther.

Enjoy this pleasant spot and then head back the way you came. For a change of scenery, take the turnoff for the optional streamside fork (signed as Bear Canyon Loop Trail), the path you didn't take on the way uphill.

Options

Another easy-to-moderate hike in the Mount Baldy Village area is the trip to 5,796-foot Sunset Peak. From Mount Baldy Road in the village, turn west on Glendora Ridge Road and drive 4.3 miles to the start of Forest Service Road 2N07, on the left. Park near the gate and hike uphill on the road/trail. Bear right at a fork almost two miles up, then left at a second fork a mile farther. At Sunset Peak's summit, the foundation of an old fire lookout tower can be seen, plus great views of Mount Baldy and the San Gabriel Valley. This seven-mile round-trip has only 1,300 feet of elevation gain.

Directions

From I-210 in Upland, take the Mountain Avenue/Mount Baldy exit and drive north for 4.3 miles (Mountain Avenue becomes Shinn Road). At a T junction with Mount Baldy Road, turn right and drive 4.9 miles to the Mount Baldy Visitor Center on the left side of the road. Park alongside the road in front of the visitor center or in the lot behind it, but, if you choose the latter, note that the parking lot gates are locked at 4:30 P.M. each day. The start of the trail is Bear Canyon Road, which begins about 50 yards below the Mount Baldy Visitor Center. Access it from the parking lot behind the visitor center (signed as Mount Baldy Trail) or by walking downhill on Mount Baldy Road.

Information and Contact

A national forest adventure pass is required; see page 297 for more information. Dogs are allowed. A trail map of the Angeles High Country is available for a fee from Tom Harrison Maps, 800/265-9090, www.tomharrisonmaps.com. For more information, contact Angeles National Forest, San Gabriel River Ranger District, 110 N. Wabash Avenue, Glendora, CA 91741, 626/335-1251, www.fs.fed.us/r5/angeles. Or contact the Mount Baldy Visitor Center, 909/982-2829.

37 ICE HOUSE CANYON TO ICE HOUSE SADDLE

BEST C

Angeles National Forest/Cucamonga Wilderness

Level: Strenuous

Total Distance: 8.8 miles round-trip

Hiking Time: 5 hours

Elevation Gain: 2,600 feet

Summary: A streamside canyon hike through alpine scenery leads to a 7,580-foot saddle with trail access to multiple peaks.

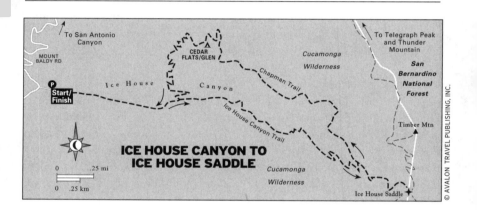

Ice House Canyon got its name in the 1850s, when 100-pound blocks of ice were carved from its frigid stream canyon and carried by mule-drawn wagon to satisfy the thirst of the growing city of Los Angeles. Beyond its use in the ice trade, the canyon held tourism appeal; it was the site of a popular resort in the 1920s. Even today, Ice House Canyon remains one of the most inviting and frequently visited places in the higher San Gabriel Mountains. Its 5,000-foot elevation, cool mountain air, crystal-clear stream, and stately conifers make it a fine place to go for a walk on a summer's day.

The multitudes who hike here are heading for a variety of destinations. The vast majority simply stroll for a mile or two up the picturesque canyon, pick a pretty spot by the stream, and call it a day. Many hikers make Ice House Saddle—a high point at 7,580 feet and a major trail hub—their destination. Those out for a strenuous all-day hike can choose from a smorgasbord of nearby peaks (see Options, below).

You can get a good taste of the beauty of this place by hiking the Ice House Canyon Trail to Ice House Saddle, then looping back on Chapman Trail.

Heading up Ice House Canyon, you'll reach the saddle in 3.6 miles with a 2,600-foot elevation gain. The 7,580-foot saddle can be very cold and windy, even when it is warm at the start of the hike, so carry some extra layers.

The hike is fairly strenuous, with a steady climb right from the start over fairly rocky terrain, but the scenery is so inspiring that you won't mind a bit. In addition to its rushing stream, Ice House Canyon is home to a huge variety of trees. The live oaks and incense cedars at the lower elevations quickly give way to stately, Yosemite-style conifers, including giant Jeffrey pines, big-cone Douglas firs, and white firs.

In the first mile of trail, you'll pass many small cabins perched near the stream. Some are still used as vacation homes; others are merely the crumbling memories of happy summers long past. You'll reach the turnoff for the alternate Chapman Trail at one mile out; this is where your loop will return. Continue on Ice House Canyon Trail to the Cucamonga Wilderness Boundary at 1.8 miles. You must fill out a free day-hiking permit here if you have not already done so at the Mount Baldy Visitor Center in town.

Once you pass the wilderness sign, the canyon becomes noticeably more wild. All signs of human habitation and development disappear. After the heavy snowfall and rains of 2005, a 20-foot-deep avalanche of snow and debris covered a portion of the trail for several months. After two miles, the trail leaves the canyon floor and starts to switchback uphill. The trail surface actually gets easier as you ascend; the rocky trail gives way to a smoother tread beneath

© ANN MARIE BROWN

Uprooted trees and a lot of snow and rock came tumbling down Ice House Canyon during an avalanche in the winter of 2005.

your feet. As you continue the climb, be sure to stop occasionally to check out the ever-changing views behind you. You'll be amazed both at how high you have climbed and also how visibly steep these canyon walls are. If you've ever visited Mineral King Valley in Sequoia National Park, the experience is surprisingly similar. The higher you go, the better your views of neighboring Telegraph and Thunder Peaks.

You'll pass trickling Columbine Spring at 2.8 miles, then a second junction with Chapman Trail at 3.0 miles. Bypass it for now to reach Ice House Saddle at 3.6 miles from the start. Here, with expansive views to the east and west, is a fine place for a picnic and a rest, before heading back down the trail to pick up Chapman Trail for your loop return. Chapman Trail charts a longer, more meandering course back downhill to lower Ice House Canyon. Along the way, the trail camp at Cedar Flats (also called Cedar Glen) offers another fine rest stop.

Options

From the major junction of trails at Ice House Saddle, you can make a hard right and hike to 8,693-foot Ontario Peak (2.7 miles from Ice House Saddle) or a soft right and hike to 8,859-foot Cucamonga Peak (2.5 miles from Ice House Saddle). Or, go left instead for the Three Ts—Timber, Telegraph, and Thunder Peaks (0.9, 2.8, and 3.9 miles from Ice House Saddle, respectively).

Directions

From I-210 in Upland, take the Mountain Avenue/Mount Baldy exit and drive north for 4.3 miles (Mountain Avenue becomes Shinn Road). At a T junction with Mount Baldy Road, turn right and drive 6.4 miles, then bear right on Ice House Canyon Road. Drive 100 yards to the parking lot at the end of the road.

Information and Contact

A national forest adventure pass is required; see page 297 for more information. A free wilderness permit is also required; they are available at the Mount Baldy Visitor Center in Baldy Village or along the trail at the Cucamonga Wilderness boundary. Dogs are allowed. A trail map of Mount Baldy and the Cucamonga Wilderness is available for a fee from Tom Harrison Maps, 800/265-9090, www.tomharrisonmaps.com. For more information, contact Angeles National Forest, San Gabriel River Ranger District, 110 N. Wabash Avenue, Glendora, CA 91741, 626/335-1251, www.fs.fed.us/r5/angeles. Or contact the Mount Baldy Visitor Center, 909/982-2829.

38 MOUNT BALDY
(EASY WAY OR HARD WAY)   BEST ◖
Angeles National Forest

🏞 🦌 🐕

Level: Strenuous or Butt-kicker   **Total Distance:** 6.4 or 13.6 miles round-trip

Hiking Time: 4 or 7 hours   **Elevation Gain:** 2,200 or 3,500 feet

Summary: An epic trek to the highest summit in the San Gabriel Range and the third highest summit in Southern California.

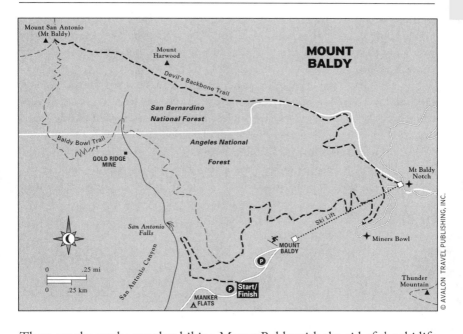

There are those who say that hiking Mount Baldy with the aid of the ski lift is just plain cheating. Although we admire their honorable work ethic, we respectfully submit that the ski lift "handicap" can be just plain fun. Check with your conscience and decide for yourself. You can hike the entire 13.6-mile round-trip to the summit, conquering a 3,500-foot elevation gain, or you can ride the ski lift to Mount Baldy Notch, then hike the remaining 6.4 miles round-trip with a more forgiving 2,200-foot elevation gain. Take your pick—we won't judge you either way.

To do the trip the long, hard way, start hiking at the junction of Mount Baldy Road and San Antonio Falls Road, 0.3 mile beyond Manker Flats

Campground. Park in the dirt pullout by Falls Road and begin hiking on the gated road, which is the ski lift maintenance road. After passing San Antonio Falls at 0.5 mile out (the waterfall is impressive only in spring, a mere dribble by summer), continue three more miles to a trail junction at Baldy Notch, where a restaurant is open on summer weekends. Make a mental note of the menu for your victory dinner on the way back downhill.

At Baldy Notch, views of the desert to the north will inspire you onward. Go left and follow another fire road 1.4 miles, mostly in the shade of stately conifers, to the upper end of the ski lift. At the top of the upper lift, you access the infamous Devil's Backbone, a steep and jagged ridge. Some hikers find this section of trail, with its sheer drop-offs on both sides into the Lytle Creek Canyon and San Antonio Canyon, to be rather hair-raising. Certainly this is not the place to be after having a few cocktails, but, otherwise, it's safe enough as long as you watch your footing.

Soon you leave the Jeffrey pines and incense cedars behind for the smaller, more hardy conifers—mostly lodgepole pines. You'll pass the south side of Mount Harwood at 9,552 feet (really just a high bump on Baldy's ridge) and then reach a wind-blown saddle between Harwood and Baldy. A few gnarled, wind-sculpted limber pines eke out a living in this barren terrain. From the saddle, it's only a short tromp to the top, but this is the steepest stretch of the entire day. In the last few hundred yards, you'll comprehend the aptness of

© LONNIE DECLOEDT

The Devil's Backbone Trail runs up the narrow spine of Mount Baldy.

Mount Baldy's nickname. The mountain's official name is Mount San Antonio, named for Saint Anthony of Padua, a Franciscan priest and miracle worker. But ask anyone who has been there: the peak's barren, boulder-strewn summit looks more like a Baldy than a saint. A few windbreaks made of rock provide some shelter from the frequent wind.

What about the summit view? If it's a clear day, it's the best vista in the San Gabriel Mountains. Just about everything comes into view—desert, city, ocean, the peaks of the San Bernardino Mountains, even a few high summits of the southern Sierra and Death Valley, 130 miles distant. The earlier in the season you take this hike, the better your chance for good visibility. But there's a caveat: unless you are an experienced mountaineer, don't think about making the trip until the Devil's Backbone is snow and ice free. Although some intrepid hikers head for the summit in the winter and early spring months, proper equipment such as an ice ax and crampons, and the training to use them, are a vital necessity. Most years, Memorial Day is the start of the recreational hiking season on Baldy, although it varies. Check with the Mount Baldy Visitor Center (909/982-2829) before you plan your trip.

If you opt to do the trip the easier way, you simply drive your car a few miles farther to the end of Mount Baldy Road and the parking lot for Mount Baldy Ski Area. The ski lift only operates on weekends and holidays during the summer months, so you must time your trip carefully to take advantage of this convenient hikers' handicap. If you catch the first lift at 8 A.M. (call 909/981-3344 to confirm current operating times), you'll likely be on the summit by 10—still early enough to beat the worst of the San Gabriel Valley haze, which obscures much of the view later in the day.

No matter which way you do it, this is arguably the most popular hike in the San Gabriel Mountains, so plan on having plenty of company. Hundreds of hikers sign the summit register every summer weekend. The crowds are justifiable; after all, Mount Baldy is the highest peak in the San Gabriels at 10,064 feet. It's also one of the three highest peaks in Southern California, one-third of the great triumvirate that also includes 11,502-foot Mount San Gorgonio and 10,834-foot Mount San Jacinto. Climb all three peaks at some point in your career, and you can pat yourself on the back for being a tried-and-true Southern California hiker.

Options

If you'd rather hike to Mount Baldy via an even steeper route than either of those described above, help yourself. The 5.1-mile one-way San Antonio Ski Hut Trail is another possible route. Start at San Antonio Falls Road and, in just shy of a mile, leave the road and turn left on a trail. At 2.4 miles, you reach the San Antonio Ski Hut, owned by the Sierra Club and used in winter by backcountry skiers. From the hut, follow the trail west across Baldy Bowl, then north to Baldy's summit. Most hikers choose to turn this into a loop, returning via the Backbone Trail/Baldy Notch route for an 8.3-mile round-trip utilizing the ski lift, or an 11.9-mile round-trip entirely on foot.

Directions

From I-210 in Upland, take the Mountain Avenue/Mount Baldy exit and drive north for 4.3 miles (Mountain Avenue becomes Shinn Road). At a T junction with Mount Baldy Road, turn right and drive 9.0 miles to San Antonio Falls Road on the left, 0.3 mile past Manker Flats Campround. (If you choose to use the ski lift "handicap," drive a total of 9.7 miles on Mount Baldy Road to its end at the ski lift parking area.)

Information and Contact

As of 2005, the Mount Baldy ski lift costs $12 per adult. Phone 909/981-3344 or go to www.mtbaldy.com for current operating hours and fees. A national forest adventure pass is required; see page 297 for more information. Dogs are not allowed on the ski lift, but they are allowed on the trail. A trail map of Mount Baldy and the Cucamonga Wilderness is available for a fee from Tom Harrison Maps, 800/265-9090, www.tomharrisonmaps.com. For more information, contact Angeles National Forest, San Gabriel River Ranger District, 110 N. Wabash Avenue, Glendora, CA 91741, 626/335-1251, www.fs.fed.us/r5/angeles. Or contact the Mount Baldy Visitor Center, 909/982-2829.

HOLLYWOOD HILLS, PALOS VERDES, AND CATALINA ISLAND

© ANN MARIE BROWN

BEST HIKES

If your hiking sensibilities run more toward sunset

walks along the beach than summit ascents of snow-capped mountains, the region south of downtown Los Angeles – including the Hollywood Hills, Palos Verdes, and Catalina Island – has your kind of trails.

Although this area has some of the most developed real estate in the L.A. basin – from the tall buildings of downtown L.A. to the mega-mansions of the Palos Verdes Peninsula – there is still wild land to be found here, if you know where to look. From the urban-edge parks of the Hollywood Hills to the coastal headlands of "PV," the tranquillity of nature is never very far from the nearest freeway.

If you are seeking the true L.A. experience, head for Griffith Park and ascend to the top of Mount Hollywood, or to the world-famous Hollywood sign on neighboring Mount Lee. You'll never be far from the nearest water fountain – or the sounds and sights of the city – but you will be pleasantly surprised by the abundant bird life and spring wildflowers. And, who knows, you might just see a movie star on the trail.

Hikers strolling with their dogs will be among their ilk in Wilacre, Coldwater, and Fryman Parks in the Hollywood Hills, where views of the city — especially at sunset — are sure to inspire. Or, take a walk with the young, restless, and beautiful (dogs and people alike) in nearby Runyon Canyon Park, a tiny, 130-acre "urban wilderness" located just two blocks from Hollywood Boulevard. For those inclined toward more serious nature study, pack along a pair of binoculars and a birding guide and check out the Audubon Center trails at Debs Park near Highland Park.

Coast lovers will want to make a beeline for the Palos Verdes Peninsula, which was once an island but is now firmly connected — at least on one side — to the mainland. This distinct block of land offers excellent hiking possibilities on its high bluff tops as well as its rugged, rocky shore. Or, hop on a ferry and pay a visit to Catalina Island, 20 miles from the mainland but still a part of Los Angeles County. Rising 2,000 feet above sea level, the island is more than 20 miles long, making it one of the largest of the eight Channel Islands. Over the years, Catalina has been used for ranching, mining, military occupation, and as a playground for the rich and famous. Today, visitors can hike or backpack to a variety of destinations, including seaside campgrounds, grassy summits, and lonesome beaches.

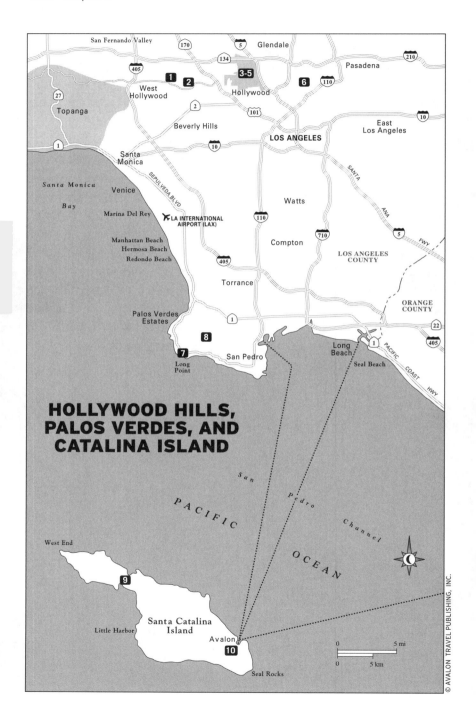

HOLLYWOOD HILLS,
PALOS VERDES, AND
CATALINA ISLAND

Hollywood Hills, Palos Verdes, and Catalina Island Hikes

1 BETTY B. DEARING TRAIL
Wilacre, Coldwater, and Fryman Parks

Level: Moderate

Hiking Time: 3 hours

Total Distance: 6.6 miles round-trip

Elevation Gain: 700 feet

Summary: Explore pockets of rugged natural beauty bounded by freeways and hillside homes in Studio City.

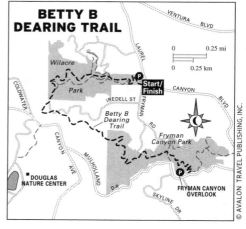

The three parks in Fryman Canyon in the eastern Santa Monica Mountains straddle the psychological boundary between the San Fernando Valley and the ritzy communities "over the hill" in the Los Angeles basin. With this fortunate geography, hikers here are treated to views of rugged, scenic canyons and the ingeniously constructed homes that cling to their hillsides. The Betty B. Dearing Trail, named for a conservationist who was instrumental in the formation of the Backbone Trail across the Santa Monica Mountains, is your ticket to visiting all three parks.

Pick up the trail at Wilacre Park, located on Fryman Road, just off Laurel Canyon Boulevard. The route is paved at first, as it passes the foundation of the former estate of silent movie star Will Acres, for whom Wilacre Park is named. The trail then turns to dirt and heads steadily uphill.

Before long, you'll start to notice some architecturally impressive houses precariously perched on the steep slopes outside the park boundaries. Oak, bay laurel, and walnut trees along the trail provide shade. Look skyward to catch a glimpse of the red-tailed hawks that cruise the canyon and perch along the trail. On a clear day, you can see across the Valley to the Verdugo Mountains and San Gabriel Mountains.

After the first hill, the trail flattens out in a meadow and continues straight ahead before beginning to climb and head to the south. You top a small pass—unfortunately it's not all that dramatic—and emerge looking down at a lush valley. The trail then descends to a junction at 1.5 miles, where you'll find a doggie watering fountain on the left side of the trail. Across from the fountain, a stone staircase leads to Coldwater Canyon Park, which has its own hiking trails and is the headquarters of TreePeople, the citizen forestry organization that enlists volunteers to plant trees around the city. The park is also home to the S. Mark Taper Foundation Amphitheatre, an outdoor performance venue that offers concerts, plays, children's shows, and environmental presentations.

Continue straight on Betty B. Dearing Trail, descending 0.5 mile to a gate at Iredell Lane. About 50 yards down the street is the continuation of the dirt road/trail, on the right. Follow it as it edges along a chain-link fence, then bear left at the fork. Mulholland Drive comes into view; your trail will soon parallel it. The path climbs steeply up, then drops back down to a eucalyptus-shaded creek. A few more trail forks must be negotiated but all are signed. More up-and-down undulations follow as you make your way up to the white gate that marks Fryman Canyon Overlook on Mulholland Drive, four miles from your start. Sure, most people drive to this high vista point with its sweeping views over the San Fernando Valley, but it's so much more satisfying to get there on two feet.

It is possible to loop back down to your starting point from the overlook, but we prefer a partial backtrack and a semiloop. Head back the way you came to Iredell Lane, then turn right on Iredell and follow it to Fryman Road. A left turn brings you back to your car.

Hiking dogs get a special drinking fountain on the Betty B. Dearing Trail near the Coldwater Canyon Park junction.

Options

At the intersection with the dog water fountain, walk up the stone staircase and make a detour into Coldwater Canyon Park. Pick up a brochure for the park's self-guided nature trail, the Magic Forest Nature Trail.

Directions

From U.S. 101 in Studio City, exit on Laurel Canyon Boulevard and head south. Drive 1.6 miles and turn right on Fryman Road. Turn right into the Wilacre Park parking lot at 3431 Fryman Road or continue south on Fryman Road and park on the street. Begin hiking at the gated road.

Public transportation: Metro Bus 218 stops on the northwest corner of Laurel Canyon Boulevard and Fryman Road.

Information and Contact

A $3 day-use fee is charged per vehicle at Wilacre Park, or you can park on the street for free. Dogs are allowed. Download a park map at www.lamountains.com; click on "hiking trails" and choose "Wilacre Park in Fryman Canyon." For more information, contact Santa Monica Mountains Conservancy, 5750 Ramirez Canyon Road, Malibu, CA 90265, 310/589-3200 or 310/858-7272, www.lamountains.com.

2 RUNYON CANYON
Runyon Canyon Park

Level: Easy   **Total Distance:** 3.4 miles round-trip

Hiking Time: 1.5 hours   **Elevation Gain:** 700 feet

Summary: Here is one of L.A.'s most social hikes – a heart-thumping trek high above Hollywood providing some of the best people- and dog-watching in the City of Angels.

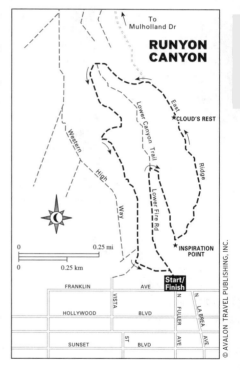

Spend enough time in L.A., and you're bound to discover a favorite neighborhood escape where the young and fit socialize while staying in shape. Places like Santa Monica's Fourth Street stairs, for example. Runyon Canyon Park is Hollywood's version, minus the stairs and with a lot more chaparral, tattoos, and dogs.

It's a star-studded locale. Sheryl Crow's house is in the neighborhood. Celebrities spotted on the trail include Orlando Bloom and his dogs and Brad Pitt (dogless).

If you adore *canis familiaris,* this is the hike for you. With much of the main hiking loop off-leash for dogs, Runyon Canyon has become a de facto city dog park. There are plenty of deliriously happy pooches here, as well as poop-bag dispensers, trash cans, and doggie-watering stations along the route—a welcome relief on the warm, dusty parts of the trail.

In case you haven't yet gotten the idea, this hike is not a wilderness experience. Footwear seen on this trail includes gym shoes and even flip-flops. Because of its proximity to so much humanity—it's literally blocks from bustling Hollywood Boulevard—this 133-acre urban park gets hit hard by its users.

Once you find street parking around the Fuller entrance—not an easy task on weekends—enter the park, where you'll see a sign for "The Pines,"

An oversized bench at Cloud's Rest is a popular place for humans and canines to hang out.

evidence of the canyon's colorful past. Runyon Canyon has been the location of several estates, including one owned by George Hamilton Hartford II, heir to the A&P grocery fortune. In the 1940s, Hartford planned to build a resort in the canyon and commissioned Frank Lloyd Wright to design it. The plan was nixed by neighbors. Erroll Flynn once lived in the Hartford estate's pool house. The city acquired the estate and made it a park in 1984.

At the entrance, take the main trail to the right. Doing the hike counterclockwise provides a steep climb in the beginning, then a longer, gradual descent. The trail ascends about a half mile to the first overlook, dubbed Inspiration Point (like so many other high points in the Los Angeles area). The point offers good views of Hollywood, but it gets even better. The dirt trail narrows and ascends steeply up some steps to Cloud's Rest, the second and main overlook. Here you can catch your breath and sit on an oversized bench so high your feet won't touch the ground. This is a great spot to take in views near and far. You'll get an eyeful, from the tattooed and pierced locals, to views of the Hollywood sign, Griffith Observatory, and, on exceptionally clear days, the distant ocean and even Catalina Island.

After quenching your visual appetite, continue on the trail, which now heads downhill. Almost immediately there's a turnoff to the right, which will lead to a third overlook in about 0.75 mile, at Mulholland Drive. Or, finish the loop by skipping the third overlook and continuing on the main trail downhill. At the bottom, on your way back to the Fuller entrance, you'll pass the Vista Street entrance. You can keep going and exit the park back at Fuller, or exit at Vista and finish the hike on sidewalks, walking past the beautiful homes, hoping to catch a glimpse of celebrity inhabitants. From Vista, turn left onto Franklin, then left on Fuller.

There's no parking on Vista, but the street gets plenty of foot and paw traffic, much to the distress of neighbors, who have lobbied in the past to close the busy entrance. A hotly contested plan is underway to pave part of the Fuller entrance and provide metered parking there, to relieve street parking for Runyon Canyon users.

Options

A lesser-used trail along the far west side of the park starts at the Vista Street entrance and is a 1.5-mile, steep ascent along the spine of a ridge to the north end of the canyon. Another trail that originates at the canyon bottom and branches off the main loop begins 0.25 mile from the Fuller entrance and ascends 0.75 mile through the middle of the canyon, passing an old reservoir, dam, and building ruins. It hooks up with the main loop trail about a half mile northwest of Cloud's Rest.

Directions

From U.S. 101 in Hollywood, exit at Highland Avenue and head south 0.5 mile to Franklin Avenue. Turn right (west) on Franklin. Drive 0.6 mile and turn right (north) on Fuller Avenue. Runyon Canyon Park is 0.25 mile ahead at the end of Fuller. Street parking fills up quickly on weekends; beware of permit parking zones on surrounding streets. There is also a walk-in entrance at Vista Street, two blocks west of Fuller, and an entrance with parking at Mulholland Drive, at the park's far north end.

Public transportation: There is a Metro Red Line subway stop at Hollywood Boulevard and Highland Avenue; from there, walk west on Hollywood Boulevard 0.6 mile and turn right on Fuller Avenue. Walk 0.25 mile until it ends at the park. Or, take the Metro 212 bus from Hollywood/Highland to Hollywood and LaBrea and walk 0.75 mile to the park (north two blocks on LaBrea, west two blocks on Franklin, north three blocks on Fuller to the park).

Information and Contact

There is no fee. Dogs are allowed. There is a map behind glass at the entry kiosk at Fuller Avenue. A trail map of the Santa Monica Mountains is available for a fee from National Geographic/Trails Illustrated, 303/670-3457 or 800/962-1643, www.trailsillustrated.com. A map can also be found at www.runyon-canyon.com. For more information, contact Runyon Canyon Park, 2001 North Fuller Avenue, Los Angeles, CA 90046, 323/913-7390 or 323/666-5046, www.laparks.org.

3 HOLLYRIDGE TRAIL TO HOLLYWOOD SIGN
Griffith Park

Level: Easy	**Total Distance:** 3.0 miles round-trip
Hiking Time: 1.5 hours	**Elevation Gain:** 500 feet

Summary: Here's your chance to get as close as legally possible to L.A.'s famed landmark, the big white letters of the Hollywood sign.

The first thing you should know: The Hollywood sign is not on top of Mount Hollywood, it's on top of Mount Lee. A combination of trail, fire road, and paved road brings you to a spot behind the infamous 450-foot-long sign, with a view of the Los Angeles basin in the background.

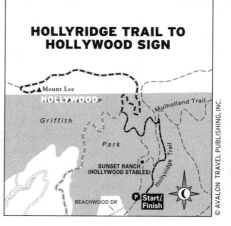

Trailhead parking is at a pullout just before the entrance to Sunset Ranch stables. As soon as you park, look for a sign for the Hollyridge Trail, the first leg of this short, view-filled hike. The trail is a fire road, although some maps erroneously show it as a footpath. From the parking area, the trail ascends steeply and rounds a bend, soon allowing your first glimpse of the epic sign's letters. Be sure to look left as you pass the Sunset Ranch sign, near a short spur trail to the stables. This is a good photo opportunity for shooting the sign. Here you will also start sharing the path with horseback riders, but you'll soon leave them behind.

After about a half mile up Hollyridge, take a sharp left—almost a hairpin turn—onto another fire road that heads moderately uphill. This is Mulholland Trail, but don't expect to see a trail sign; the initial Hollyridge sign is the only one visible on this hike. The trail continues another 0.5 mile before dropping slightly to an intersection with paved Mount Lee Road. Turn right on the blacktop, which is a maintenance road for workers driving to the radio transmission towers atop Mount Lee. The park doesn't encourage hikers on this road, but, technically, you are allowed to be here. Just mind your manners.

The road begins climbing steadily up Mount Lee and then winds around its north side, allowing views of the Verdugo Mountains and beyond, the San Ga-

© JULIE SHEER

view of the Hollywood sign from Hollyridge Trail

briel Mountains, including Mount Wilson and Mount Baldy. After the last trail bend, the peak's radio towers come into view. Voila. You have nearly summited 1,680-foot Mount Lee and are now directly above the Hollywood sign.

A chain-link fence lines the trail between you and the sign, but that doesn't block one of the best views around: you can peek through the sign's "O" to clear views of the Hollywood Hills neighborhood and Hollywood Reservoir. Strategic placement of a small lens camera between the fence's chain links will yield dramatic images of the sign looming in the foreground, with the L.A. basin stretching before you.

But don't even think of scaling the fence to sneak a "head-through-the-O" photograph. Surveillance cameras erected in 2002 complement a gauntlet of security measures designed to keep intruders from accessing the sign. These include alarms, motion detectors, and audio warning systems. These folks mean business.

First erected in 1923 as an advertisement for a housing development called Hollywoodland, the sign has undergone a number of renovations and tranformations over the years, including the dropping of the last syllable in 1949. By the 1970s, the sign was in various stages of disrepair. A campaign to raise money to replace each of the letters included celebrity donors Hugh Hefner, Alice Cooper, and Gene Autry. In 1978, the new, steel letters were unveiled. The old letters sat in storage for years, and then in 2004 portions of the original sign were auctioned on eBay.

Over the years, the sign has been the site of various stunts. In what was touted with great fanfare but ended up being little more than a yawn, the sign was lit up on New Year's Eve 1999 to celebrate the new millennium. A plan to paint a flag on the sign to salute Veterans Day was nixed in 2001. Today's hiker can salute Hollywood's most glamorous symbol with a swig of bottled water and, after taking in the view, head back down to the flatlands.

Options

To add some mileage, instead of turning back on Mulholland Trail, continue down Mount Lee Road, which ends at Mulholland Drive and Deronda Drive, an alternate starting point for this hike. You can also take Mulholland Trail to Mount Hollywood Trail.

Directions

From northbound U.S. 101 in Hollywood, exit at Gower Street, take the Beachwood Drive ramp, and head north. Go 1.8 miles on Beachwood Drive until it ends just short of Sunset Ranch stables. Turn right into the parking area, near the Hollyridge Trail sign.

From southbound U.S. 101 in Hollywood, exit at Gower Street. Take Gower Street north one block and turn right on Franklin Avenue. Drive one block and turn left on Beachwood Drive. Go 1.8 miles on Beachwood Drive until it ends just short of Sunset Ranch stables. Turn right into the parking area, near the Hollyridge Trail sign.

Public transportation: Take the Red Line subway from downtown L.A. to the Hollywood/Vine stop. Take the Dash bus north on Beachwood Canyon Drive. From the last stop, walk about 0.75 mile to the trailhead.

Information and Contact

There is no fee. Dogs on leash are allowed. A free trail map is available at the ranger station on the east side of the park or at the Fern Dell Nature Museum. Or download a park map at www.griffithobs.org/GriffithPark-Map.html. For more information, contact Griffith Park Ranger Station, 4730 Crystal Springs Drive, Los Angeles, CA 90027, 323/913-4688 or 323/913-7390, www.laparks.org. Or contact the Hollywood Chamber of Commerce, 323/469-8311, www.hollywoodchamber.net.

4 GRIFFITH OBSERVATORY WEST TRAIL LOOP
Griffith Park

🏛 🏕 🚌

Level: Easy

Hiking Time: 1 hour

Total Distance: 2.5 miles round-trip

Elevation Gain: 500 feet

Summary: An easy trek from the lush Fern Dell picnic area to historic Griffith Observatory, with the option to continue to Mount Hollywood.

GRIFFITH OBSERVATORY

West Observatory Loop

GRIFFITH OBSERVATORY WEST TRAIL LOOP

Start/Finish

FERN DELL DR

HOBART BLVD

LOS FRANCISCOS WAY

LOS DIEGOS WAY

LOS BONITOS WAY

LOS FELIZ BLVD

NOTTINGHAM AVE

0   250 yds
0   250 m

© AVALON TRAVEL PUBLISHING, INC.

You can drive to Griffith Observatory to catch a star show, but why burn gasoline when you can hike there? This short loop starts at Fern Dell, a delightful picnic spot at the southwest end of Griffith Park, near Los Feliz Boulevard. Before setting out on the trail, explore around a bit. There are picnic tables, restrooms, a playground, quaint footbridges over ponds, and, of course, ferns. There are even coastal redwoods that were planted here decades ago. Not bad, considering Hollywood Boulevard is minutes away.

To get to the start of the trail, follow the creek north from Fern Dell, past the restrooms. This hike makes a counterclockwise loop, taking the lower trail first, then returning on the upper trail. Stay on the right side of the creek to pick up the lower trail. The trailhead on the left is where you'll end up on the return leg.

The trail, which is a fire road, begins to climb immediately, rising up and away from Fern Dell. Right away, the dome of the observatory pops into view amidst trees and shrubby chaparral. As the trail steepens, look left for views of the Hollywood sign on Mount Lee.

At the first major intersection, make a hard right and head uphill toward the observatory. The trail flattens at the top of the loop and reaches a tree-dotted plateau, offering great views of the city. Looking south, the neighborhoods of Los Feliz, Hollywood, and Silver Lake are in the foreground. You can also

© JULIE SHEER

the West Trail Loop as it approaches the Griffith Observatory

see Echo Park, with downtown L.A. just beyond. To the west are Mid-City, Westwood, and, on a clear day, the Palos Verdes Peninsula and Catalina Island. Look east for views of Mount Wilson and other San Gabriel peaks, including Mount Baldy, 30 miles distant.

An obvious side trail leads 0.25 mile from the plateau straight to Griffith Observatory. The photogenic white dome has been a popular film locale, providing the setting for memorable scenes in movies such as *Rebel Without a Cause* and *The Terminator*. Built in 1935, the observatory has been undergoing a facelift since 2002. It is expected to reopen in summer 2006, after an extensive renovation that includes restoring the copper domes, rebuilding the planetarium theater and interior dome, earthquake repair, and other expansion work.

You might want to bring along your wallet and time your trip for the observatory's open hours so you can take in a star show. Nearly two million visitors a year enter the observatory's astronomy museum. Museum entry is free; there is a fee for star shows.

To loop back to Fern Dell, retrace your steps for 0.25 mile, then bear right at a trail junction. The trail curves to the north and then back west as it heads downhill to Fern Dell.

Options

From the observatory turnoff, you can continue east on the East Observatory Trail 0.5 mile until it ends at Vermont Canyon Road. Or you can hike to Mount Hollywood from the observatory parking lot, starting at the Charlie Turner trailhead (1.5 miles to the summit; see the next listing, Mount Hollywood from Griffith Observatory).

Directions

From I-5 in Los Feliz, exit at Los Feliz Boulevard and head west. Drive 2.4 miles and turn right (north) on Fern Dell Drive. Drive 0.3 mile to the parking area on the right. It's just past the stop sign at Red Oak Drive.

Alternatively, from U.S. 101 in Hollywood, take the Sunset Boulevard exit and drive east three blocks to Western Avenue. Turn left and go north on Western Avenue for 0.4 mile; the road veers right and becomes Los Feliz Boulevard. Turn left immediately on Fern Dell Drive and drive 0.3 mile to the parking area on the right.

Public transportation: The Hollywood/Western Metro Rail stop is 0.8 mile from the trailhead at Fern Dell. From the stop, walk north 0.5 mile on Western Avenue, which turns into Los Feliz Boulevard. Go left (north) on Fern Dell Drive and walk 0.3 mile to Fern Dell picnic area. Or the Metro 26 bus stops on Franklin Avenue at its intersection with Western Avenue. Follow the same walking directions as above to the trailhead.

Information and Contact

There is no fee. Dogs on leash are allowed. A free trail map is available at the ranger station on the east side of the park or at the Fern Dell Nature Museum. Or download a park map at www.griffithobs.org/GriffithParkMap.html. For more information, contact Griffith Park Ranger Station, 4730 Crystal Springs Drive, Los Angeles, CA 90027, 323/913-4688 or 323/913-7390, www.laparks.org. Or contact Griffith Observatory at 323/664-1191.

5 MOUNT HOLLYWOOD FROM GRIFFITH OBSERVATORY
Griffith Park

Level: Easy

Total Distance: 3.0 miles round-trip

Hiking Time: 1.5 hours

Elevation Gain: 500 feet

Summary: This easy hike leads to far-reaching views of the Los Angeles basin from the highest point in Hollywood.

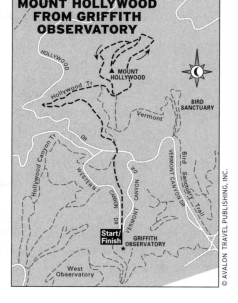

Griffith Park is as much a part of Los Angeles legend as Mann's Chinese Theater or the Santa Monica Pier. In all of the park's many acres, no trail is more frequently hiked than the path to the top of Mount Hollywood. Out-of-towners need to be told that this is not the peak that bears the famous "Hollywood" sign; that's Mount Lee, although you can easily see that sign from this peak. Rather, Mount Hollywood is the highest point in all of Hollywood at 1,625 feet in elevation, and, even for those who greatly prefer a sea of conifers to a sea of civilization, its summit view is sublime.

It's just about impossible to get lost on this wide, easy trail. Start hiking at the Charlie Turner trailhead, directly across from Griffith Observatory. In case you need to be reminded that you're in Los Angeles and not the Ansel Adams Wilderness, a tree at the trailhead is dedicated to Beatles star George Harrison. The road/trail meanders on a gentle grade over sage- and chaparral-covered slopes, offering worthwhile city views at every curve. You'll experience an interesting mix of man versus nature here. On the one hand, you can hear the happy "chi-ca-go" call of native quail. Simultaneously you may hear jackhammers tearing up a nearby sidewalk, or sirens racing down the valley streets below.

The wide fire road/trail is simple and straightforward, with no junctions

© ANN MARIE BROWN

a sweeping view from the concrete-railed summit of Mount Hollywood

to negotiate until you near the top, where a half-mile loop circles the summit. We suggest you take the right fork first, passing a small terraced garden and picnic area called Dante's View, thus hiking the loop counterclockwise. Just beyond Dante's View is a short spur trail that leads 100 yards to a lower, brushy peak, but you might as well skip the small stuff and head straight for Mount Hollywood. You'll reach a four-way junction just below, and north of, the summit. Turn left to walk the final few steps to the top.

As flat as a pancake and about half the size of a football field, the summit of Mount Hollywood is decorated with hitching posts, trash cans, a few concrete picnic tables, a concrete railing, and, well, more concrete. But the attraction is not the amenities here; it's the view, which stretches from downtown L.A. all the way to the ocean. The San Gabriel Mountains loom large in the background, and on the clearest days it is possible to pick out Southern California's big three peaks, far off to the east: Mount Baldy, Mount San Gorgonio, and Mount San Jacinto.

A close look at the summit survey marker embedded in—guess what? concrete—tells you that Mount Hollywood is actually 1,619 feet high, but Griffith Park officials insist it is actually 1,625. Give or take a few feet, it's a great view.

Options

You can nearly double the length of this hike by starting from the parking lot near the Fern Dell Museum, then hiking on the trail/fire road to Griffith Observatory instead of driving on the paved road.

Directions

From U.S. 101 in Hollywood, take the Sunset Boulevard exit and drive east three blocks to Western Avenue. Turn left and go north on Western Avenue for 0.4 mile; the road veers right and becomes Los Feliz Boulevard. Turn left immediately on Fern Dell Drive and drive two miles (it becomes Western Canyon Road) to West Observatory Road. Turn right and drive 0.3 mile; park near the observatory. The trail begins across from the observatory at the Charlie Turner trailhead.

Alternatively, from I-5 in Los Feliz, exit at Los Feliz Boulevard and head west. Drive 2.4 miles and turn right (north) on Fern Dell Drive. Continue as above.

Information and Contact

There is no fee. Dogs on leash are allowed. A free trail map is available at the ranger station on the east side of the park or at the Fern Dell Nature Museum. Or download a park map at www.griffithobs.org/GriffithParkMap.html. For more information, contact Griffith Park Ranger Station, 4730 Crystal Springs Drive, Los Angeles, CA 90027, 323/913-4688 or 323/913-7390, www.laparks.org.

6 SCRUB JAY TRAIL   BEST (

Ernest E. Debs Regional Park

Level: Easy   **Total Distance:** 2.5 miles round-trip

Hiking Time: 1 hour   **Elevation Gain:** 200 feet

Summary: An in-city hike in a park with an eco-friendly visitor center, located a few car honks from a major freeway.

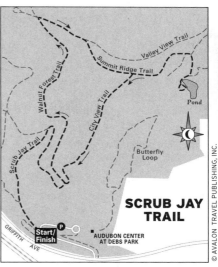

Want to get a kid interested in hiking? Grab a backpack, map, nature guide, binoculars, bug traps, and maybe a picnic basket and hit the trail at Debs Park just north of downtown Los Angeles.

You can borrow gear from the park's new eco-friendly Audubon Center, which opened in November 2003 at a cost of $4.8 million. When kids return from hiking, they can report on their wildlife discoveries for an ongoing survey of the park's wildlife, which includes 137 species of birds and the usual reptiles and mammals that reside in the foothills. They may even get a close-up look at critters such as captive snakes, which Audubon employees sometimes bring out for demonstrations.

The 17-acre Audubon Center is considered one of the greenest buildings in Los Angeles. It is 100 percent solar powered, constructed mostly of recycled materials—including countertops made of crushed sunflower seeds—and landscaped with native trees and plants. It was built by the National Audubon Society with one primary goal in mind—introducing urban children to nature. More than 50,000 school-aged children live within a two-mile radius of the Center, and Audubon's goal is to have nature inspire each and every one.

There are about two miles of trails at the Audubon Center and an additional 8.5 miles in the rest of 282-acre Debs Park. You can hike on your own or hook up with one of the guided hikes offered by Audubon, which include bird-watching hikes and native plant landscape tours.

Hiking here isn't exactly a wilderness experience, but there are plenty of

a view of downtown Los Angeles from City View Trail at Debs Park

hills to get the heart pumping and views to enjoy. A pleasant hour or two can be spent on a 2.5-mile trail loop from the Audubon Center to a pond in Debs Park. After picking up a map at the Audubon Center, start out on the Scrub Jay Trail. Walk through the parking lot and turn right out of the lot on the main fire road (unsigned) heading uphill. Don't be put off by the freeway noise; it disappears as you head farther into the park.

Scrub Jay Trail is more fire road than trail—it is basically two strips of dirt with grass growing in the middle and scrubby shrubs on both sides. About 500 yards up Scrub Jay, take a hard right. Again, there's no sign, but this is the start of the Walnut Forest Trail. The trail heads south and then west for about 300 yards. Soon there is another trail intersection, heading straight ahead and uphill. This is City View Trail, the return leg of your loop. Stay on Walnut Forest for now. True to its name, the trail heads through a forest of Southern California black walnut trees, which are most common in the foothills below 4,500 feet. The species is dwindling because of urbanization.

You'll emerge onto a black-topped road, Summit Ridge Trail, and turn right. A stone picnic shelter on the left, labelled "Gazebo" on the trail map, offers abundant city vistas. Look northeast toward Pasadena for views of Mount Baldy. To the northwest, you'll spot radio towers on Mount Lukens, the highest point in the city of Los Angeles. Visible immediately south are downtown L.A. and even City Hall.

Continue on Summit Ridge Trail for about 0.4 mile to a right turn on a narrow trail that leads to a tree-shaded pond, stocked with bass, bluegill, and catfish. This spot is popular with families and provides a first fishing experience for many children. A path leads around the pond's edges. Walk to the opposite shore for views of Long Beach, the Palos Verdes Peninsula, and the ocean. Scale the grassy knoll next to the pond trail for good views of the San Gabriel Mountains.

Head back to Summit Ridge Trail and retrace your steps north. In 0.25 mile, go left on unsigned City View Trail. At first a narrow, brushy single-track that heads downhill, the path widens as it heads back to Scrub Jay Trail. Along the way are more views of downtown L.A., the lights of Dodger Stadium, and the Southwest Museum across the 110 freeway in Mount Washington.

Go left on Scrub Jay Trail and head back to the Audubon Center. If you still have time and excess energy, take your young hiking companions to the 1.5-acre Children's Woodland, where they can paint, draw, climb a tree, and learn a lot about nature in this small wilderness set amidst the big city.

Options
Scrub Jay Trail can be hiked as a loop by turning left instead of right at the Walnut Forest Trail. Walk about 0.2 mile, then turn back west on Scrub Jay Trail and head 0.5 mile back to the trailhead.

Directions
From southbound I-110 in Highland Park, exit at Avenue 52 and head south, veering west as the street turns into Griffin Avenue, for a total 0.7 mile. Turn left into the entrance gate at 4700 N. Griffin Avenue and park at the Audubon Center.

From northbound I-110 in Highland Park, exit at Avenue 43 and go right. Turn left on Griffin Avenue and in 0.5 mile turn right into the park entrance at 4700 N. Griffin Avenue.

Public transportation: The Gold Line rail Southwest Museum stop is about a quarter mile from the park entry. Metro Bus 81 stops at Sycamore Grove Park; cross the park and footbridge to Debs Park. Metro Bus lines 46 and 255 stop at Avenue 43 and Griffin Avenue; walk north on Griffin, past Montecito Drive. The Audubon entrance is the second driveway on the right.

Information and Contact
There is no fee. Dogs on leash are allowed. A trail map is available for $1 at the Audubon Center, which is open 9 A.M. to 5 P.M. Wednesday through Sunday. (Park trails are open daily.) For more information, contact Audubon Center at Debs Park, 4700 N. Griffin Avenue, Los Angeles, CA 90031, 323/221-2255, www.audubon-ca.org or www.laparks.org. Or contact the Los Angeles Department of Recreation and Parks at 323/913-7390, or Arroyo Seco Recreation and Parks District at 323/255-0370.

7 POINT VICENTE BEACH WALK BEST ℂ
Palos Verdes Peninsula

Level: Easy

Total Distance: 3.0 miles round-trip

Hiking Time: 1.5 hours

Elevation Gain: 250 feet

Summary: Access a piece of the Palos Verdes Peninsula's highly coveted shoreline on this rocky coastal walk.

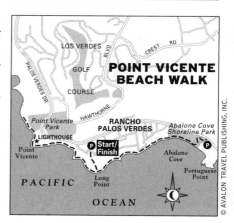

The Palos Verdes Peninsula, an up-lifted marine terrace forced out of the sea millions of years ago, is by any standard a beautiful stretch of Southern California shoreline. Million-dollar homes and manicured golf courses rub elbows on its 100-foot-high, ocean-view bluff tops. Sunday drivers regularly tour the loop around "PV Drive" to enjoy the world-class coastal vistas. The Peninsula's protruding landform is so distinct that gray whales use it, in conjunction with Catalina Island, to help them navigate on their 5,000-mile annual migration from the Bering Sea to Baja, Mexico. Too bad that hikers and beach lovers don't have more and better access to this pristine stretch of coast. Instead, we are too often confronted with "no beach access" signs.

But here's one place on the Peninsula where you can get some sand under your shoes: Point Vicente Fishing Access at Long Point. This ecological preserve has a free public parking lot right along Palos Verdes Drive, less than a mile east of the Point Vicente Lighthouse.

An easy half-mile trail descends to the beach, but pause for a moment before you hike down. At the top, you are rewarded with views across the sea and out to Catalina Island. This is a perfect location for spotting migrating gray whales during their winter and spring travels (best from December through April). Throughout the migration season, volunteers from the Point Vicente Interpretive Center are often seated on the bluff top, keeping track of the whale census.

After descending to the beach, you can hike out and back in either direction. The going is slow no matter which way you choose; the beach is littered with rounded rocks that must be navigated with care. To your right, about a

© ANN MARIE BROWN

The rock-lined shore of the Palos Verdes Peninsula can be explored from the trail at Point Vicente Fishing Access.

half mile away, is Point Vicente. Getting past the lighthouse's point of land is possible only at low tides. To your left is Long Point and Abalone Cove. Most beach walkers head left, but, again, a reasonably low tide is required to get around the point. Not that it matters much. Your choice of destination, and the distance you travel, is almost irrelevant. On a walk like this, every step is a rich experience, as pelicans soar overhead, gray whales spout and dive, and an endless series of breakers head for dissolution on the rocky beach.

Options

Abalone Cove Shoreline Park (310/377-1222) is 1.2 miles farther east along Palos Verdes Drive. If you are willing to fork over the $6 parking fee, you can follow the main trail across the bluffs to a wooden railing, then head left along the railing to a trail that descends to the beach. Head left along the beach to access the best tidepooling in the area, by Portuguese Point.

Directions

From Highway 1/Pacific Coast Highway in Torrance, turn left on Palos Verdes Boulevard which becomes Palos Verdes Drive. Drive 7.2 miles south and then east to the Point Vicente Fishing Access on the right (0.8 mile east of Point Vicente Lighthouse). The trail begins by the restrooms.

Information and Contact

There is no fee. Dogs are not allowed. No trail map is available. For more information, contact the Rancho Palos Verdes Recreation and Parks Department, 30940 Hawthorne Boulevard, Rancho Palos Verdes, CA 90275, 310/544-5260. Or contact the Point Vicente Interpretive Center, 310/377-5370 or 310/544-5264.

8 PEACOCK FLAT
Rancho Palos Verdes

Level: Easy

Total Distance: 2.0 miles round-trip

Hiking Time: 1 hour

Elevation Gain: 400 feet

Summary: An easy trek on the Palos Verdes Peninsula that leads to a knoll with spectacular 180-degree ocean views.

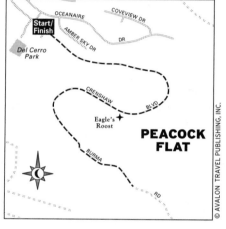

Hiking on the Palos Verdes Peninsula isn't very user-friendly. Made up of a handful of exclusive residential communities, the Peninsula is laced with trails—many well used by equestrians—which are often unmarked and, in some cases, can only be accessed if you're a resident.

Nonetheless, there are several excellent options for hikers, if you know where to go. Probably the easiest hike, and one of the most scenic in Los Angeles County, is the short trek along a fire road to Peacock Flat in Rancho Palos Verdes. The hike starts where Crenshaw Boulevard ends at its southernmost point. Back in the 1950s, there were plans to extend Crenshaw all the way south to Palos Verdes Drive and build homes all over these coastal bluffs and rolling grasslands. A major landslide in 1956 at Portuguese Bend put an end to the developers' dreams. The landslides have continued; in some places, the earth moves three feet per year on average. (Road signs on Palos Verdes Drive prohibit stopping or parking in a one-mile stretch because the land is so unstable.) Crenshaw Boulevard's proposed extension was never paved or developed, and the dirt right-of-way became a de facto hiking trail.

The dirt road doesn't have an official name, but you'll hear or see references to it as old Crenshaw Road, Crenshaw Extension, Burma Trail, and, on Thomas Guide maps, as Crenshaw Boulevard/Burma Road. The trail, which is technically on private land, will hopefully get an official name once a deal is completed to bring it into the public domain. Negotiations are underway between landowners, the city of Rancho Palos Verdes, and the Palos Verdes Land Conservancy to purchase the land and turn it into the Portuguese Bend

Nature Preserve. Once that happens, the Conservancy will oversee the trails and, at long last, print some user-friendly trail maps.

The lack of a name, or even of a map, won't matter much when you hike here and enjoy the nearly constant cerulean blue Catalina Channel views. Park on the street or at nearby Del Cerro Park. Walk south on Crenshaw Boulevard past some million-dollar homes. Just past Burrell Lane, you'll come to a gate marked "private property," a sign which hikers and cyclists simply ignore and walk around. Pay attention to other signs warning of ticks and rattlesnakes; they're abundant here in the spring and summer. The road/trail is all downhill from the gate, so pace yourself if the weather is warm. There's not much shade, and the return hike back uphill can be a grind.

Before long, you'll have a clear view of Catalina Island, about 17 miles distant. Even the isthmus at Two Harbors is visible on the best air-quality days. Mustard, sages, and bright yellow sunflowers abound along the trail, and the surrounding brush-covered hills are emerald green in the spring.

In about a mile you'll come to a meadow referred to as Peacock Flats, named for the showy-feathered fowl that once roamed the area. To the left is a short path to a knoll called Eagle's Roost, decorated with about a dozen pine trees. Expansive coastal views are yours for the taking here. Gray whales are sometimes seen from this point as they make their way north during the spring migration. This is also a popular picnic spot.

From the knoll, you can take another path to the left, back to the fire road.

© JULIE SHEER

A large expanse of Catalina Island is in view from the Crenshaw Extension Trail.

Turn left again on the fire road to continue to Badlands Slide, an area that signifies what the Peninsula's geology is all about—dramatic land movement. Geologists say that a fault at the north end of the Peninsula got pushed up by tectonic activity, forming the Peninsula's familiar dome. A layer of ash from an ancient volcano settled on the land. This unstable layer below soil and rocks gets slippery when water (rain) is added, causing the familiar slides along the Peninsula's coast. For developers who want to build multimillion dollar homes, this is a bad thing. For hikers and nature lovers, it's a good thing.

Options

If you continue on the road/trail past the overlook at Eagle's Roost, you'll pass Portuguese Canyon and head toward Palos Verdes Drive South. You can hike as much as three miles one-way on the fire road before nearing Palos Verdes Drive South (it's impossible to cross the busy road). Many loops are possible on the footpaths that connect with the fire road.

Directions

From I-110 in Wilmington, exit at Highway 1/Pacific Coast Highway, heading west. Drive three miles to Crenshaw Boulevard. Go left (south) on Crenshaw until it ends in four miles in Rancho Palos Verdes. Park on the street or in Del Cerro Park, on the right.

Public transportation: The Metro 225 bus stops on the southwest corner of Crest Road and Crenshaw Boulevard in Rancho Palos Verdes. From there, walk south on Crenshaw about 0.4 mile until it ends.

Information and Contact

There is no fee. Dogs on leash are allowed. A booklet of equestrian trail maps is available for sale at Rolling Hills General Store, 26947 Rolling Hills Road, Rancho Palos Verdes, 310/541-3668. For more information, contact Rancho Palos Verdes Recreation and Parks Department, 310/544-5260, or Palos Verdes Peninsula Land Conservancy, P.O. Box 3427, Palos Verdes Peninsula, CA 90274, 310/541-7613, www.pvplc.org.

9 TWO HARBORS' WEST END ROAD   BEST (

Catalina Island

Level: Moderate

Hiking Time: 5 hours

Total Distance: 9.0 miles round-trip

Elevation Gain: 500 feet

Summary: Stow away to an island off the coast of Los Angeles and hike to secluded beaches on Catalina's north side.

When first-timers make the trip to Catalina Island, they usually head for the city of Avalon, Catalina's largest destination. Although Avalon is a fun place—plenty of nightlife, restaurants, hotels, and shops—it's a bit too much like Newport Beach to feel like a true "getaway." For a more out-of-the-ordinary adventure, take the ferry to Catalina's second city (really a small village), Two Harbors. There

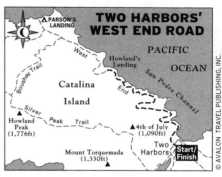

© AVALON TRAVEL PUBLISHING, INC.

you'll find a more authentic taste of Catalina Island, as well as a terrific hiking or backpacking trail.

When you make your ferry reservation, be sure you book a direct boat to Two Harbors. The ferry ride becomes interminably long if the boat goes to Avalon first, then stops at multiple private campgrounds around the island. An express boat will get you there in about an hour.

Next, be aware that you can do this hike as a day trip from the mainland, but you must plan your ferry shuttles carefully to allow enough time. Except for during the summer season, ferries run infrequently to Two Harbors, so, if you're visiting in the off-season, you may have to stay overnight to catch the next boat. A few accommodations exist in Two Harbors, including a campground and a lovely old hotel called the Banning House, both requiring advance reservations. You can also arrange a bus shuttle across the island to Avalon, where there are dozens of hotels.

Your ferry from the mainland will drop you off at Two Harbors' Isthmus Harbor. Stop in at the general store to stock up your day pack, then start hiking on West End Road, a dirt road that is nearly level and follows the contour of the coastline. Access West End Road from the pier by walking to your right along the beach. Take the dirt path at the beach's end and make a

© JULIE SHEER

Huge, shaggy bison are a common sight on Catalina Island.

quick, steep ascent past some tiny shoreline cottages. When you join the dirt road, go right (northwest).

West End Road's wide and mostly level treadway makes it ideal for holding hands with your hiking partner, or gazing at the coastside beauty without worrying about your foot placement. You are treated to eyefuls of oceanfront scenery, including rocky outcrops, steep headlands, and beckoning coves. Prickly pear cactus is ubiquitous, and a few palm trees wave their fronds above the coastal scrub. Peer down into the emerald waters below the bluff-top trail, and you'll spot flashes of bright orange: They're garibaldis, California's state saltwater fish.

At 1.25 miles you reach Cherry Valley and Cherry Cove, named for the native Catalina cherry tree, which erupts into a display of showy white flowers in the spring. The road/trail turns inland to detour around the long, narrow cove. A private camp is located here, and a flotilla of colorful kayaks often lines the beach. You'll pass many more private camps as you continue your languid coastal stroll. The route remains almost completely level, with only a negligible elevation change.

Watch for the camp at Howland's Landing, 4.5 miles from your start. Shortly beyond it is a marvelous stretch of white sand, marked by a couple of tall, rocky sea stacks about 150 yards offshore. An obvious spur trail leads from the main road down to the beach, where you will surely want to take a swim. Now is a good time to pull a lunch out of your day pack and ponder how lucky we are to have this scenic island so close to Los Angeles. If you start to feel homesick for the mainland, just squint your eyes. You should be able to make out the Orange County coast, a hazy blur of land some 20-plus miles away. Most people feel quite content seeing "civilization" from such a distance.

Options

If you want to hike farther, the sandy cove at Parson's Landing is another 2.5 miles (seven miles from the start). This beautiful, rocky pocket beach has six campsites right on the beach, each equipped with a picnic table and fire grill. Bottled water and firewood are included with your camping reservation fee (they are stored in lockers at the beach; you are given a locker key with your reservation). For camping reservations, call 310/510-8368 or go to www.catalina.com. Even if you aren't prepared to camp, Parson's Landing makes a fine destination for a day hike, and the 14-mile round-trip is surprisingly easy because of the level terrain.

Directions

Catalina Express provides ferry service to Two Harbors from San Pedro Harbor. Call 800/618-5533 or visit www.catalinaexpress.com for a departure schedule, reservations, and fee information. The Catalina–Marina Del Rey Flyer provides ferry service to Two Harbors from Marina Del Rey. Call 310/305-7250 or visit www.catalinaferries.com for a departure schedule, reservations, and fee information.

Information and Contact

A free Santa Catalina Island hiking permit is required and can be obtained from Two Harbors Visitor Services; phone 310/510-0303 for more information. Dogs are not allowed. A free trail map is available when you pick up your hiking permit. An online trail map is available at www.scico.com/camping/home.html. A trail map is also available from Franko's Maps, 808/834-6887, www.frankosmaps.com. For more information about Catalina Island, visit www.catalina.com or www.catalinaconservancy.org.

10 COTTONWOOD-BLACK JACK TRAIL TO LITTLE HARBOR

BEST ◖

Catalina Island

Level: Moderate

Total Distance: 8.0 miles (one-way)

Hiking Time: 4 hours

Elevation Loss: 1,650 feet

Summary: This hike across Catalina Island's interior to a secluded beach campground traverses undeveloped wilderness that only a small fraction of Catalina visitors ever see.

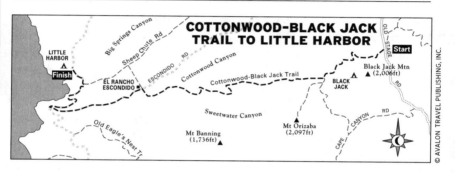

For many people, a trip to Catalina Island means shopping in Avalon and taking a glass-bottom boat ride. But if you'd rather spend your time on a trail than in a T-shirt shop, the island's backcountry interior beckons. How does it sound to be stranded on your very own tropical island?

The logistics of this trip are a bit more complex than your average day hike, but the payoff is well worth the extra effort. It's best done as a one-way hike with an overnight campout at Little Harbor, but it is possible to make it a day hike in one very long day.

First, there is a one-hour boat ride to Catalina Island from Long Beach or San Pedro. Then, you need reservations for bus transportation to the Cottonwood–Black Jack trailhead, located about seven twisty, steep miles inland from Avalon. Buses leave twice a day in the summer, once a day in the winter. If you aren't backpacking, you also need a free hiking permit, which can be obtained from the Catalina Island Conservancy. Reserve a permit by calling the conservancy before you go (310/510-1421).

When you get off the boat, pick up your bus tickets at Pavilion Lodge, about a block away from the Avalon ferry landing. (Go right on Crescent Avenue; the lodge is at the corner of the first street on the left, Claressa Avenue.) To get to the bus stop, keep going north on Crescent Avenue and then go left on Catalina Avenue to Island Plaza. The bus ride takes about 20 minutes and drops you off at the trailhead, Black Jack Junction, elevation 1,350 feet. From here on in, you're likely to see more bison than people.

Before setting out, snap some ocean shots. Once you head inland, it will be a while before you see water again. The first mile is a steep 350-foot climb on a fire road. To the south is Black Jack Mountain, topped with a radio tower. At 2,006 feet, it's a shade shorter than the island's highest point, 2,097-foot Mount Orizaba. In 1.3 miles, go right at the sign for Cottonwood Camp/ Little Harbor. (If you get to the turnoff for Black Jack Campground, you've gone too far.) You'll pass through an unlocked cattle gate; be sure to close the gate behind you. For the next 6.7 miles, you'll be hiking through the best of Catalina's backcountry.

It shouldn't be too hard to spot bison. A herd of 14 were brought to the island for a film shoot in the 1920s. They took well to the climate and multiplied. Because of overpopulation and destruction of native vegetation, more than 100 were removed from the island in 2003 and transported to Indian reservations in South Dakota. The bison population numbers about 150 these days. The shaggy beasts graze on the grassy hillsides and also use the Black Jack Trail as a thoroughfare, so watch your step.

© JULIE SHEER

a view of Little Harbor on the final leg of the Cottonwood-Black Jack Trail

The trail ultimately descends, but there are plenty of ups and downs along the way. As you wander, you'll have expansive views of oak woodlands scattered over the hills. Bush poppy, Catalina mariposa lily, and Catalina daisy are abundant in the spring. Big bunches of prickly pear cactus sport bright yellow blooms. Keep your eyes peeled for deer bounding through the brush.

The ocean views return about 3.4 miles in, where the trail meets a road at El Rancho Escondido, a ranch once owned by the Wrigley family. As you walk down a path through the ranch, take a look at their sleek Arabian horses. The Wrigleys bred Arabians and used them for ranching in the 1930s. The rest of the ranch is off-limits except for visitors on special tours.

Beyond the ranch, you'll turn left onto an unsigned dirt road marked on maps as Escondido Road. The ocean is straight ahead. It's still 3.3 miles to Little Harbor, but the road is well graded and mostly flat. In two more miles you'll reach an ocean overlook with a breathtaking view of your destination. This is the photo opportunity of the day. Waves crash on the rugged shoreline below. Little Harbor Campground is set just beyond the beach under a canopy of palm trees.

Continue 1.2 miles to the camp. If you have reservations to spend the night, the campground has water, picnic shelters, fire rings, chemical toilets, outdoor showers, and a pay phone. There are two beaches, one that's perfect for swimming and the other with more surf.

Whether you are camping or day hiking, the return trip is easy. The Safari Shuttle bus picks you up right at the campground then drops you off in Avalon. Feel free to buy a T-shirt when you return. You've earned it.

Options

To get to 2,097-foot Mount Orizaba, the highest point on the island, from Black Jack Junction, hike 1.3 miles, past the turnoffs for Black Jack Campground and Cottonwood–Black Jack Trail. After those turnoffs, take a left off the Black Jack Trail and from there it's 1.1 miles to Mount Orizaba. From Little Harbor Campground, you can also hike to Two Harbors, 5.7 miles north; take the main trail north out of the campground for 2.5 miles, turn left on Banning House Road, and it's 3.2 miles to Two Harbors.

Directions

Catalina Express provides ferry service to Avalon from Long Beach Harbor. Call 800/481-3470 or visit www.catalinaexpress.com for a departure schedule, reservations, and fee information. Reservations and a fee are required for bus service across the island; call 310/510-8368 or go to www.catalina.com.

Information and Contact

For camping reservations and fees, call 310/510-8368 or go to www.catalina.com. Dogs are not allowed. For more information, contact the Catalina Island Conservancy, 310/510-1421 or www.catalinaconservancy.org. Hiking permits can be picked up at the conservancy office at 125 Claressa, at the Wrigley Garden, or Airport-in-the-Sky. A free trail map is available when you pick up your hiking permit. An online trail map is available at www.scico.com/camping/home.html. A trail map is also available from Franko's Maps, 808/834-6887, www.frankosmaps.com.

ORANGE COUNTY

© ANN MARIE BROWN

BEST HIKES

Mention "Orange County" and most people think of the lifestyle depicted on the television drama that has made the initials "O.C." a household acronym. But there's a lot more to this 800-square-mile county than its 42 miles of beaches and seemingly endless supply of shopping malls and beautiful people. The "O.C." might not be the first place you think of when you crave a wilderness experience, but there's a lot more nature here than most people realize.

Although nearly three million people inhabit Orange County, a vast expanse of its land is protected – and safeguarded from future development – by a patchwork of county, state, and federal parklands. Consider the inland area of the county, for example, where a tumble of deep canyons in the Santa Ana Mountains is home to hawks, lizards, coyotes, and shady copses of sycamores and oak. The Santa Ana range is mostly contained within Cleveland National Forest, the southernmost national forest in California. In the summer months, this is a forbidding land, where temperatures frequently soar to three digits, and wildfires are a frequent occurrence. But, in the cooler seasons of the year, the chaparral- and sage-covered slopes of the Santa Anas turn green, and seasonal creeks and waterfalls flow with abandon. A federally designated wilderness area – the San Mateo Canyon Wilderness – is found here, as well as one of

Southern California's largest waterfalls, 150-foot Tenaja Falls. Except for a few popular spots, this wilderness area is one of the least visited in the state. Lace up your hiking boots, pack plenty of water and snacks, and you can easily "get lost" in these hills for an afternoon or longer.

Bordering Cleveland National Forest is Orange County's largest county-managed parkland – Ronald W. Caspers Wilderness Park. Its 8,000 acres and 30 miles of trails provide an appealing outdoor playground for hikers, mountain bikers, and equestrians.

But if chaparral-clad hillsides and woodsy canyons don't suit your hiking mood, you can always take a break from the "Orange Crush" traffic and pay a visit to Laguna Beach, where seaside sands give way to view-filled coastal hills at Crystal Cove State Park and Laguna Coast Wilderness Park. Or take a trip to the "951," on the far eastern edge of Orange County, where there is still plenty of country left at Chino Hills State Park. Here, miles of wide-open grasslands provide critical habitat, and a wildlife corridor, for the critters who dwell within.

It may take some effort to travel to the more remote parks of Orange County, but do so and you'll be pleasantly surprised. Disneyland? Knott's Berry Farm Theme Park? That's the "other" Orange County. You won't find anything like that out here.

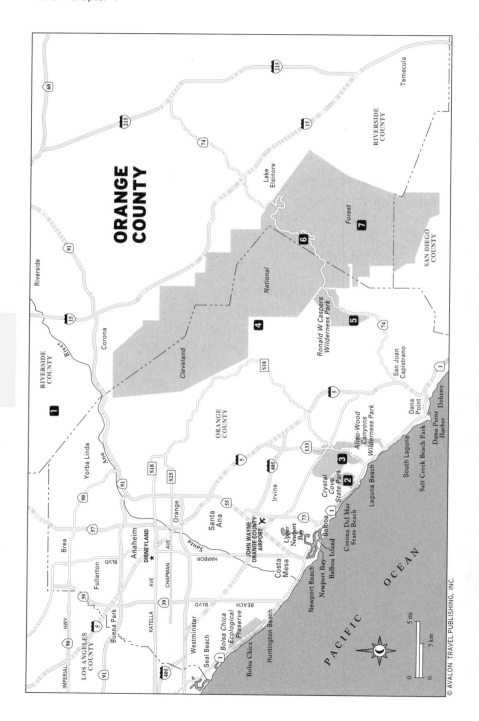

© AVALON TRAVEL PUBLISHING, INC.

Orange County Hikes

1 SOUTH RIDGE TRAIL AND TELEGRAPH CANYON LOOP

Chino Hills State Park

Level: Moderate

Hiking Time: 2.5 hours

Total Distance: 5.0 miles round-trip

Elevation Gain: 1,070 feet

Summary: A pleasant cool-weather trek to a high point in a park that serves as an urban oasis for the Inland Empire and an important habitat link for wildlife.

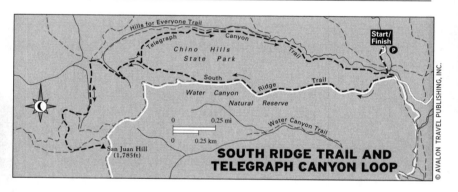

SOUTH RIDGE TRAIL AND TELEGRAPH CANYON LOOP

Pity the poor coyotes, bobcats, and other critters that try to roam between the Santa Ana Mountains in Orange and Riverside Counties, and the Puente Hills 15 miles north. As a result of encroaching humanity in the form of subdivisions and strip malls, creatures that travel by paw have been increasingly hemmed in. But thanks to local environmentalists, wildlife corridors are being created to link these increasingly isolated islands of habitat. Chino Hills State Park, opened in 1984, is just such a link.

The South Ridge Trail traverses the south end of the 12,452-acre park, stretching from the Rolling M Ranch entrance off Bane Canyon Road at the park's east end, west to the Rimcrest entrance in Yorba Linda. A nice workout for a day hike is the 2.4-mile stretch of South Ridge Trail from the trailhead near Rolling M to San Juan Hill. The hike passes through hillsides lush with grasses in the spring, with clear-day views all the way to Mount San Jacinto. A loop return on Telegraph Canyon Trail follows a seasonal creek graced by sycamores and oaks.

But make no mistake: This is definitely a winter or spring hike. The majority of Chino Hills State Park is completely without shade, and, as soon as the weather warms up, the verdant hillside grasses bake into the classic SoCal brown.

Expect to come across plenty of mountain bikers if you hike on a weekend. If you can't stand to share the trail with two-wheelers, stick to weekday visits or hike on one of the park's single-track trails instead, where bikes are not allowed (see Options, below).

Start your trip at Rolling M Ranch, 1,720 acres of land that were leased to area landowners for cattle grazing in the mid-1800s. The ranch is now the park's headquarters, with restrooms, a ranger residence, amphitheatre, barn, and other historic buildings. A new 25-site campground opened in spring 2005 and replaces the aging Aliso Canyon Campground directly

California sycamores or "buttonballs" grow in Telegraph Canyon; their fruit hangs on long stalks.

south. After parking, walk out of the lot, back to the road. Turn left and walk to the signed South Ridge trailhead, about 100 feet up on the right.

The ascent on South Ridge is gentle. Birds flit through the trailside grasses—more than 200 species have been spotted in the park—and lizards and rabbits scurry across the trail. Oak woodlands dot some of the hillsides. The only downside is that overhead power lines are rarely out of view. In about two miles, you'll come to a signed trail junction. To the right is Telegraph Canyon Trail, your loop return. Keep to the left to continue on South Ridge, now heading south. This is the prettiest section of trail, especially in spring when the oak-studded hillsides are painted yellow with flowering black mustard and wild radish.

The turnoff to San Juan Hill isn't obvious. At a trail fork about a half mile past the Telegraph Canyon junction, head left on a trail that is signed "Not a through trail." After a short distance, bear right at another fork and head up a faint, unmarked path to a knoll. The summit is just west of the humming powerlines and marked by a hexagonal concrete marker engraved "San Juan Hill 1896." This may have been left from one of the old land surveys done in the late 1800s, when private land acquisition began. The land had previously been used as spillover grazing from surrounding Mexican ranchos. Driving through the park, you'll notice windmills dating back to the ranching era.

Views from the hill include distant Mount San Jacinto, Cleveland National Forest to the south, and in the foreground the 241 Tollway to Orange County. It's a reminder that Chino Hills is truly an island in a sea of civilization.

For your return trip, hike back downhill and retrace your steps to the Telegraph Canyon junction you passed previously. Turn left and follow Telegraph Canyon Trail east, following a seasonal creek, for two miles back to the trailhead.

Options
You can also continue on South Ridge Trail past San Juan Hill to the Rimcrest entrance, which adds another three miles and 981 feet of elevation loss. Or, to avoid sharing the trail with mountain bikes, park near the now-closed Aliso Canyon Campground and follow the old road to the start of Water Canyon Trail, about a half mile out. The trail travels about 1.5 miles up Water Canyon through an increasingly dense thicket of oaks, sycamores, willows, and occasional native California walnut trees.

Directions
From the Highway 71 and Highway 91 junction in Corona, take Highway 71 north 6.4 miles. Exit at Soquel Canyon Parkway and drive south 1.3 miles. Turn left on Elinvar Road, drive to its end, then turn left on Sapphire Road and right into the park entrance. Proceed three miles to the trailhead parking, which is just past the South Ridge and Telegraph Canyon trailheads.

Information and Contact
A $4 day-use fee is charged per vehicle. Dogs are not allowed. A trail map is available online at www.parks.ca.gov. For more information, contact Chino Hills State Park, 1879 Jackson Street, Riverside, CA 92504, 951/780-6222, www.parks.ca.gov or www.hillsforeveryone.org.

2 EL MORO CANYON TRAIL
Crystal Cove State Park

BEST ◖

Level: Easy/Moderate	**Total Distance:** 5.2 miles round-trip
Hiking Time: 2.5 hours	**Elevation Gain:** 850 feet

Summary: Birds, butterflies, and bunnies await hikers on this lush canyon trail on the Orange County coast.

Crystal Cove State Park is a miraculous chunk of public land lying smack in the midst of some of the most overdeveloped coastline in California. Considering how much money could be made by turning the park's 2,500 coastal acres into condos and townhouses, it's amazing to see this slice of heaven remains open and protected in Orange County.

El Moro Canyon is one of the park's many scenic wonders. On average, only 12 inches of rain fall at Crystal Cove each year, but when

you see how lush and overgrown the foliage is in El Moro Canyon, you won't believe it. Although El Moro Creek flows only in the wet season, its banks are lined with oaks, sycamores, and willows. Birds and butterflies flock to its edges. The trail through El Moro Canyon is a pleasant walk at any time of the year but is best seen after winter and spring rains.

To access the trail, walk from the ranger station parking lot down the road to the entrance kiosk, then turn left on a dirt fire road. The road leads past the trailers of the El Morro Mobile Home Park, which, if funding is secured and all legal documents are completed, will soon be converted to a park campground and picnic area. The scenery quickly improves at 0.7 mile as you veer left on El Moro Canyon Trail and head up the shady, tree-lined canyon. The vegetation thickens and thins as you walk, alternately allowing the sun in, then creating a tunnel of cool shade.

Many hikers prefer a simple out and back on El Moro Canyon Trail, but loop lovers will want to follow what the park calls its "Red Route." Head up El Moro Canyon Trail to a right turn on East Cut Across Trail, 1.6 miles from your start. Follow East Cut Across for a mile to Moro Ridge Trail, turn right again, and enjoy some lovely ocean views from up high, plus glimpses into the rugged canyons that are now preserved as Laguna Coast Wilderness Park. Be sure to take the 0.25-mile detour off Moro Ridge Trail to Emerald Vista (a left fork just before Moro Ridge begins to descend steeply). This ocean overlook is a perfect spot for a lunch break before heading back downhill. On clear days, you can pick out Catalina and San Clemente Islands.

Continuing on Moro Ridge Trail, a final right turn on BFI Trail (don't ask what it stands for because we can't print it) will bring you back downhill on a rather steep grade, but the trail delivers more fine coastal vistas along the way. BFI connects with El Moro Canyon Trail near the mobile home park, where you turn left and retrace your steps for the final 0.5 mile back to your car. It's pretty hard to get lost in this park; every major junction is marked with a "you are here" trail map.

The most obvious wildlife you are likely to see are dozens of rabbits hopping along the trail in lower El Moro Canyon. Bird-watchers usually fare well here, spotting an abundance of songbirds, hawks, quail, and roadrunners. On the upper side of the loop, the riparian habitat gives way to grasslands, which are covered with wildflowers in spring. With the bloom of the flowers comes the butterflies. Common varieties include the anise swallowtail (yellow and black) and the red admiral (brown, red, and black).

© ANN MARIE BROWN

El Moro Canyon is lush with oaks and dense coastal sage scrub, creating a haven for birds and butterflies.

And, yes, Crystal Cove State Park is a well-known hot spot for mountain biking, but the cyclists we have met here have all been very respectful of hikers. This park is proof positive that when bikers and hikers mind their manners, everybody gets along just fine.

Options

When you've completed your canyon exploration, be sure to pay a visit to Crystal Cove's 3.5 miles of Pacific coastline. Beach access is available at Reef Point, Pelican Point, and Los Trancos. Reef Point is the best spot for swimming and bodysurfing. If you'd like to spend the night at Crystal Cove, there are three backcountry campsites, two on Moro Ridge and one in Deer Canyon, that are accessible via a three-mile-plus hike. You must pack everything in, including water. Call the park for reservations and details.

Directions

From Corona del Mar, drive south on Highway 1 for three miles to the entrance to Crystal Cove State Park on the inland side of the highway. Park near the ranger station, then walk downhill to the entrance kiosk and turn left on the dirt road.

Public transportation: Orange County Transportation Authority local bus route 1 stops at the park entrance; contact them at 714/636-7433, www.octa.net.

Information and Contact

A $10 day-use fee is charged per vehicle. Dogs are not allowed. A map of Crystal Cove State Park is available for a fee at the ranger station. For more information, contact Crystal Cove State Park, 8471 Pacific Coast Highway, Laguna Beach, CA 92651, 949/494-3539 or 949/492-0802, www.parks.ca.gov or www.crystalcovestatepark.com.

③ LAUREL LOOP

Laguna Coast Wilderness Park

Level: Easy

Hiking Time: 2 hours

Total Distance: 4.0 miles round-trip

Elevation Gain: 625 feet

Summary: A scenic loop in an Orange County coastal park that is a treasure of open space in an area being rapidly gobbled up by expensive housing.

If you're a nature lover living in Southern California, Orange County is probably not the first place you think about when it comes to hiking. Shopping, maybe. The beach, definitely. But in recent years the county, several cities, and land conservation agencies have scooped up valuable property wedged

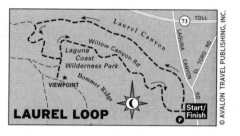

between Newport Beach and Laguna Niguel that stretches from the beach inland to I-405, saving it from the clutches of developers. These 17,000 acres of coastal canyons and ridgelines are preserved as wilderness parks, open space preserves, and land reserves under the umbrella title of South Coast Wilderness.

Laguna Coast Wilderness Park is one of the parks. Its 6,400 acres include miles of trails for hikers, bikers, and equestrians. Created in 1993, the park's land has long been coveted by developers, who have so far been successfully held at bay by the city of Laguna Beach and nonprofit groups such as the Laguna Canyon Foundation.

Check your calendar and your watch before you go: The park is open only on Saturdays and Sundays, 8 A.M.–4 P.M. Start at the main park entrance on Laguna Canyon Road, just south of El Toro Road. Make your first stop the park office, which is currently just a trailer that houses maps, park habitat information, and wildlife displays such as animal scat samples. Rangers are usually stationed at a tent outside the trailer. They are sure to warn you about rattlesnakes, which are frequently seen slithering across the trails in this coastal canyon. Plant identification signs scattered near the trailhead help botany newbies polish their skills. California wild rose, oak and sycamore trees, and vibrant orange California poppies are some of the natives residing here.

Our suggested route heads north on Laurel Canyon Trail, takes a brief detour to an ocean viewpoint at Bommer Ridge, then returns on Willow Canyon Fire Road. In the spring, a creek flows alongside Laurel Canyon Trail, and

taking in the views from the Bommer Ridge/Willow Canyon junction

the grasses are dotted with monkeyflower. The annoying buzz of traffic noise fades as you head west. Although the trail is exposed and can get hot in the summer (when it's best to hike in the early morning), several stands of oaks near the creek provide shade. There's also plenty of poison oak, so beware if you step off the trail to check out the creek.

A short distance from the start, as the trail gently ascends, look to the left for a large cave carved out of the sandstone by wind and water. Just past the first big stand of oaks, look right for a rock formation known as Caspers Rock, which looks like a big gray ghost with a tongue sticking out of his mouth.

For the most part, the trail rises gradually, but there is one steep stretch, clearly marked by Xs on the park's detailed handout map. Luckily this section is mostly shaded by oaks and sycamores. In rainy years, there's a small waterfall about a mile in, just off the left side of the trail. Above the falls are big, flat rocks to stretch out on to take a rest.

At 1.8 miles from the start, you'll turn left at a wooden post marked "10" that is the junction with the Laurel spur trail, a 0.5-mile connector to the next leg of the loop. The spur is a steep fire road that heads south, deeper into the park's finest coastal chaparral habitat. In the spring, this trail is lined with head-high black mustard. It is accompanied by big bunches of pale orange monkeyflower and huge stands of yellow and orange deerweed, a California native in the pea family that is valuable for erosion control and helping to balance nitrogen in the soil.

This scenic stretch ends at Willow Canyon Fire Road, the final leg of the loop. Before turning left to finish the loop, turn right for a 100-yard detour to the junction with Bommer Ridge Fire Road, where there's a nice ocean view from 875 feet above sea level. Cast a few admiring glances at the sea, then follow Willow Canyon Fire Road as it winds north and then east 1.4 miles back to the trailhead. As you head downhill, you'll enjoy fine mountain views and interesting sandstone rock formations just off the trail, but sadly, the vista also includes the San Joaquin Hills Tollway and an Irvine subdivision just beyond. It's an unfortunate reminder that wherever you are in this coastal county, civilization is never far away.

Options
From the Willow Canyon/Bommer Ridge junction, you can drop into Emerald Canyon and do a loop, or access Crystal Cove State Park. To access Emerald Canyon, at the junction (wooden signpost No. 3), turn right, go about 0.1 mile, and turn left on Emerald Canyon Road. The road descends 375 feet in a little over a mile to Old Emerald Trail, on the left (post No. 14). Follow it 0.5 mile to Bommer Ridge Road (post No. 13). Turn left on Bommer and hike one mile north, back to the Bommer/Willow junction. This loop adds about 2.5 miles to the Laurel Loop hike. To get to Crystal Cove State Park, turn right on Bommer Ridge at the Bommer/Willow junction. Take Bommer Ridge 0.5 mile to Moro Ridge fire road, then go left on Moro Ridge to access the state park.

Directions
From Highway 1 in Laguna Beach, turn north on Laguna Canyon Road. Drive 3.1 miles and turn left into the Laguna Coast Wilderness Park parking lot.

Public transportation: Orange County Transportation Authority local bus route 89 stops at the park entrance just south of El Toro Road; contact them at 714/636-7433, www.octa.net.

Information and Contact
A $3 day-use fee is charged per vehicle. Dogs are not allowed. A free map is available at the ranger station at the trailhead. A detailed map of Orange County parks is also available for a fee from Franko's maps, 808/834-6887, www.frankosmaps.com. For more information, contact Laguna Coast Wilderness Park, 20101 Laguna Canyon Road, Laguna Beach, CA 92651, 949/923-2235, www.ocparks.com.

Special note: The park is open on Saturdays and Sundays only, 8 A.M.–4 P.M.

◢ HOLY JIM FALLS

Trabuco Canyon/Cleveland National Forest

Level: Easy

Total Distance: 3.0 miles round-trip

Hiking Time: 1.5 hours

Elevation Gain: 550 feet

Summary: A family-friendly hike through a sylvan canyon leads to a petite but charming waterfall.

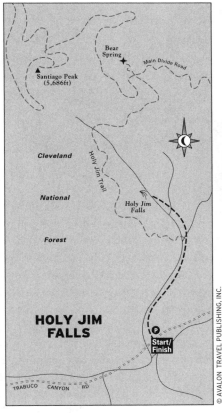

Holy Jim Falls has one of the most intriguing names and interesting histories of any Southern California waterfall. The fall and its canyon were named for James T. Smith, better known as "Cussin' Jim," a beekeeper who lived in the canyon in the 1890s. Apparently Smith earned his nickname through his bad temper and colorful language. Since honey-loving grizzly bears were plentiful in the area in those days, a beekeeper might have plenty of reasons to be angry.

But conservative mapmakers who plotted Trabuco Canyon in the early 1900s found Smith's moniker in bad taste. Lacking much imagination, they arbitrarily changed it to "Holy Jim." The sanitized name stuck.

The canyon's waterfall has made its own name for itself. A favorite destination of Orange County hikers, the Holy Jim Trail is quite busy on winter and spring weekends when the fall is flowing strong. The drive to the trailhead can be a bit of a challenge (five miles on a rocky dirt road, manageable by most passenger cars but high clearance is strongly advised, especially in the wet season), but the hike is a breeze. It's a mellow stroll through a forest of shady oaks and alders, keeping close company with Holy Jim Creek. Even in the dry late-summer months, when the waterfall is less

Holy Jim Falls cascades into a secluded rock grotto in the Santa Ana Mountains.

than ebullient, this leafy canyon is a pleasure to walk through. The only tricky part is that the waterfall isn't right along the main trail; you must follow a spur off the main trail to reach it. A few hops, skips, and jumps along and in the streambed, and you're there. Of course, if you hike here immediately following a period of hard rain, the hike is a lot more challenging, because of the numerous stream crossings along the way.

A free brochure that describes the Holy Jim Trail is available at the Corona Forest Service office; it corresponds to numbered guideposts along the route and provides interesting facts about the natural and human history of the canyon.

Start by walking down the dirt road that leads to some leased Forest Service cabins, passing an array of big cacti and succulents, until at 0.5 mile you reach the official Holy Jim trailhead. Leaving the dirt road for a narrower trail, you're surrounded by a lush canyon filled with oaks, alders, spring wildflowers, and even a few ferns—all thriving in the shade alongside Holy Jim Creek. The trail crosses the creek several times, passes numerous small check dams, and gently gains elevation as it heads upstream.

After nearly 30 minutes of walking, the trail steepens noticeably. As you pass an old, massive oak tree on your left, paths branch off in every direction. Stay on the main route by continuing upstream for about 40 yards, then cross the creek again (on your left). Immediately after crossing, follow the trail's right fork, which sticks alongside the stream. The left fork switchbacks uphill to the summit of 5,687-foot Santiago Peak, seven miles away.

Now you have only a 10-minute scramble through the rapidly narrowing canyon to reach Holy Jim Falls. A petite but picturesque 20 feet high, the waterfall is set in a small, intimate grotto that forms a nearly circular rock amphitheater. Maidenhair ferns cling to the walls on both sides of the watercourse. You won't want to leave this special place too quickly.

Options

After visiting the falls, backtrack to the junction with the Holy Jim Trail to Santiago Peak, and follow that route as far as you like. The summit is a long and arduous seven miles away, but you can always head for Bear Springs instead, only 3.5 miles from the junction.

Directions

From I-5 at Laguna Hills, exit on El Toro Road and drive six miles east. Turn right on Live Oak Canyon Road at Cook's Corner and drive 4.5 miles (two miles past O'Neill Regional Park). Turn left on Trabuco Canyon Road, a dirt road just beyond the paved Rose Canyon Road turnoff. (The road is usually suitable for passenger cars, but high clearance is recommended.) Drive five miles to the well-signed parking area for Holy Jim Trail. The trail leads from the parking lot's left side.

Information and Contact

There is no fee, but a national forest adventure pass is required; see page 297 for more information. Dogs are allowed. For more information and/or a map of Cleveland National Forest, contact the Trabuco Ranger District, 1147 East Sixth Street, Corona, CA 92879, 909/736-1811, www.fs.fed.us/r5/cleveland.

5 BELL CANYON AND EAST RIDGE LOOP
Ronald W. Caspers Wilderness Park

Level: Moderate

Total Distance: 5.2 miles round-trip

Hiking Time: 2.5 hours

Elevation Gain: 900 feet

Summary: A varied loop in this peaceful wilderness park offers expansive views, a walk through a riparian woodland, and spring wildflowers.

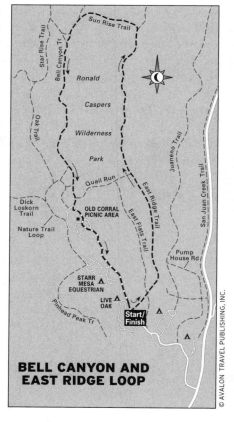

BELL CANYON AND EAST RIDGE LOOP

© AVALON TRAVEL PUBLISHING, INC.

Ronald W. Caspers Wilderness Park is Orange County's largest public parkland, covering a whopping 8,000 acres in the western Santa Ana Mountains. Its lush valleys are complemented by expansive groves of coast live oak and stands of California sycamore. Wildlife—particularly deer, rabbit, coyote, and a wide variety of birds—is abundant in the park and easily spotted (birders, don't forget your binoculars). The park's trails are well built and well maintained. A hike here is a near guarantee of a good experience.

Unfortunately, Caspers received a bad rap in 1986 when two children were attacked by a mountain lion. After a controversial and expensive lawsuit in which the family of one of the children sued the county over the cougar attack, the park was closed to all minors for a decade. In 1996, this ludicrous regulation was lifted, and the park was reopened to visitors of all ages. Still, even today, park signs request that adults keep children under close supervision at all times.

The fact is, you have a better chance of getting hit by lightning in Orange County than getting attacked by a mountain lion. The vast majority of hikers in this park—as well as the rest of Southern California—will never spot a

© ANN MARIE BROWN

Blue-eyed grass is a common springtime sight among the ridgetop grasslands on East Ridge Trail.

mountain lion, even from a very long distance. But you'd never guess it from the number of mountain lion warning signs now posted in Caspers Wilderness Park (and rattlesnake warning signs, too). The powers that be are clearly doing everything possible to prevent another lawsuit.

While some people may be scared off by this terrible piece of history, many locals consider Caspers to be the best park in Orange County. Even the drive to reach it is a pleasure—a winding cruise inland from the coast, past ranches, nurseries, and long stretches of open space.

Bell Canyon runs through the southern heart of the park, allowing many options for a variety of loops and out-and-back hikes. The five-mile Bell Canyon and East Ridge Loop is a great introduction to the park's myriad charms. Start on the East Ridge Trail across from Live Oak Campground. The initial steep climb will get your heart pumping, but in spring you are rewarded with a colorful display of monkeyflower, blue-eyed grass, yucca, pincushion, and fiesta flower. At any time of year, you'll gain panoramic views of Bell Canyon below and the surrounding peaks and ridges of Cleveland National Forest. On clear days, the town of San Juan Capistrano comes into view, as well as the coast beyond, and sometimes even San Clemente Island. If you find this first leg of the hike to be a bit too hot and/or strenuous, relax, because it gets easier from here.

After two miles on East Ridge Trail, turn left on Sun Rise Trail and hike 0.6 mile through grasslands and coastal sage scrub to connect to Bell Canyon

Trail (via a short stint on Cougar Pass Trail). A left turn on Bell Canyon Trail will lead you through the canyon's lush, leafy canopy of oaks and sycamores. You'll cross Bell Creek a few times, then pass through a gate that leads into the Old Corral picnic area. Here you'll find the park's often-photographed old windmill, a reminder of this fertile valley's cattle ranching days in the 1940s. The windmill is still used today to pump water for wildlife.

Bell Canyon Trail continues past the park's equestrian campground and then winds its way back to Live Oak Campground. When you return to your car, you'll most likely find that this loop has whetted your appetite for further explorations in Caspers Wilderness.

Options
If you'd prefer a more mellow hike, just head out and back along Bell Canyon Trail for as long as you please. The trail parallels the creek much of the way and has an almost negligible change in elevation. Or you can extend this loop by following East Ridge Trail for another 0.5 mile to its end at Cougar Pass Trail, then turning left on Cougar Pass to connect to Bell Canyon Trail.

Directions
From I-5 at San Juan Capistrano, take the Ortega Highway (Highway 74) exit and drive northeast for 7.6 miles. The park entrance is on the left at 33401 Ortega Highway. Park near Live Oak Campground; the trail begins there.

Information and Contact
A $5 day-use fee is charged per vehicle on weekends, $3 on weekdays. Dogs are not allowed. Free trail maps are available at the trailhead, or you can download one at www.ocparks.com/caspers/. For more information, contact Ronald W. Caspers Wilderness Park, 33401 Ortega Highway, San Juan Capistrano, CA 92675, 949/923-2210, www.ocparks.com.

6 SAN JUAN LOOP TRAIL
Cleveland National Forest

Level: Easy

Hiking Time: 1 hour

Total Distance: 2.2 miles round-trip

Elevation Gain: 150 feet

Summary: This easy nature trail is located right alongside scenic Highway 74 and makes a perfect leg-stretching hike for Sunday drivers.

Highway 74 from Lake Elsinore to San Juan Capistrano takes visitors through the heart and soul of Orange County. It begins in the lowlands, climbs across the rolling ridgeline of the Santa Ana Mountains, and comes to a scenic denouement at the Pacific Ocean. Most of the countryside through which the road traverses is Cleveland National Forest, and it is some of the least-visited public land in Southern California. Why? Because it's hot, that's why. If you visit in summer, you'll bake your boots for sure.

On the other hand, if you time your trip for immediately following a winter rain, or during the spring wildflower bloom from late February to early May, you'll think you've found paradise right here in Orange County.

A great leg-stretching break on Highway 74 is the San Juan Loop Trail. This easy, informative walk is a perfect introduction to the landscape of the Santa Ana Mountains. Don't be put off by the warning sign at the trailhead, which explains in doomsday style about the dangers of mountain lions, rattlesnakes, poison oak, and rugged terrain. Although this sign has surely inspired some would-be hikers to get back in their cars and head for Disneyland instead, it's highly unlikely that you'll meet up with any of those hazards, except for the rugged terrain, of course.

Begin hiking on the San Juan Loop Trail from the north side of the parking lot. The sandy trail is well maintained and easy to follow. It parallels the highway for its first 0.5 mile, but you'll forget about the road noise as you discover a cornucopia of plant life along the path. In spring, you'll enjoy the blooms of monkeyflower, purple nightshade, and tall yuccas with their silky, milk-white flowers on long spikes. Lizards dart here and there among the foliage. Although dry and exposed, the desertlike terrain is lush and laden with flora.

At 0.3 mile, the trail passes a railing and overlook above a small seasonal waterfall on San Juan Creek. Scramble down to the water's edge, if you like, to get a better look at the 15-foot-high falls. (A short spur trail leads down to the waterfall from the railing's left side.) The polished, light gray, granite walls of this narrow gorge and the creek's ultraclear pools invite a closer look.

A yucca whipplei prepares to burst into bloom along the San Juan Loop Trail.

Back on the trail, you'll soon pass the turnoff for Chiquito Trail. One more highlight awaits as you continue on the San Juan Loop Trail: a lovely grove of ancient oaks, which provide a cool, shady contrast to the open exposure along the rest of the trail. The oak canopy provides enough shade for ferns to grow. In early spring, they unfurl their new fronds.

Beyond the oak grove, the path heads out into the sunshine again and skirts the edge of Upper San Juan Campground. Exposed slopes from here to the trail's finale encourage more spring wildflowers. Your loop finishes out on the opposite side of the parking lot from where you started.

It's worth noting that this trailhead is right across the road from the Country Cottage and General Store, the only game in town for filling your day pack with supplies. The shop is known as "The Candy Store" because that was its original name, but of greater importance to hikers, the woman who runs the place stocks a good supply of handmade chocolates. If you load your pack with them, don't wait too long to indulge. It gets pretty warm around here.

Options

The Bear Canyon Trail begins across the road near the store. You can follow that trail out and back over the chaparral-covered hillsides. A high point two miles out provides wide views into the San Mateo Canyon Wilderness.

Directions

From I-5 at San Juan Capistrano, take the Ortega Highway (Highway 74) exit and drive northeast. In 21 miles, you'll reach the Country Cottage store on the right (0.75 mile past Upper San Juan Campground). The trailhead is across the road from the store; turn left and park in the large parking lot. Start hiking from the north side of the parking lot.

Information and Contact

There is no fee, but a national forest adventure pass is required; see page 297 for more information. Dogs are allowed. For more information and/or a map of Cleveland National Forest, contact the Trabuco Ranger District, 1147 East Sixth Street, Corona, CA 92879, 909/736-1811, www.fs.fed.us/r5/cleveland.

TENAJA FALLS

San Mateo Canyon Wilderness/Cleveland National Forest

Level: Easy

Total Distance: 1.5 miles round-trip

Hiking Time: 1 hour

Elevation Gain: 300 feet

Summary: A short, easy hike leads to a surprising waterfall in the brushy lands of the San Mateo Canyon Wilderness.

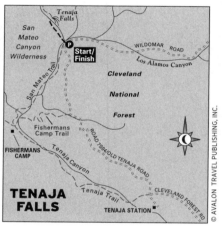

Tenaja Falls might be the most popular swimming hole in all of Orange County. At 150 feet high, it's definitely the county's most impressive waterfall. See it when it is running full with water, and you'll be astonished at the power and beauty of its cascading silver spray.

The hike to reach the falls is easy—maybe too easy, judging from the amount of litter which too often soils this special place. Take a cue from the Boy Scouts who frequent this area and bring an extra plastic bag with you to carry out some of the junk. (A big thank you to those hardworking Scouts.) The only hard part in getting there is the long drive to the unsigned trailhead; follow the directions below exactly. After parking, go around the metal gate that blocks the old road/trail into the San Mateo Wilderness to vehicles, and cross the creek on a concrete apron. If the apron is too flooded to cross, that's good news—it means the waterfall will be flowing hard. You'll have to wander upstream a ways to find a spot where the creek is narrower and you can cross more easily. Just be sure to rejoin the main trail, a wide dirt road, as soon as possible. If you keep following the informal trails that run alongside the creek, you'll soon wind up hopelessly lost in a tangle of ceanothus and other assorted spiny shrubs. (Guess how we know.) The poison oak around here is so prolific that it looks like it is being grown commercially.

The dirt road heads northward, rising gently out of the canyon and along slopes of sage and chaparral. You're high above Tenaja Creek here, not alongside it. In only a few minutes, you'll round a curve and be treated to a partial view

© ANN MARIE BROWN

Mighty Tenaja Falls drops 150 feet in five tiers.

of the waterfall ahead. Keep walking toward it; the trail deposits you at the falls' lip.

At full flow, Tenaja Falls is a treat for the senses. It is huge, by Orange County standards, with five tiers dropping a total of 150 feet. Unfortunately, you never reach a vantage point where you can see the whole thing in one glance. When the water level is low enough, you can cross over the top of the falls and gain a different perspective, looking downstream. Some people jump off the rocks and into the waterfall's deep pools, but this is probably only a good idea if you're young and foolhardy. Remember that the granite is even more slippery than it looks. Still, there's no harm in taking off your shoes and socks for a little cool-water wading.

Tenaja Falls' season is short, so you must visit early in the year. Average annual rainfall in the San Mateo Canyon Wilderness is only about 15 inches per season, and it's usually all over by March.

Options

You can take a longer hike to Tenaja Falls by starting at the Tenaja trailhead (you'll pass it on the way to the trailhead for the hike described above). From the Tenaja trailhead, it is a 5.4-mile hike to the falls.

Directions

From Lake Elsinore, drive south on I-15 for about 12 miles to the Clinton Keith Road exit. Drive south on Clinton Keith Road, which becomes Tenaja Road, for 4.5 miles. At a signed intersection with Tenaja Road, turn right and drive 4.3 miles west to Cleveland Forest Road. Turn right and drive one mile to the Tenaja trailhead. Stay right, passing the trailhead parking area. Reset your odometer and drive 4.4 miles on Road 7S04 to a hairpin turn and a parking pullout on the left.

Information and Contact

There is no fee, but a national forest adventure pass is required; see page 297 for more information. Dogs are allowed. For more information and/or a map of Cleveland National Forest, contact the Trabuco Ranger District, 1147 East Sixth Street, Corona, CA 92879, 909/736-1811, www.fs.fed.us/r5/cleveland.

RESOURCES

MAP SYMBOLS

- - - - - - ·	Featured Trail	(80)	Interstate Freeway	○	City/Town
- - - - - - -	Other Trail	(101)	US Highway	✕ ✈	Airfield/Airport
═══════	Expressway	(29)	State Highway	⌘	Golf Course
━━━━━━	Primary Road	66	County Highway	🖎	Waterfall
━━━━━━	Secondary Road	❶	Trailhead	▱	Swamp
= = = = = = =	Unpaved Road	★	Point of Interest	▲	Mountain
··············	Ferry	℗	Parking Area	⚑	Park
━ ·━ ·━ ·	National Border	⋀	Campground	⑂	Pass
━ ·· ━	State Border	▪	Other Location	✛	Unique Natural Feature

Resources

PARK INFORMATION SOURCES

Angeles District of California State Parks
1925 Las Virgenes Road
Calabasas, CA 91302
818/880-0350
website: www.parks.ca.gov

Angeles National Forest
701 N. Santa Anita Avenue
Arcadia, CA 91006
626/574-1613
website: www.r5.fs.fed.us/angeles

Big Pines Visitor Center
760/249-3504

Catalina Island information
www.catalina.com or
www.catalinaconservancy.org

Chilao Visitor Center
626/796-5541

Chino Hills State Park
1879 Jackson Street
Riverside, CA 92504
951/780-6222
website: www.parks.ca.gov or
www.hillsforeveryone.org

Conejo Recreation and Park District
403 West Hillcrest Drive
Thousand Oaks, CA 91360
805/381-2741 or 805/495-6471
website: www.crpd.org

Crystal Cove State Park
8471 Pacific Coast Highway
Laguna Beach, CA 92651
949/494-3539 or 949/492-0802
website: www.parks.ca.gov or
www.crystalcovestatepark.com

Grassy Hollow Visitor Center
626/821-6737

Laguna Coast Wilderness Park
20101 Laguna Canyon Road
Laguna Beach, CA 92651
949/923-2235
website: www.ocparks.com

Los Angeles City Parks
2001 North Fuller Avenue
Los Angeles, CA 90046
888/527-2757
website: www.laparks.org

Los Angeles County Department of Parks and Recreation
433 S. Vermont Avenue
Los Angeles, CA 90020
website: http://parks.co.la.ca.us

Los Angeles River Ranger District
12371 N. Little Tujunga Canyon Road
San Fernando, CA 91342
818/899-1900
website: www.r5.fs.fed.us/angeles

Monrovia Canyon Park
1200 North Canyon Boulevard
Monrovia, CA 91016

National Forest Adventure Pass

Angeles National Forest requires an Adventure Pass for each parked vehicle. Daily passes cost $5; annual passes are available for $30. Adventure Passes can be purchased at national forest offices in Southern California and dozens of retail outlets and online vendors. Holders of Golden Age and Golden Access (not Golden Eagle) cards can purchase the Adventure Pass at a 50 percent discount at national forest offices only, or at retail outlets for the retail price. When you purchase an annual Adventure Pass, you can also buy up to three additional annual Adventure Passes for $5 per family vehicle. Credit cards are accepted at most retail and online outlets, but not at Forest Service offices.

More information about the Adventure Pass program, including a listing of retail and online vendors, can be obtained at www.fsadventurepass.org.

626/256-8282
website: www.ci.monrovia.ca.us

Mountains Restoration Trust
3815 Old Topanga Canyon Road
Calabasas, CA 91302
818/591-1701
website: www.mountainstrust.org

Mount Baldy Visitor Center
909/982-2829

**Palos Verdes Peninsula
Land Conservancy**
P.O. Box 3427
Palos Verdes Peninsula, CA 90274
310/541-7613
website: www.pvplc.org

**Rancho Palos Verdes Recreation
and Parks Department**
30940 Hawthorne Boulevard
Rancho Palos Verdes, CA 90275
310/544-5309

San Gabriel River Ranger District
110 N. Wabash Avenue
Glendora, CA 91741
626/335-1251
website: www.r5.fs.fed.us/angeles

**Santa Clara/Mojave Rivers
Ranger District**
30800 Bouquet Canyon Road
Saugus, CA 91390
661/296-9710
website: www.r5.fs.fed.us/angeles

**Santa Monica Mountains
Conservancy**
5750 Ramirez Canyon Road
Malibu, CA 90265
310/589-3200
website: www.lamountains.com

298   Moon Take a Hike Los Angeles

Santa Monica Mountains National Recreation Area
401 W. Hillcrest Drive
Thousand Oaks, CA 91360
805/370-2301
website: www.nps.gov/samo

MAP SOURCES
Always obtain a detailed map of the area in which you will be hiking. Particularly helpful are maps that include trails, streams, peaks, and topographic lines. These are some excellent map sources:

Earthwalk Press
5432 La Jolla Hermosa Avenue
La Jolla, CA 92037
800/828-MAPS (800/828-6277)

Map Center
2440 Bancroft Way
Berkeley, CA 94704
510/841-6277

Map Link
30 South La Patera Lane, Unit 5
Santa Barbara, CA 93117
805/692-6777
website: www.maplink.com

National Geographic/ Trails Illustrated
P.O. Box 4357
Evergreen, CO 80437-4357
800/962-1643
website: www.trailsillustrated.com

Tom Harrison Maps
2 Falmouth Cove
San Rafael, CA 94901
415/456-7940 or 800/265-9090
website: www.tomharrison-maps.com

U.S. Geological Survey
Branch of Information Services
P.O. Box 25286
Federal Center
Denver, CO 80225
303/202-4700 or 888/ASK-USGS (888/275-8747)
website: www.usgs.gov

SOUTHERN CALIFORNIA HIKING CLUBS

Looking for some friends to hike with? Check out these Southern California hiking clubs:

Angeles Chapter of the Sierra Club (Los Angeles and Orange Counties):
www.angeles.sierrraclub.org

California Canine Hikers:
http://caninehikers.com

Ivy League Association of Southern California, Hiking Group:
www.ivy.hiking.info

Jewish Outdoor Adventures:
www.jewishoutdooradventures.com

Outdoors Club:
www.outdoorsclub.org

OTHER SOURCES FOR L.A. OUTDOOR INFORMATION

High/low tide schedules:
www.tidelines.com

Hiking expertise and gear reviews:
www.adventure16.com
www.rei.com

Hiking gear for your dog:
www.youractivepet.com or www.ruffwear.com

Los Angeles-area birding opportunities:
www.laaudubon.org

Los Angeles Astronomical Society:
www.laas.org

Wildflower information:
www.theodorepayne.org/hotline/hotlinelinks.html

Tidepool walks at Cabrillo Aquarium:
www.cabrilloaq.org

Index

MOON TAKE A HIKE LOS ANGELES

Avalon Travel Publishing
An Imprint of
Avalon Publishing Group, Inc.

AVALON
publishing group incorporated

1400 65th Street, Suite 250
Emeryville, CA 94608, USA
www.moon.com

Editor: Erin Raber
Series Manager: Sabrina Young
Acquisitions Manager: Rebecca K. Browning
Copy Editor: Donna Leverenz
Graphics Coordinator: Stefano Boni
Production Coordinator: Darren Alessi
Cover Designer: Gerilyn Attebery
Interior Designer: Darren Alessi
Map Editor: Kevin Anglin
Cartographers: Suzanne Service, Chris Markiewicz
Cartography Manager: Mike Morgenfeld
Proofreader: Erika Howsare
Indexer: Deana Shields

ISBN-10: 1-56691-764-6
ISBN-13: 978-1-56691-764-3
ISSN: 1557-7171

Printing History
1st Edition—March 2006
5 4 3 2 1

Text © 2006 by Ann Marie Brown, Julie Sheer.
Maps © 2006 by Avalon Travel Publishing, Inc.
All rights reserved.

Title page photo: Eagle Rock, Santa Monica Mountains © Ann Marie Brown
Front cover photo: Sandstone Peak, Backbone Trail, Santa Monica Mountains National Recreation Area © Peter Bennett/California Stock Photo
Back cover photo: © Peter Cade/Getty Images

Printed in the United States by Malloy, Inc.

KEEPING CURRENT

We are committed to making this book the most accurate and enjoyable hiking guide to Los Angeles. You can rest assured that every trail in this book has been carefully reviewed in an effort to keep this book as up-to-date as possible. However, by the time you read this book, some of the fees listed herein may have changed and trails may have closed unexpectedly.

If you have a favorite gem you'd like to see included in the next edition, or see anything that needs updating, clarification, or correction, please drop us a line. Send your comments via email to feedback@moon.com, or use the address above.